New American Poets
of the 80's

NEW
AMERICAN POETS
OF THE 80's

Edited by
Jack Myers
&
Roger Weingarten

A WAMPETER PRESS / POETRY INTERNATIONAL BOOK

Book Design by George E. Murphy, Jr.
Composition by Coastal Composition, Box 2600, Ocean Bluff, MA 02065

The editors and the publisher would like to acknowledge the assistance of
Nadell Fishman, Carol Hamilton, Rene Harlow, Susan Harper, and Rosemary
Murphy in the preparation of this manuscript.

Printed in the U.S.A.

The publication of this book is supported by grants from the Massachusetts
Council on the Arts & Humanities and Norwich University.

Wampeter Press is a tax-exempt, non-profit publisher supported by funding
from the National Endowment for the Arts, the Massachusetts Council on
the Arts & Humanities, IBM, by donations from private individuals, and by
the work of volunteer editors and services provided by the business community.

ISBN: 0-931694-35-3

Wampeter Press, Box 512, Green Harbor, MA 02041

CONTENTS

INTRODUCTION

When W. H. Auden said "Poetry makes nothing happen," he did not mean that poetry is merely a decorative grace note to a pragmatic, modern age; but rather he meant the opposite—that poetry has the power to transform the emptiness within us into substance, and that language pushed to its aesthetic limits creates experience and therefore does not merely represent an event, but is an event in itself. In other words, poetry makes things happen.

Over the past five thousand years, the poet's function has not changed measurably. He still labors to make complex inner states of mind and heart concrete; to record, understand, and celebrate experience; and to articulate, and thereby fix his insights so that the life within and around him will not seem so fleeting, chaotic, and illusory. Where else is there to turn except to art to explore and affirm the inner limits of being alive?

The task of anthologists, aside from evaluating, selecting, and organizing work from the field, seems rather an awesome one when one considers the self-evident truism that generally what is published is what is passed on and implicitly authorized, that what is passed on is what is taught, and that what is taught is what most likely will be remembered. So, as editors, we quickly make the claim that this anthology could easily have included two or three times as many poets as are included here. There are that many fine young American poets writing today. And that while we hope we have made our selections with an objective eye toward an eclecticism regarding styles, concerns, and forms; inevitably, given equal levels of skill and achievement, the matter will reduce itself to editorial preference. We are certain of the worth of the work included here, and we remain apologetic for the work that has been necessarily omitted.

Nearly a decade has passed since there has been any significant anthology of younger American poets published. That, and the fact that a number of strong, new voices have emerged during that time, has created the need for this present volume. We see its function to be the introducing of promising new poets, the showcasing of poets who have been writing for a number of years but who have not yet been included in an anthology, and the updating of work by poets who have been previously anthologized and who have gone to establish their reputations. For the most part, the poets included here are between thirty and forty-five years of age, and have produced at least one volume of poetry. The Contributors Notes at the back of the book lists their bio/bibliography, but the work of the poets speaks best for itself. It is our further intention here to whet the reader's appetite so that he or she will go on to read more work by these authors.

Since the publication of George Orwell's *Nineteen Eighty-Four* in 1934, there has been a tremendous curiosity and interest in what events and changes to our life and language this nightmarishly painted year of 1984 might bring. Let it be noticed that the event of this gathering of poets, to whom the legacy and gift of language has been passed on so generously, is one of them.

Jack Myers
Roger Weingarten

JON ANDERSON

Each Day Does That

It seems, before sleep, something has been dishonest;
I'd like it to have been the day.

It is the recognition of a circle, some mild agreement
made as a child to behave, by which I could assign
myself the center of all things: a passive nature.

I sometimes write from an "occupation" —mailman—cardiac—
those whose lives are honest because without perspective.
They begin to value their loneliness. They grow tragic
and beautifully antique.

If these could meet, say in a conspiracy designed to fail,
they might agree: "I never met a man I didn't like."
Of all confessions, the worst!

Had I arrived, I'd say: "Resignation, the acceptance of
the reasonably tragic, is why I made you." They would
tear up their former maxims and begin to compete.

Once I wanted my readers to cry; now it's my personae.
Things are getting hot.

But the truth is I'm getting older. Most of my definitions
turn out to have been early promises, now more and
more forgettable.

Just before sleep, when I'm afraid, a few of those poems
which I had thought to be distant turn their small,
interested faces.

Never plain enough, or true enough, but their intention
turns my body, which had been weak with stubbornness,
toward home.

My parents lie like children in the dark. I'm not close
enough to hear them speak. But their love for each other,
which once seemed small to me, is there, and I can sleep.

The Face of Dürer

Is, perhaps, the face of Christ,
Had he a moment alone in the jail
At the City of Jerusalem, just
Before his deliverance to another
Intelligent enough to both ritualize
The judgment & absolve himself. Thus,
Perhaps the honest face of Pilate, also.
Men like this recognize each other,
Are aware of the burden of another's
Seriousness which justifies their own.

I, Albrecht Dürer the Northerner,
Have painted my own portrait here
In the proper colors at the age of 28.
Outside, it is 1500: the world is crazed
With its own ending, is allowed
No believable consolation. Sometimes
At midday only the rumble of carts
May be heard. All he is doing
Is bearing witness to himself, though
He will be the 1st and last of us to do so.

No revelation, none at all.
Unless his genius is itself
The progress of revelation.
The figure emerges from its black
Background. The hand's singular
Gesture, the face it helps identify,
Identify the future: there will be no
Plague, no further wars or oppressors.
We shall stand like this a long time,
As before a mirror, as before one another.

for Gail Orlen

2

Ye Bruthers Dogg

Hodain D. Dogg
& Toolie Orlen

Ye dogg, O'Toole,
Who hath not work
At love nor arte
Nor goeth schule
Sayeth with fart
At Gulden Rulle,
"Be it bitch or bisquit
Or platter stewe,
Ye palate alone shal guide yu."

Ye dogg, Hodain,
Forgoeth bone
Nor doth distain
To moanne,
". . . for winde & raen,
Ye snow & fogg,
Ye seasons, sunn,
& world roll on,
But ye dayes a' dogg be not longe."

Bruthers Tew,
Ye slimm Hodain
& fatte O'Toole,
Beneath fense
Diggeth hole.
Into ye world
Ye Bruthers danse;
Nor wuld return
Ye fatte O'Toole & slimm Hodain.

Sune is report
Bruthers Tew
Doth run amok
I' neighborhude.
Cautions O'Toole,
"Hodain, ye may barke,
May scowle & be rude,
But do not bitte
Ye hand what giveth dogg fude."

3

Tho all complane
A' Bruthers Tew,
No winde nor raen
Doth drive them homme.
Then sayeth Hodain
To Bruther, "O'Toole,
Tho we hath been frende
Thru thik & thinn,
Dogg needeth sume love from Mann."

So ende ye song
A' Bruthers Tew.
Away they had flown
& back they flewe.
Reclineth i' yard
Thru seasons & sunn,
Thru winde & raen,
Ye snow, ye fogg,
O'Toole, Hodain, ye Bruthers Dogg.

The Cypresses

Of the leaning cypresses,
Franconati says, *These*
Feathers constitute an evidence
Or inclination of God's breath.
Seeing them from my study window
They are a gesture I begin
To understand: as the raised
Open hand, in farewell,
Salutes a depth of feeling.
Now the great ocean of wind moves,
Again the cypresses lean

& whatever their meaning,
It is a dignification, a rational
Grace, because the weight
Of even the topmost parts moves
In its own time. The wind
Is an ocean. A great armada
Of ships, pennants awash, rushes

To the horizon. They are on
An important errand, but will return
Bearing men haggard with war &
Having lived too long with the quick,
Bright meaningless striking of oars.

So this story, or poetry, first told
Among savages who were kings
In a land of cypresses by a man
Who was blind, unwinds its
Thousands of cadences: the dead are
Risen & the imagined countenanced.
When the cypresses lean again
I notice their light, slow
Tracings upon a sky full of clouds
Assuming familiar shapes;
In time, upon all the possible
Faces of all possible things.

The Time Machine

In *Pandora's Box,* a silence of almost
        Two hours, conceived largely
By its meticulous director, G. W. Pabst,
        There is a moment (perhaps
Of thirty frames, a second or two) when
        A woman who is on trial—
Because she both has & has not
        Murdered the lover she
Had married earlier that same day,
        But that is another story—

Sits. Her name is Louise Brooks;
        She is still alive & was
Then one of the most beautiful
        Naturally animated images
Which has been memorized by the
        Motion of film. She appears,
As those few we sometimes notice,
        Usually in passing, who
Wholly belong to this particular planet
        We've set afloat. I think

Of them as animals. They are beyond
    My envy, they are almost
Beyond my comprehension, so I think
    Wherever she lives, an
Elderly woman, she is doing well.
    Two men have just spoken
Passionately—of her, almost *to* her—
    One raised his hand, pointed,
Then swept her from the earth, for
    She is its abomination,

Is the world hurling its massive will,
    Again & again, around its
Fiery sun and it will have its way.
    To the other man I think
She is like the animals I described:
    He sees her in passing.
Both are accurate. The film is proof.
    And the film's silence
Is now accurate, for she has risen
    For judgment, hears perhaps

The projector's whirring revolutions
    Only, & they are distant.
When the word is spoken, we *see* it,
    It casts her down so
Swiftly, not even a moment. Then,
    For a moment, the veil she
Has earlier let down upon her face—
    And you will not ever,
Having seen it, forget her face—
    The veil, though dark, so

Delicate it *seems* transparent,
    Turns lightly to one
Side, as if an afterthought of
    Her body's downward
Momentum—its edge, momentarily
    Taking the graceful shape
Of that loop by which we signify
    Infinity. Though, of
Course, it is meaningless, only
    The film's perfect memory.

for Patrick Hoctel

In Sepia

Often you walked at night, house lights made
    Nets of their lawns, your shadow
Briefly over them. You had been talking about
    Death, over & over. Often
You felt dishonest, though certainly some figure
    Moved in the dark yards, a parallel
Circumstance, keeping pace. By Death, you meant
    A change of character: He is
A step ahead, interlocutor, by whose whisper
    The future parts like water,

Allowing entrance. That was a way of facing it
    & circumventing it: Death
Was the person into whom you stepped. Life, then,
    Was a series of static events,
As: here the child, in sepia, climbs the front steps
    Dressed for winter. Even the snow
Is brown, &, no, he will never enter that house
    Because each passage, as into
A new life, requires his forgetfulness. Often you
    Would explore these photographs,

These memories, in sepia, of another life.
    Their use was tragic,
Evoking a circumstance, the particular fragments
    Of an always shattered past.
Death was process then, a release of nostalgia
    Leaving you free to change.
Perhaps you were wrong; but walking at night
    Each house got personal. Each
Had a father. He was reading a story so hopeless,
    So starless, we all belonged.

GEORGE BARLOW

Stacademia

Lot of folks
don't know it
but Stagolee
used to go to college

didn't like it
too much though
said none of them
professors & deans
seemed to have
they heads on tight

no style
stack said
wrinkled suits
& desert boots
no soul nowhere
punch-drunk pundits
lettered loons
that's what stack
called 'em

One day
Stack was sittin up
in a philosophy class
& the prof said:
> *I am a liar*
> *I always tell lies*
> *& i am lying about*
> *being a liar*
> *now Mr. Stagolee*
> *tell me how and/or*
> *why my last statement*
> *is true or false*

Stack didn't say nothin
just reached in his pocket
pulled out his .44
& blowed the professor away

Said he was just
puttin the old fool
out of his misery
& doin everybody a favor

You know ole Stack dropped out
the day before
they was to give him
his B.S.
in analytical euthanasia
& he never went back again

Old Man Sweeping

I drive through zero
each morning
Look for me

in the primal vacuum
between one moment
& the next

I come & go
in the
A.M. magic show

Commuting magicians
only vanish
only to appear

more like
the doughnut's hole
than the doughnut itself

everywhere & nowhere
more abstract than
a left turn

more absurd than

a right
nothing really nothing

I move from here
to there
& read the signs blindly

My speed is checked by radar
I merge left my right lane
is closed ahead

I usually see no kinship
in the clock-punching mugs
a fat man

true smoke
swirling in his cockpit
a woman yawning desperately

a car-pooler
catching his rightful winks
in the back seat

nothing nothing
mad transit &
a lane change

a truck bearing down
& the glass eye of the CHP
nothing nothing

But this morning's
light has caught me
in front of Mickey's Blue Room

where an old man
is slowly pushing a big broom
through last night's hoopla

Cold cold morning air
chill in his face
& hands

How many magicians

have vanished
before him this morning

He seems
unaware of me
unaffected by my gaze

Maybe he was young once
Maybe he glanced over
at an old man once

on a cold morning
like this
& thought he saw his life

run quickly down
a broom handle
like a mouse

Maybe he squashed
the vision in the same instant
with a blink of his eye

Now he sweeps
& doesn't his floppy old hat
tattered fatigues

slow careful moves
make more sense
than

my clock
my steering wheel
my corny routine

Isn't he past
present
future

the chill
that clutches
my idling bones

the light that

will change in a moment
naturally absolutely

He is

Little Half-Brother, Little Black Star

When I see him
gliding gazelle-like
stealing the white
out of third base

pulling a fly ball
from the sky
like a star from
his very own galaxy

bobbing his bushy head
to a new beat
digging the ancient sorrow
of an ancient song

taking his breaths
his cuts
his love
& his freedom

I see
runagate blacks
stealing their way
by the north star

&
cosmic blood
running through his
night train veins

& a woman
we found

some time ago
in an old family bible

Harriet
an aunt of his
a black woman
they called *The General*

                         for Mark

MICHAEL BURKARD

A Feeling from the Sea

I was feeling all this magic
and so I wrote this thing
and I made it up as I went along.
And two days later, actually a day,
I thought it must have seemed silly, and untrue,
that I attributed it to magic and to voices
in the air, in the room, and a feeling
from the sea. But it was not bravado
and I believed it.

I believed her too. And the face
of Pasternak, and the book I borrowed,
and half read, and the streets I half walked
and half looked while walking.

And then today I read some lyrical poems,
just a few, and a portion, a small piece,
from another one which was not so lyrical.
And I thought these lyrics were a truth,
equal to many, and I thought of disappointment
at these feelings. They are made this way, these lyrics,
like a hill you are meant to take into yourself,
and so better understand the world and fools.
And the power of people when they truly believe.

And I wrote some letters, and made some calls,
and tried to write, and it seemed falsely
lyrical. And I put it away. And I felt that in closeness
there is still something, many things, I don't understand,
or am afraid of, or find, later, unexpected.
And I thought myself foolish.

I could not find a tone for things.
I could not find a moment.

Time When the Day Ended

The mind went away
when I saw the snow
falling among love's
snow, on that afternoon
in New York City, —

and I wondered why
I was still haunted
by the picture of the "lost"
man you sent to me,
in a February, in a long

time when the day ended
with him next to me
just as it had begun.
I wanted to keep that
picture, I didn't think

it was me but thought
I had something to do with
his loss, I was responsible,
or I wanted to be his thin
self on one of those days, —

so now it is summer, and
the picture is boxed away:
Diane sent me this wanted
poster, and I have packed
it away. A little note

here, a little note there,
a note to this unknown
family about love's snow.
Are you still alive, are
you broken, is there a pause

of love's farness there?
Who were you when you went
talking about the summer
moon, July's, over and over
again. It was July

and there was no end
to the haunting, to the
mind or its farness.
The yellow is a good evening,
the cruel orange moon breaks.

There was a feather for his
life, and it erupted in a
brief illusion. I was his,
he was mine, we exchanged
identities in July.

The Story of Marie

There were many sounds I was raised with —
hammers, coughs, exhaust — exhaust creates
a hiss in the brain following morning coughs,
the cars close by the window, father coughing,
mother sneezing, brother playing hammer with a fist . . .

— and then there were the sounds of Marie,
slow tablets I listened to as the morning progressed,
tablets of song and smoke, smoke I felt in the back of my brain
behind the hiss, the song I felt beneath her heart . . . heart
which was a city, city of forged letters, forged secrets:

secret passages to my secret sister, my secret brother . . .
phantoms which hovered and dropped over the glasses my mother wore.

And there was the stillness
after the sound, not unlike the story
my uncle told me, the head beheaded, the head
lolling and trembling off. The depths
of such a story interfered with an otherwise

contented life. These depths were plumbed also:
by Marie, so named by her family
for the pheasants which fell from the sky
on the day of her birth
pheasants which pursued her childhood:

there, in the shoes she wore,
in the braids in her hair:
pheasants, braille pheasants, which recited
the songs before they were sung by her attuned blind voice.

It seems now there is a singular condition behind the life,
mine and hers. It separates one from another like a bridge
separates a side of the river from the other side,
and the river is of course always flowing, starlit
under the bridge.

And the singular condition drives one into the other:
stars driven into the river, shoes driven into songs,
life driven into another life. If the sounds are not dead
then they must be living,

and Marie's sober ghost locks up the white afternoon
upon the bridge, her father is almost home when he reaches
the bridge's midpoint: the relics hear him stopping, looking over,
and the pins and buttons and stuffed pheasants fall from the shelf . . .

here is Marie at work, so put off by her death her ghost is sober,
white like a false eye, an eye which never divides its gaze
and thus continually welcomes the pheasants back, and the braille
bridge, the braille water, the pounding of the braille upon the bridge.

Who can say my brother killed her,
who can say she killed my uncle,
who in their longing can say?

Within the stillness there is a cough, cough
from a white car passing by. I see her hand
murmur at the window, heading off
over the singular condition of what must be
an afterlife. There is no other reason

for the smoke, for the song which went:
one day my uncle took my head in his hands
and took it off, one day I heard a car sing.
Give me the ring from your finger,
give me the pheasant which sleeps in your bed . . .

the song is that condition,
like the condition of my brother,

my brother the tailor, forging the pheasant life,
never expecting my visit . . .

and I walk in as singular as the bridge I think,
and then the past coughs,
and Marie sings a song for my dead uncle.

Your Voice

It began here, on the horned road,
it began here, because I am not your father,
my answer is not your answer. It might be the light
beside the blackberry box, it might be the tone
of the heated song of the hot bird, singing, still
singing at 2 a.m. And it might be the ghost
ambling over the few tracks in the road, and the ghost's
voice which murmured out I am nervous in the night
because of being nobody, no one, no thing.

It began here as no thing, as an arm which fell
from your face, as the truer thing, — not the truth,
but a small true thing. And depending upon where
you were standing, were you sitting in the tree or not,
you either saw the cart far away on the road or you say
nothing but a different turn in the road, and each was
some part of the road and was true.

Tell me what to see — I will stay beside, tell me,
I will listen. The other side of the true story, then
another. Your voice, tell it in your voice.
A human voice of desire and snow and roads.

Strangely Insane

I could not eat much
as a child.
Now I eat and I have debts.
No child acquires debts like mine

and I find this unfortunate.
For if my debts were a child
I could pay in rain,
I could pay in repetition
I could pout like a garbage can
between two garages.
I could sell berries, cheaply,
to my dead neighbors.
I could make them undead.
I could make half the city sun,
half the city fog, so everyone (there)
could sigh, except for some unfortunates
upon whom my visitations would most
selfishly beat. And they could
drive me away to stars in apogee,
to corner stores, to market places
where death is an eerie island.

I am waiting for your portrait.
That will please me. That will please
the ghost I presumptuously ate for you.
Help me. Hold me. I am inside a light
I cannot recall. Skyless.
Strangely, as they say, insane.

In here it reads: orange leaf,
misunderstanding the ways we were lost,
there is no we which trembles.
It reads and reads . . .

I could not eat much as a child.
Go away, go away, go away.

PETER COOLEY

For Alissa

This is a poem for my daughter,
her of the topaz eye reflecting mine
eight years into the world.
Women have told me my eyes are like a statue's,
unmoving, cold. Hers never stop dancing.

Nor does her little body
lost to a plié or the dark woods
in the midst of Brothers Grimm
surrender its sharp grip
on the ground under it, spinning.
Nor on the wind over her always lifting.

Who from her mother was ripped
before her time and clung to Death
three days until he fell.
Who cocks her head like a bear cub
at my approach, moving too fast
that I should touch her with my expectation.

Who in a night season
seven years back
when I lay in terror of myself
cried out and drew me to her
hours while I walked her.
That tiny head pressed to my shoulder
downed with hair fine as cowslip
or the soft, white fire of milkweed
spilling over my skin—
and lifted these wings here
nubby, oracular, stubborn,
which brought me to morning,
nudging their small way upward.

Such Comfort As The Night Can Bring To Us

A man and a woman walk out into the summer night.
All evening they have been fighting
and now, arms intertwined, their bodies
wrung with sweat, they ache
numb, to be speechless,
delivered of each other.

Let the night speak then.
First to the woman that she turn to him
here, by the river lifting already to them
the face of its black depths. Then to the man
that he draw her down beneath the willows
where they trade shadows, trade them back
as in the falling light they bartered words,
swapping the coinage weightless.

Let the night sing then.
Let it ring dumb the chorus
of that other life, echoless
in root and vein, rock sucking at the wave
or in midair a note struck warbling.

As in that other time the night played, mute,
walking the garden noons—
where it strolled later in the cool—
before men, before women,
language, their shadows known to them
in parting only, and all flesh ravaging.

The Sparrows

By the time it comes to me
I will have ceased speaking
even to myself, the woman thinks.
On the window evening deepens
beyond her yard, and at the river
the willows, in the shallows waist-high,
already lie down with the first dark.

Her cold palms lift her breasts.
Lighter, they slip from her.
At her belly the fingers web
over this child, unmoving now
she will surrender tomorrow, still.

Yet how this first appeared,
the river gone over to the dark,
the acanthus and jasmine little flames
the pane divided up, she cannot put away.
How the frost parted and the grass
flickered, then stood still
that first instant, quickening,
And after that, how the light fell
on the sparrows she had not seen before.
How, without echo, their screams arose
before them, and the shrub gave up
blossom to seed that they might sing,
each bearing upward before it
the token moment of its survival.

The Unasked For

There, at the other side,
where afternoon steps down,
fluted between the willows,
and draws its shape from them
till stem, bole, root
become the night, invisible,
the Mississippi is another river.

Here, it is this minute.
Or this one, scummed, lapping, empurpled.
From the highroad of the levee
I stare out over the depths,
a small daughter at each hand.
Sundays are glass jars
on our side, sapphire, emerald
fluttering wings inside them.
They are bouquets of open air.

The barge's pearl wake, the bargemen
muttering their arcane tongue,
the sky over my shadow, violet,
and the noon, scintillant, breaking across it—
I have brought them up here
that they remember years from now
nothing of this, nothing but this:
when the light staggers on our side
and on that other, across the water
unasked for, darkness starts.
And then, trembling, the willows
follow, to bear us down
with their wind, headfirst, staggering.
And take such night to us
that only the fingers inside mine
assure me we are here together,
a day they may remember if at all
a lightning bug, a father shadowless, this starless water.

The Last Gift

Tonight my mother, dinner over
alone or with the widows
she names friends,
walks the shingle of gulf water,
the twilight violet on her rings.
Far from my father,
the old house in the North,
she is barefoot, halfway through her seventies,
and the water is emerald and then clear
this mid-December as she stoops
to claim a shark tooth, a sand dollar.

The voice which walked above me
by the cold waters of Lake Huron
resinous with pine and parted them
to take me in, who named the stars,
the roaring at the Royal Oak Zoo,
the first seedling in the garden

23

streaked with frost and sang the night asleep,
rests now within her finally.
What last word did it bend to give me
in the garden by the fishpond?
Was it forsythia which at that moment fell?
What name did she give me for the rock?
What kind of luminescence did she spell into my hand?

The Other

When you come to the other side
of lust the body lays itself
down in others as itself
no longer and the fields till now
fallow, bloom, vermillion.

When you cross to the other side
of pride the heart withers
into tinder, the wind blesses it.
Your body flares, white sticks
this side of anger.

Arriving at the other side
of terror the voice is a dark flame
walking evenings in the garden,
your name unknown to it
if the last light calls you.

And when you have passed the other side
of hope the shore will blaze
finally. We are all light here.
Do not look for me or ask.
You will never have known me.

PHILIP DACEY

Skating

Skating on the surface of my life,
I saw myself below the ice,
another me, I was moving fast
above him, he was moving slow,
though he kept up. There must have been
some warp of being twisting
us together so, two different speeds
head to head, or feet to feet, or,
better, shoulder to shoulder, brothers,
that's the way it felt, but separated
by a death, an ice, a long wall
laid down upon the world to lock us
into rooms. Knock, knock. Are you
there? He was, and waving, though
it was a distant wave, an outer-space
wave, as if he were umbilicaled
and drifting off between the stars. The stars
skated on that ice, too, and went so fast
they seemed not to move at all. Perhaps
he was the one sped swerveless home,
an arrow, while I dream-skated,
my two blades, for all their dazzle,
leaving the ice unchanged, and top was
bottom and bottom top, but who could say?
I only knew I wanted to break through.
I wanted the ice to melt to let
us sink together, two lovers in a bed,
or crack, a warning sign missed, while
the stars swam around us like fish
lit up from within by something
we could never name, nor wished to,
lest the light fade. But the ice held,
because it was wiser than I was,
because two is more than twice one,
because the air and water made a pact
to disagree while I skated on
the surface of a life I thought was mine.

Wild Pitches

You've been holding back
long enough, Son.
Stop aiming the ball.
Let your power,
that animal,
out. Don't worry
about hurting me.
I'm in my father-squat
behind homeplate, like a frog,
the soon-to-be-a-prince frog,
nothing and nobody
can stop that story.
Not even you. The whole world
squats so, just waiting
for you to throw the ball
as if you meant it,
an angry word,
an idea
to change the world,
a declaration
of love. It's true
some pitches will go wild.
At first a lot will.
But remember,
God is somewhere
with a mask and protector
for his chest and nuts
and catches every
wild pitch there is.
He's a scrambler.
So let that arm uncurl
and snake out
like the snake that girdles
the world. Whip-snake,
diamonded and poisoned
to the point where
the wildest pitch
is the one that stays
in the hand.

The Winter Thing

We were going to
but the storm came.
It would have been the first time
for either of us.
The place and hour were set.
Everything was ready.
The storm said no.

The storm poured out of us,
white denial,
white reticence.
We filled the road between us
with that whiteness.
No cars could move,
they wondered so
at the elaborate system
of beautiful roadblocks
people are as good
as wind at creating,
drifts this high
from shoulder to shoulder.

So we left our homes
and went out into it,
the Thing we had made
our environment, she there,
I here, and made
snow-angels, touching,
at all points,
one on top of another,
you couldn't tell them apart.

Crime

She lies at the side of the road, naked,
having been raped, beaten, tossed from a car.
You made her up. She is your soul's image.
Who are the men speeding away? You are.

The No

The condom salesman tries them on like shoes.
He'll find the size and style for you. He has
the practiced eye and hand, the sense of what

confines just so, that you can live in,
a way to breathe without the need to breathe.
He'll see it fits you like a pair of shoes

to go anywhere in, and touch nothing,
always a sole away, or skin, the fashion
nowadays for those who'd stay clean

cleaner, cleanest in the face of faces
close enough to catch. The condom salesman
looks you in the eye a thin film protects

and asks you how it feels, the size he found
to help you make your disappearance perfect
while seeming not to disappear at all.

But you've no feeling left to tell him,
or just enough to make a sign: you'll buy.
Today the going-out-of-business sale,

and he, the salesman of the means
of going out of business, smiles to turn
aside a question about price. Who can't

afford protection such as this? Sometimes,
as any schoolboy knows, you have to lose
your life to save it. And there's the beauty

of the thing itself, whatever the style,
the sleek and shining sleeve, a work of art,
finer than a shoe, and looking—this No

manufactured in accordance with
the highest standards—just like you.

Pac-Man

Sometimes the best move is not to,
is to wait and see how the ghosts
are behaving. They'll flutter away
if you pick the right place to be still

and you can clear one entire
side of your life before they return.
They will. They always do. The deadly
butterflies. The delicious

deadly butterflies. You have a mouth
like a wedge of pie that's missing
and you come from the Japanese word
for eat. Paku, paku. And

sayonara. The power pill
in each corner, swallowed,
gives you a chance at the ghosts:
you'd swear to watch them run

they didn't regenerate every time
at the reincarnation center.
But be quick: electricity is just lightning
pretending to be permanent. Soon

there's that moment when the balance
of power shifts again and the open
mouth of the devourer translates
to a silent scream: get out of here!

It's then your touch on the joy-stick
matters to take you around corners
and down speedways, all the while
what's counting are the video wafers

you can call your own, one communion
after another, little lines
like hyphens connecting the parts
of a life, compounding it. Even

when you die, the total stays,
a ghost itself whose only imperative

is haunt, which means eat
or be eaten, which means

a strange music as a sign
transformation is taking place
which means eyes set free
to float, and see.

STEPHEN DOBYNS

Bleeder

By now I bet he's dead which suits me fine,
but twenty-five years ago when we were both
fifteen and he was camper and I counselor
in a straight-laced Pennsylvania summer camp
for crippled and retarded kids, I'd watch

him sit all day by himself on a hill. No trees
or sharp stones: he wasn't safe to be around.
The slightest bruise and all his blood would simply
drain away. It drove us crazy— first
to protect him, then to see it happen. I

would hang around him, picturing a knife
or pointed stick, wondering how small a cut
you'd have to make, then see the expectant face
of another boy watching me, and we each knew
how much the other would like to see him bleed.

He made us want to hurt him so much we hurt
ourselves instead: sliced fingers in craft class,
busted noses in baseball, then joined at last
into mass wrestling matches beneath his hill,
a tangle of crutches and braces, hammering at

each other to keep from harming him. I'd look up
from slamming a kid in the gut and see him watching
with the empty blue eyes of children in sentimental
paintings, and hope to see him frown or grin,
but there was nothing: as if he had already died.

Then, after a week, they sent him home. Too much
responsibility, the director said.
Hell, I bet the kid had skin like leather.
Even so, I'd lie in bed at night and think
of busting into his room with a sharp stick, lash

and break the space around his rose petal flesh,
while campers in bunks around me tossed and dreamt
of poking and bashing the bleeder until he

was left as flat as a punctured water balloon,
which is why the director sent him home. For what

is virtue but the lack of strong temptation;
better to leave us with our lie of being good.
Did he know this? Sitting on his private hill,
watching us smash each other with crutches and canes,
was this his pleasure: to make us cringe beneath

our wish to do him damage? But then who cared?
We were the living children, he the ghost
and what he gave us was a sense of being bad
together. He took us from our private spite
and offered our bullying a common cause:

which is why we missed him, even though we wished
him harm. When he went, we lost our shared meanness
and each of us was left to snarl his way
into a separate future, eager to discover
some new loser to link us in frailty again.

Black Dog, Red Dog

The boy waits on the top step, his hand on the door
to the screen porch. A green bike lies in the grass,
saddlebags stuffed with folded newspapers. The street
is lined with maples in full green of summer, white houses
set back from the road. The man whom the boy has come
to collect from shuffles onto the porch. As is his custom,
he wears a gray dress with flowers. Long gray hair
covers his shoulders, catches in a week's growth of beard.
The boy opens the door and glancing down he sees yellow
streaks of urine running down the man's legs, snaking
into the gray socks and loafers. For a year, the boy
has delivered the man's papers, mowed and raked his lawn.
He's even been inside the house which stinks of excrement
and garbage, with forgotten bags of groceries on tables:
rotten fruit, moldy bread, packages of unopened hamburger.
He would wait in the hall as the man counted out pennies
from a paper bag, adding five extra out of kindness.
The boy thinks of when the man's mother was alive.

He would sneak up to the house when the music began
and watch the man and his mother dance cheek to cheek
around the kitchen, slowly, hesitantly, as if each
thought the other could break as simply as a china plate.
The mother had been dead a week when a neighbor found her
and even then her son wouldn't let her go. The boy sat
on the curb watching the man hurl his fat body against
the immaculate state troopers who tried not to touch him
but only keep him from where men from the funeral home
carried out his mother wrapped in red blankets, smelling
like hamburger left for weeks on the umbrella stand.

Today as the boy waits on the top step watching the urine
trickle into the man's socks, he raises his head to see
the pale blue eyes fixed upon him with their wrinkles and
bags and zigzagging red lines. As he stares into them,
he begins to believe he is staring out of those eyes,
looking down at a thin blond boy on his front steps.
Then he lifts his head and still through the man's eyes
he sees the softness of late afternoon light on the street
where the man has spent his entire life, sees the green
of summer, white Victorian houses as through a white fog
so they shimmer and flicker before him. Looking past
the houses, past the first fields, he sees the reddening
sky of sunset, sees the land rushing west as if it wanted
to smash itself as completely as a cup thrown to the floor,
violently pursuing the sky with great spirals of red wind.

Abruptly the boy steps back. When he looks again into
the man's eyes, they appear bottomless and sad; and he
wants to touch his arm, say he's sorry about his mother,
sorry he's crazy, sorry he lets urine run down his leg
and wears a dress. Instead, he gives him his paper
and leaves. As he raises his bike, he looks out toward
red sky and darkening earth, and they seem poised
like two animals that have always hated each other,
each fiercely wanting to tear out the other's throat:
black dog, red dog— now more despairing, more resolved.

Cemetery Nights

Sweet dreams, sweet memories, sweet taste of earth:
here's how the dead pretend they're still alive —
one drags up a chair, a lamp, unwraps
the newspaper from somebody's garbage,
then sits holding the paper up to his face.
No matter if the lamp is busted and his eyes
have fallen out. Or some of the others
group together in front of the TV, chuckling
and slapping what's left of their knees.
No matter if the screen is dark. Four more
sit at a table with glasses and plates,
lift forks to their mouths and chew. No matter
if their plates are empty and they chew only air.
Two of the dead roll on the ground,
banging and rubbing their bodies together
as if in love or frenzy. No matter if their skin
breaks off, that their genitals are just a memory.

The head cemetery rat calls in all the city rats
who pay him what rats find valuable —
the wing of a pigeon or ear of a dog.
The rats perch on tombstones and the cheap
statues of angels and, oh, they hold their bellies
and laugh, laugh until their guts half break;
while the stars give off the same cold light
that all these dead once planned their lives by,
and in someone's yard a dog barks and barks
just to see if some animal as dumb as he is
will wake from sleep and perhaps bark back.

Under the Green Ceiling

Two men walk along the edge of a country road.
One is joking and talking about girls, describing
the abrupt curve from waist to buttocks and how
it sometimes seems the whole world lives there.
As he talks, he idly tosses rocks into the field
on his right, a field of purple clover spotted
with yellow flowers. The rocks clip the flowers or

green leaves, then disappear into the darkness beneath.
It is a cloudless afternoon in midsummer
and in the distance a green locomotive drags
a string of red box cars toward the horizon.

The other man has hardly eaten for two days.
He is silent and has almost made up his mind
that when they reach the shelter of the woods
half a mile distant, he will rob his companion
who he met only that morning. He has a knife
and intends only to show it, but if the other man
wants to fight, well, so much the worse for him.
And he imagines how the knife will slide up
under the ribs, how he'll drag the body off the road,
then escape over the field to the railway line.
So, while the one man talks about girls,
the other tries to steel himself and feel hatred
for his companion, tries to make him the focus
for all that has gone wrong in his life—
the loss of his job, desertion of his family.

Shortly, the man talking about girls begins
to think of his wife who he hasn't seen
for nearly a month. And partly he talks
to keep from thinking about her and partly
to keep her a teasing question in his mind.
Will she still love him? Has she found someone else?
He thinks of times they made love when he would
sit back on his haunches straddling her ankles
and see how her body was spread out beneath him;
and as he talks the memory of his wife naked
upon the bed fills his mind, while the rocks he
tosses into the field become the fears of betrayal
and desertion that he one by one pushes from him.

Days later the other man is arrested in the city
and as he awaits the slow unfolding of justice
he tells himself how foolish his companion
had been with his constant talk about girls
and how he deserved all that had happened.
He has no sense of himself as a fragment.
He has no sense of how he and his dead companion
made up one man. Add a third and he's still
one man; add a fourth, likewise. But by himself,

he's a fragment of wall, part of a broken pot;
he's like the quivering rodent under its
protection of leaves, terrified when the chance
rock crashes through its green ceiling, victim
of a world that is endlessly random and violent.

MARK DOTY

Gardenias

In Puerto Rico in 1939 my mother has leaned
against a garden gate, her hands in the black
dotted pockets of her dress. In one she holds
a small bitter orange she's picked today.
She is waiting for my father, who's perhaps
stopped again for gardenias at the market; his khaki truck
might be mired in this afternoon's rain.
When he does come home he will carry beside him
his leather case of tools: level and T-square,
compass, a little gray Testament of trigonometric functions,
the rolled prints of a bridge, thunderhead blue.
She would like to ride on the seat
beside him, its cracked upholstery cool against
the straight seams of her hose. She watches the road,
pokes a black, strapped heel at the foot
of a clump of lilies blaring their whiteness
above the fence, taller than anything at home.
Here green is magnified, the blooms more headily fragrant
than everything she's known. She would like him
to regard her as he does the tools,
each set in place in its polished, latched case.
Instead she is part of this garden
and its dense, florid heat, its lack of boundaries,
its insistent green. I will not be conceived for fourteen years,
though perhaps I am in some form imagined,
the outline of "son" like a vacancy
in a picture, some unpainted section a muralist
has saved for last, unable to imagine
how the space remaining might be filled.
She may imagine the nimbus forms of my sister,
my shadow brother who'll die at birth.
(She will tell me where he's buried,
but I cannot remember.) What I can construct
of this scene rises from snapshots and the recollection
of snapshots, a hybrid of memory and invention.
For the moment's dreamed duration,
this is the height of summer, the southern cross
already rising, not yet visible, behind the deep blue rim
of the afternoon's storm. She stands with her back

to the garden of melons and rampant mint,
dizzy as if overpowered by perfume, and leans
into the gatepost with all her weight,
her eyes closed, waiting into evening
for the truck grinding gravel at the foot of the hill.

Late Conversation

From the window 28th is slick with rain,
the corner shop's displays doubled
and rippling. I imagine you,
student of skies, standing
in the hallway. From the landing
you watch blue as I watch myself
— the way one studies a caged fortuneteller
move her wax palm over cards,
pause over a future . . .
Even after it's eluded us for years,
it's motion we look for in the mirror,
the weather beneath the skin.
I'm content to talk to you
through the barely open door.

> *— you there — I here*
> *with just the Door ajar*

Today the slow-witted boy
across the street told me
he hears me typing at night;
how my attic window must look,
evenings, those low barred frames
glowing down through the crabapple . . .
A child who lived across the road
from your high hedges remembered
your lit blind upstairs, how sometimes
she'd glimpse with a shiver
"Miss Emily's shadow." To others,
undaunted by legend — the apparition
of your white dress moving, afternoons,
in the orchard — you lowered cakes

in a basket tied to a length of rope.
You carried them upstairs,
breathless as ever, from the kitchen
where you kneaded flour
bleached as your sleeves

> *that white Sustenance*
> *Despair*

eggs, butter. Daisy,
you called yourself to a man
who'd always elude you.
A more solitary bloom, I'd say;
white delphinium, calla.
You were no eyeful of sun.

> *but bold, like the chestnut burr —*
> *and my eyes, like the sherry*
> *in the glass that the guest leaves*

And the guests left, one after another,
or else you saw them through a slit
in the door. A few occasions, a few
occasional visitors: a friend from school
whom you offered her choice between a glass
of wine and a rose, a faculty wife
invited to the back stairs "alone,
by moonlight," a seamstress
who spent a week sewing
—bridal gowns, shrouds, bakers' uniforms
pure and severe? Your appetite for silence grew,
and the pastry's perfection: silver to stir,
glass to measure — the troche,
the loved, liberal dash,
the glancing rhyme of *pearl*
and *alcohol* exact as cake.
What a lonely circling,
the trade of Circumference!
Once your father rang church bells,
summoned sleepers to view an aurora;
who heard your carillon, all of space
tolling beneath your steady weather?
Shall we discuss a monumental loneliness?
A common attraction to unattainable

objects? till the heart
would choke on it — that bird

small, like the wren

wrapped in such choiring . . .

Split the lark and you'll see the music

or an aversion to silence,
granting us this business:
to encircle. So sing,
shadow in the hall, from behind the door.
I will not open it. No intrusions. Like you,
like stars, I am retreating year by year,
and these rooms seem enough:
midnight to north and south, and the mirror
I study from this bed filled,
in its upper reaches, with
silvered light, vacant.

— bright Absentee

Like a fontanelle, Emily, like a door,
my face, yours, closing.

Latin Dances

My father writes from Arizona:
two weeks rain, the longest in memory,
broke an earthen dam in the foothills.
Four feet above ground, his Airstream
was the center of an island. "There's nothing to do
in the garden or orchard till February."
Always distant, he's used labor
as the heart's disguise. I picture him pacing,
restless as ever, the rows of skinny pecans
and peaches in his new grove. Over days
the surrounding sheet of water perked down,
left the desert an unexpected cinnabar.
"We found a trout in the road," he writes

"We have a tape cassette on Spanish
and I've been spending an hour a day
listening. Also we have an Arthur Murray record
on latin dances. We do a fair samba,
box-step and tango, but flunk out on the mambo.
Could you find good instructions in a bookstore?
Also we need a good cha-cha." Fish in the chaparral
don't surprise more than this sudden flaring
of small festivities; at seventy the man
who held himself so far away
he seemed hazy and remote as foothills
now throws my stepmother across the trailer floor
in a "fair tango." Chairwoman
of the county Bell Collectors' Society,
President of the District Homemakers
— whose headquarters, the letter goes on,
are now under two feet of mud, needlework
and recipe files sodden with rain
and the occasional lost minnow — does she pin
a plastic rose in her chignon
while he whirls her in circles growing
closer and closer to the shining windows,
rocking the foundations of the trailer?
Which stands, in the flood that's decked
the desert in speckled trout, given to my father
and stepmother's arms and boxstepping feet
the rhythmic and reeling pleasure of survivors.

RITA DOVE

The Great Palaces of Versailles

Nothing nastier than a white person!
She mutters as she irons alterations
in the backroom of Charlotte's Dress Shoppe.
The steam rising from a cranberry wool
comes alive with perspiration
and stale Evening of Paris.
Swamp she born from, swamp
she swallow, swamp she got to sink again.

The iron shoves gently
into a gusset, waits until
the puckers bloom away. Beyond
the curtain, the white girls are all
wearing shoulder pads to make their faces
delicate. That laugh would be Autumn,
tossing her hair in imitation of Bacall.

Beulah had read in the library
how French ladies at court would tuck
their fans in a sleeve
and walk in the gardens for air. Swaying
among lilies, lifting shy layers of silk,
they dropped excrement as daintily
as handkerchieves. Against all rules

she had saved the lining from a botched coat
to face last year's gray skirt. She knows
whenever she lifts a knee
she flashes crimson. That seems legitimate;
but in the book she had read
how the *cavaliere* amused themselves
wearing powder and perfume and spraying
yellow borders knee-high on the stucco
of the *Orangerie.*

A hanger clatters
in the front of the shoppe.
Beulah remembers how
even Autumn could lean into a settee

with her ankles crossed, sighing
I need a man who'll protect me
while smoking her cigarette down to the very end.

The Oriental Ballerina

twirls on the tips of a carnation
while the radio scratches out a morning hymn.
Daylight has not ventured as far

as the windows—the walls are still dark,
shadowed with the ghosts
of oversized gardenias. The ballerina

pirouettes to the wheeze of the old
rugged cross, she lifts
her shoulders past the edge

of the jewelbox lid. Two pink slippers
touch the ragged petals, no one
should have feet that small! In China

they do everything upside down:
this ballerina is not rising but drilling
a tunnel straight to America

where the bedrooms of the poor
are papered in vulgar flowers
on a background the color of grease, of

teabags, of cracked imitation walnut veneer.
On the other side of the world
they are shedding robes sprigged with

roses, roses drifting with a hiss
to the floor by the bed
as, here, the sun finally strikes the windows

suddenly opaque,
noncommittal as shields. In this room
is a bed where the sun has gone

walking. Where a straw nods over
the lip of its glass and a hand
reaches for a tissue, crumpling it to a flower.

The ballerina has been drilling all night!
She flouts her skirts like sails
whirling in a disk so bright,

so rapidly she is standing still.
The sun walks the bed to the pillow
and pauses for breath (in the Orient,

breath floats like mist
in the fields), hesitating
at a knotted handkerchief that has slid

on its string and has lodged beneath
the right ear which discerns
the most fragile music

where there is none. The ballerina dances
at the end of a tunnel of light,
she spins on her impossible toes—

the rest is shadow.
The head on the pillow sees nothing
else, though it feels the sun warming

its cheeks. *There is no China;*
no cross, just the papery kiss
of a kleenex above the stink of camphor,

the walls exploding with shabby tutus . . . .

(Georgianna Magdalena Hord, 1896-1979)

Pomade

She sweeps the kitchen floor of the river bed her husband saw fit
to bring home with his catfish, recalling
a flower—very straight,

with a spiked collar arching
under a crown of bright fluffy worms—
she had gathered in armfuls
along a still road in Tennessee. Even then
he was forever off in the woods somewhere in search
of a magic creek.

It was Willemma shushed the pack of dusty children
and took her inside the leaning cabin with its little
window in the door, the cutout magazine cloud taped to the pane
so's I'll always have shade. It was Willemma
showed her how to rub the petals fine
and heat them slow in mineral oil
until the skillet exhaled pears and nuts and rotting fir.

That cabin leaned straight away
to the south, took the very slant of heaven
through the crabgrass and Queen Anne's Lace to
the Colored Cemetery down in Wartrace. Barley soup
yearned toward the bowl's edge, the cornbread
hot from the oven climbed in glory
to the very black lip of the cast iron pan . . .
but Willemma stood straight as the day
she walked five miles to town for Scotch tape
and back again. Gaslight flickered on the cockeyed surface
of rain water in a galvanized pail in the corner
while Thomas pleaded with his sister
to get out while she still was fit.

Beebalm. The fragrance always put her
in mind of Turkish minarets against
a sky wrenched blue,
sweet and merciless. Willemma could wear her gray hair twisted
in two knots at the temples and still smell like travel.
But all those years she didn't budge. She simply turned
one day from slicing a turnip into a pot
when her chest opened and the inrushing air
knocked her down. *Call the reverend, I'm in the floor*
she called out to a passerby.

Beulah gazes through the pale speckled linoleum
to the webbed loam with its salt and worms. She smooths
her hair, then sniffs her palms. On the countertop
the catfish grins
like an oriental gentleman. Nothing ever stops. She feels
herself slowly rolling down the sides of the earth.

Parsley

1. The Cane Fields

There is a parrot imitating spring
in the palace, its feathers parsley green.
Out of the swamp the cane appears

to haunt us, and we cut it down. El General
searches for a word; he is all the world
there is. Like a parrot imitating spring,

we lie down screaming as rain punches through
and we come up green. We cannot speak an R —
out of the swamp, the cane appears

and then the mountain we call in whispers *Katalina.*
The children gnaw their teeth to arrowheads.
There is a parrot imitating spring.

El General has found his word: *perejil.*
Who says it, lives. He laughs, teeth shining
out of the swamp. The cane appears

in our dreams, lashed by wind and streaming.
And we lie down. For every drop of blood
there is a parrot imitating spring.
Out of the swamp the cane appears.

2. The Palace

The word the general's chosen is parsley.
It is fall, when thoughts turn
to love and death; the general thinks
of his mother, how she died in the fall
and he planted her walking cane at the grave
and it flowered, each spring stolidly forming
four-star blossoms. The general

pulls on his boots, he stomps to
her room in the palace, the one without
curtains, the one with a parrot
in a brass ring. As he paces he wonders
Who can I kill today. And for a moment

the little knot of screams
is still. The parrot, who has traveled

all the way from Australia in an ivory
cage, is, coy as a widow, practicing
spring. Ever since the morning
his mother collapsed in the kitchen
while baking skull-shaped candies
for the Day of the Dead, the general
has hated sweets. He orders pastries
brought up for the bird; they arrive

dusted with sugar on a bed of lace.
The knot in his throat starts to twitch;
he sees his boots the first day in battle
splashed with mud and urine
as a soldier falls at his feet amazed—
how stupid he looked!— at the sound
of artillery. *I never thought it would sing*
the soldier said, and died. Now

the general sees the fields of sugar
cane, lashed by rain and streaming.
He sees his mother's smile, the teeth
gnawed to arrowheads. He hears
the Haitians sing without R's
as they swing the great machetes:
Katalina, they sing, *Katalina,*

mi madle, mi amol en muelte. God knows
his mother was no stupid woman; she
could roll an R like a queen. Even
a parrot can roll an R! In the bare room
the bright feathers arch in a parody
of greenery, as the last pale crumbs
disappear under the blackened tongue. Someone

calls out his name in a voice
so like his mother's, a startled tear
splashes the tip of his right boot.
My mother, my love in death.
The general remembers the tiny green sprigs
men of his village wore in their capes

to honor the birth of a son. He will
order many, this time, to be killed

for a single, beautiful word.

NORMAN DUBIE

Dream

It was the Sung Dynasty.
They wore pleated red jackets. Virtually children —
I saw that she had concealed
In her hand a quartz blade and something
Like the dark leaves of hepatica.
There had been torrential rains
For three days. The young couple had walked
All morning to reach a waterfall and its pool;
They now knelt before one another
In an ester mist rising from pitcher plants.

It was spring and the boy's father
Would tomorrow flee with his family inland
To escape invading Tartars.
The spider who lived behind the mirror brought
Good luck, his father had said; it died
The day the rains began. The rains had weakened
Cliffs of decayed limestone that were miles
Above where the couple had knelt
Beside a waterfall to kiss. I said she opened
Her hand, she held a tiny quartz knife
And mossy stonecrop. He nodded to her,
And the distant limestone cliffs with a hillside
Of firs slid down into the river, choking it.

The stonecrop fell to her lap. The river slowed,
And then
                    the waterfall stopped.

New England, Springtime

Emerson thought the bride had one eye
Boring into the dark cellar. You stand
In the dry tub shaking powder over your shoulders.
The neighborhood is busy.

It is like anxiety: housepainters dressed in white,

Two hold a ladder while the third climbs,
Drenched in sunlight they are blind travelers
In a vertical landscape of cut ivory.

On my mother's verandah the addled missionary drinks tea.
She says
That in India if a child is bitten
By a cobra, the villagers leave at the site
A saucer of milk and hibiscus flowers. She says
That in India there is fur on a struck bell
Like fur on a bee. A toad eats a fly.
A toad sleeps. Out in the cistern

There is the great gone stomach of algae.

While the missionary speaks, we drag
An open sheet of newspaper behind us, we rise
And then kneel, with a spade we are burying
The heads of sunfish in the roots of rosebushes.
It will feed the flowers. Emerson thought

His bride
Had her one eye on the cool hams in the cellar.

Later, on a walk, we stand on a train trestle
And hold each other:
We are lost watching the hot track reach back
Under the flowering trees, the track
Has white pollen on it to the vanishing point,
It is unsustainable in the long day,

Cattle cars rattling by at sunset.

Lord Myth

A shadow through the room, a rising
Fan of violets, phenomenon
With scent, weighted with one Victorian

Iris: her long finger passes
Through the velvet drawer
Where the children's salt crystals

Are seeding along soft black threads.

In moving candlelight, still solemn,
She turns to him
And with the effort of a faint pilgrim,

At twilight, opening great barn doors
He opens her robe. She turns, he moans. There's

A rill of breast milk, a sudden sequence
Magically appearing in the deep specimen drawer.

The raven above her, on top of the oak breakfront,
Flies across the room, dragging its long tether
To the arm of the sofa. She is silent.
He whimpers.

The marble andirons cool and snap—
A pulse in the fat red crest between them.
The sun
Has set between the cliffs: inland,
And hounds are chasing something
Big across a wet sloping lawn . . .

The raven's descent to the sofa
Snuffed the storm-candle, carbon
Spackling the high ceiling above her—

A black feather plunges through the spiraling smoke.

The Sketchbook Ashes of Jehoshaphat

—Robert Lowell, 1917-1977

A painter, thin with auburn hair, works before an easel
While looking coldly into a meadow, her free hand
Raises the red gauze of her dress to scratch a pink
Spider bite that isn't there, up where the leg emerges
From the soft shadow of draping buttock muscles—

She'll do the meadow over tomorrow
With even more ghostly silica orbs of dandelions, adding the red
        spouting

Indian-pipe and tacit buttercups;
Water wells up in the painter's mouth and she swallows it . . .

Earlier in the morning, with a similar unconscious gesture,
You skimmed cream off a saucer of bread in milk, the cream
Was like petals of a buttercup
Caught in a wooden spoon, these mustard-colored flowers are shyly

Acquired by the canvas, and with that exact same gesture
Of skimming milk . . .

The painter's black dog jumped up out of the meadow,
His jaws snapping at the air-borne fleets of the wandering dandelion—

Each seed is a fading cipher
Like the invincible, numinous finger of a Balinese dancer . . .

The day of your death, a limousine will enter the cemetery
Beyond the river; there are rolling lawns landscaped with pine
And willow.

And the dead are like the nude with small breasts who poses
For students! She has knowledge of the difficult, imperceptible
Rehearsals of weight that make you steady as statuary; adjustments
Of weight, the penciled-in lines of your legs, in relationship
To your hips, which the students will justify by inches—
                              using the very last crumbs of their erasers . . .

And the large flapping sheets of paper are pinned by their elbows, as
One sketch after another is wasted, torn away and tossed up into the air
Of this cold room with its big sweeping mirrors, the nude with auburn
          hair
Has a white vaccination on her thigh beside a fresh spider bite,
          the instructor
Touches a clear cube of ice to the bite while he stutters, apologizing:
                              she steps back into her black robe, looks
Above herself to the silk hammocks of speckled brown spiders; what
          she observes
Is the first principle of weight in suspension
                              which separates the heavy cream while lifting
It to the surface, then skimming
The meadow like a breeze that carries you and the dandelion seeds into
The oblivion of the next season, *where limp*

Long greens of dandelion boil through a steamy, summer evening . . .

Einstein's Exile in an Old Dutch Winter

My theory withstood the light of the Hyades

While it passed our darkened sun. The eclipse
Was captured in Brazil and West Africa.
Here, at night, over the fields
The straight edge and compass become the severe poplar
And snowy tar-tipped spruce of Holland.
At this hour, I miss Berlin!
Descartes, too, once sat here washing oysters in milk,
The oysters of Leyden,
Laying them out over a bowl of snow,
Sprinkling pepper
Into the milk in its deep saucer,

A young mathematician
At the interior
Of a silver and gold mirror filled
With a watercolorist's impression
Of smokefall in winter.

There exists an imaginary plane, made
Increasingly solid with distance,
Like the weathered mechanical wings

Of a windmill, four pine blades
Becoming eight, becoming a bald porcelain face
In the amethyst shade
Of a cloudbank passing between sun
And the broken reeds of the lake.

Outside Leyden,
The wind is the lamp of projection!

Descartes, wintering with the armies
Of the Duke of Savoy, sat in his large furs
On the blazing bank of the Danube
Lecturing young bowmen, crying
That all of the pleasure of mathematics
Was in the one smooth pebble of *the calculus*.

There exists a flower, in Holland,
Which is not a member

Of the tremendous family of roses—
A flower which *is,* regardless,
The rose of all roses . . .

When the arrow passed through the fist
Of Cardinal Richelieu, he was dressed
In the red glove of his office; we would have said
His wound was discrete
And continuous
Like the brown burn of a canker on a rosebud.
My son has suffered a nervous breakdown!

He and I watched, in Venice, beside the old *Coq d'Or*—
In the vast relief of an exotic poverty, a barge's
Cargo of poppies was sucked down
Making sentient a geometry of water. I dreamt
Later of this vortex, in Pasadena,
In a closing circle which grew smaller,

More concentrated, until all the flowers
Fell through the bottom of their concentration
Opening into a siamese twin: two cones, black
Shifted to red, of infinite dimension—

If I enter myself with all the dignity
Of nature I will never come out again.

Descartes, in the windmill, grabbed linen
And a tarnished mothy spoon,
Sipped his peppered milk, studying himself
In the deep running mirror . . .

First light will enter his room like the powder-blue
Lepidoptera of Spring, come
To visit the mathematician
Who'll, now, sleep until evening dreaming
The triadic stream where
The opened breastbone of a swan
With its **pier-and-lintel** bones is like the window
Which contains the wintry reflection
Of the setting sun:

A waking Descartes, his red beard and smock,
Gazes out of the inferno of his window—

He is thinking of the transformative nature
Of light and symbol, he proposes

That the wasp nest up in the eaves on the windmill
Resembles the dead blossom on the lilac hedge.
Descartes is waking, he remembers the woes,
And the downcast eyes
Of his dear friend, the exiled Princess Elizabeth—
Again, in flight from emotion, he proposes . . .

The rose of all roses!

RUSSELL EDSON

The Sculptor

for Donald Hall

There is a time when the dead, not yet fully fallen from
the bone, are fleshed with a kind of soapy clay. One waits
for this certain ripening. It depends upon the soil, the
time of year . . .
Best is the digging in the early dawn, the ground wet
with dew, the air with mist. A few crows cry then, and the
screech of sea gulls. They sense the unearthing. What is work
to me is food to them . . .

Unearthed, I cut the rotten clothes from the flesh, careful
of the soft tissues, the female breasts, the male genitals,
that they are not detached nor deformed.
If it's a fat person I dig out handfuls of belly. I finish
it by smoothing it, and finally poking a new navel with my
finger.
I pinch and squeeze as mood prescribes. If driven I can
turn a man into a woman, a woman into a man!

Once I changed a man into a child by removing certain
bones. The result was less than life, yet more than death;
it was art . . .

The Love Affair

One day a man fell in love with himself, and was unable
to think of anything else but himself.
Of course he was flattered, no one had ever shown him
that much interest . . .

He wanted to know all about himself, his hobbies, his
likings in music and sports.
He was jealous he had not known himself as a child. He
wanted to know what kind of a boy he had been . . .

When asked if he thought it would lead to marriage, he said that that was his fondest wish, that he longed to have babies with himself . . .

The Rat's Legs

I met a rat under a bridge. And we sat there in the mud discussing the rat's loveliness.

I asked, what is it about you that has caused men to write odes?

My legs, said the rat, for it has always been that men have liked to run their hands up my legs to my secret parts; it's nature . . .

Good Son Jim

Poor people who do not have the price of a fence ask son Jim to be a fence for the chicken yard, that is, until their ship comes in; which no one believes because they live inland.

But what's the good of a fence around a chicken yard where there ain't no chickens?

Did you eat them chickens, Jim?

No, we ain't never had no chickens.

Then what are you doing fencing what we ain't got?

I don't know, I forgot . . .

Maybe you better be a chicken. But don't wander away, because we ain't got a fence to keep that stupid bird from wandering into the neighbor's yard and getting itself killed for Sunday dinner, said his father.

Heck, I'll just peck around the house; lots of tasty worms under the porch, said son Jim . . .

The Philosophers

I think, therefore I am, said a man whose mother quickly

hit him on the head, saying, I hit my son on his head, therefore
I am.

No, no, you've got it all wrong, cried the man.

So she hit him on the head again and cried, therefore I
am.

You're not, not that way; you're supposed to think, not
hit, cried the man.

. . . I think, therefore I am, said the man.

I hit, therefore we both are, the hitter and the one who gets
hit, said the man's mother.

But at this point the man had ceased to be; unconscious,
he could not think. But his mother could. So she thought, I
am, and so is my unconscious son, even if he doesn't know
it . . .

On The Eating Of Mice

A woman prepared a mouse for her husband's dinner, roasting
it with a blueberry in its mouth.

At table he uses a dentist's pick and a surgeon's scalpel,
bending over the tiny roastling with a jeweler's loupe . . .

Twenty years of this: curried mouse; garlic and butter
mouse; mouse sauteed in its own fur; Salisbury mouse; mouse-
in-the-trap, baked in the very trap that killed it; mouse
tartare; mouse poached in menstrual blood at the full of
the moon . . .

Twenty years of this, eating their way through the mice . . .
And yet, not to forget, each night one less vermin in the world . . .

The Thickening

A cook sleeps. On her lap a bowl of thickened material;
a wooden spoon standing in it.

As she sleeps she absentmindedly pokes her head with the
wooden spoon, and has flecks of the thickened material dotted

in her hair. She sighs and snores . . .

Her mistress says, cook, you're not doing work.
The cook nods and yawns.
But, cook, you have thickened material dotted in your
hair.
Oh, ma'am, is you drowsy, too?
No, no, I'm too excited—it's stuff from your mixing bowl.
What is that stuff that's so wonderously thick in your mixing
bowl?
I don't know, ma'am, some kind of stuff what's got thick . . .
It certainly looks thick, and you've got it dotted in
your hair . . . Will you dot it in my hair?—I command it!

Then the master comes to see the thickened material, and
wants it dotted in his hair; wonders what it would feel like
dotted in groin hair . . .
No no, cries the mistress, you cannot show cook your penis.
Of course not, cries the master, what do you take me for,
someone who shows his armpits to cooking women? Frankly,
my secondary hair is none of her business . . . Mind your own
business, cook, or I shall really have to take measures!
But the cook has fallen back asleep, and the thickened
material has grown even thicker, as has the dark of the
deepening dusk . . .

The Tunnel

I went tunneling into the earth . . .
My wife and I, going through an inventory of reasons,
found nothing sufficient to the labor.
Still, she allowed, as I, that a direction once started,
as if desire, and the desire to be desired, were mutually
igniting, drew the traveler to its end without explainable
reason . . .
Yet, does not the southern direction in extreme horizon
look to the north, even as that of the north, finding the
apex of its final arc, nods wearily south . . . ?
So I went tunneling into the earth, through darkness that
penetration only makes darker, faithful to the idea of light,
said always to be at the end of tunnels; perhaps not yet lit,

but in the universe moving in rendezvous, thus to shimmer
under the last shovelful of earth . . .

CAROLYN FORCHE

Endurance

In Belgrade, the windows of the tourist
hotel opened over seven storeys of lilacs,
rain clearing sidewalk tables of linens
and liquor, the silk flags of the non-
aligned nations like colorful underthings
pinned to the wind. Tito was living.
I bought English, was mistaken for Czech,
walked to the fountains, the market
of garlic and tents, where I saw
my dead Anna again and again,
hard yellow beans in her lap,
her babushka of white summer cotton,
her eyes the hard pits of her past.
She was gossiping among her friends,
saying the rosary or trying to sell me
something. Anna. Peeling her hands
with a paring knife, saying *in your country
you have nothing.* Each word was the husk
of a vegetable tossed to the street
or a mountain rounded by trains
with cargoes of sheep-dung and grief.
I searched in Belgrade for some holy
face painted *without hands* as when
an ikon painter goes to sleep and awakens
with an image come from the dead.
On each corner Anna dropped
her work in her lap and looked up.
I am a childless poet, I said.
I have not painted an egg, made prayers
or finished my Easter duty in years.
I left Belgrade for Frankfurt last
summer, Frankfurt for New York,
New York for the Roanoke valley
where mountains hold the breath
of the dead between them and lift
from each morning a fresh bandage of mist.
New York, Roanoke, the valley—
to this Cape where in the dunes
the wind takes a body of its own

and a fir tree comes to the window
at night, tapping on the glass like
a woman who has lived too much.
Piskata, hold your tongue, she says.
I am trying to tell you something.

Photograph Of My Room

after Walker Evans

Thirty years from now, you might
hold this room in your hands.
So that you will not wonder:
the china cups are from Serbia
where a man filled them with plum
wine and one night talked
of his life with the partisans
and in prison, his life
as a poet, Slavko, his life
as if it could not have been otherwise.
The quilt was Anna's.
There are swatches taken
from her own clothes, curtains
that hung in a kitchen in Prague,
aprons she never took off
in all her years in America.
Since her death, the stitches,
one scrap to another
have come loose.

The bundle of army letters
were sent from Southeast Asia
during '67, kept near a bottle
of vodka drained by a woman
in that same year who wanted
only to sleep; the fatigues
were his, it is she
whom I now least resemble.

In the trunk, the white eyelet
and cheap lace of underthings,
a coat that may have belonged

to a woman who approached me
on a street in April
saying, as it was spring,
would I spare her a smoke?

Under the bed, a pouch of money:
pesetas, dinar, francs, the coins
of no value in any other place.
In the notebooks you will find
those places: the damp inner thighs,
the delicate rash left by kisses,
fingers on the tongue, a swallow
of brandy, a fire.
It is all there, the lies
told to myself because of Paris,
the stories I believed in Salvador
and Granada, and every so often
simply the words calling back
a basket of lemons and eggs,
a bowl of olives.

Wrapped in a tissue you will find
a bullet, as if from the rifle
on the wall, spooned from the flesh
of a friend who must have thought
it was worth something.
Latched to its shell, a lattice
of muscle. *One regime
is like another,* said the face
of a doctor who slid
the bullet from the flat
of his blade to my hands, saying
this one won't live to the morning.

In the black cheese crock
are the ashes, flecked
with white slivers of bone,
that should have been scattered
years ago, but the thing
did not seem possible.
The rest of the room remains
a mystery, as it was
in the shutter of memory.
That was 1936, when it belonged

to someone already dead, someone
who has no belongings.

As Children Together

Under the sloped snow
pinned all winter with Christmas
lights, we waited for your father
to whittle his soap cakes
away, finish the whisky,
your mother to carry her coffee
from room to room closing lights
cubed in the snow at our feet.
Holding each other's
coat sleeves we slid down
the roads in our tight
black dresses, past
crystal swamps and the death
face of each dark house,
over the golden ice
of tobacco spit, the blue
quiet of ponds, with towns
glowing behind the blind
white hills and a scant
snow ticking in the stars.
You hummed *blanche comme*
la neige and spoke of Montreal
where a *quebeçoise* could sing,
take any man's face
to her unfastened blouse
and wake to wine
on the bedside table.
I always believed this,
Victoria, that there might
be a way to get out.

You were ashamed of that house,
its round tins of surplus flour,
chipped beef and white beans,
relief checks and winter trips
that always ended in deer

tied stiff to the car rack,
the accordion breath of your uncles
down from the north, and what
you called the stupidity
of the Michigan French.

Your mirror grew ringed
with photos of servicemen
who had taken your breasts
in their hands, the buttons
of your blouses in their teeth,
who had given you the silk
tassles of their graduation,
jackets embroidered with dragons
from the Far East. You kept
the corks that had fired
from bottles over their beds,
their letters with each city
blackened, envelopes of hair
from their shaved heads.

I am going to have it, you said.
Flowers wrapped in paper from carts
in Montreal, a plane lifting out
of Detroit, a satin bed, a table
cluttered with bottles of scent.
So standing in a platter of ice
outside a Catholic dance hall
you took their collars
in your fine chilled hands
and lied your age to adulthood.

I did not then have breasts of my own,
nor any letters from bootcamp
and when one of the men who had
gathered around you took my mouth
to his own there was nothing
other than the dance hall music
rising to the arms of iced trees.

I don't know where you are now, Victoria.
They say you have children, a trailer
in the snow near our town,
and the husband you found as a girl

returned from the Far East broken
cursing holy blood at the table
where nightly a pile of white shavings
is paid from the edge of his knife.

If you read this poem, write to me.
I have been to Paris since we parted.

Selective Service

We rise from the snow where we've
lain on our backs and flown like children,
from the imprint of perfect wings and cold gowns,
and we stagger together wine-breathed into town
where our people are building
their armies again, short years after
body bags, after burnings. There is a man
I've come to love after thirty, and we have
our rituals of coffee, of airports, regret.
After love we smoke and sleep
with magazines, two shot glasses,
and the black and white collapse of hours.
In what time do we live that it is too late
to have children? In what place
that we consider the various ways to leave?
There is no list long enough
for a selective service card shriveling
under a match, the prison that comes of it,
a flag in the wind eaten from its pole
and boys sent back in trash bags.
We'll tell you. You were at that time
learning fractions. We'll tell you
about fractions. Half of us are dead or quiet
or lost. Let them speak for themselves.
We lie down in the fields and leave behind
the corpses of angels.

ALICE FULTON

My Second Marriage To My First Husband

We married for acceptance: to stall the nagging
married friends who wanted us
to do it there and then —
with them. In the downy wedlocked bed
we ask, "Is there life after
one-day honeymoons to Kissamee Springs?
Was I all right?" The answers, woefully,
are no and no. And yes,

we lollygagged down the aisle, vowed
to forsake dallying, shilly-shallying and cleave
only onto one another, to forever romp
in the swampy rumpus
room of our eccentricities: That sanctum
sanctorum where I sport
bedsocks and never rise
till noon. What did we know?
Did you know my love for animals
has always been acute? Perhaps in time
I will become a shepherdess, a jockey.

At the reception every table was adorned
with toilet tissue twisted
into swans. When I unraveled one
to find the charm, the management
was shocked. Dismembering swans!
No bride had ever . . . And the prize, a little gizzard
of a ring, was disappointing. Oh Person,

was it worth it? Of course,
we fit at dinner parties. But as one part warbles
to be normal, another puts a spin on things.
I see you striving to frolic
in your steel-mesh tweeds as I model
chiffon voluptuaries the color of exhaust.

In the wedding album we end or commence
our revels. There we are! doing the cha-cha-cha
to the boom-chick-chick band

in our dyed-to-match togs.
We're getting fat
on the eats, foaming
white crumbs, "Honey" and "Dear"
cumbersome as live doves
on our tongues.

Bring squeezeboxes, gardenias,
a hybrid of the two. Congratulate us,
chums. Smile and freeze: Our dimples stiffen
to resolute framed stares. How adult
we look! Our eyes burn
stoplights in the Instamatic squares.

News Of The Occluded Cyclone

Night usually computes itself in stars,
cryptic as a punchcard, but now the sky is blurry
as a turp-soaked rag.

At the siren we flip through frequencies
for the latest in tornado
warnings. We lose power and light

candles, their mild spices
comforting as cookies baking.
Thunder comes, galumphing its important

gavels. I wish it could call the storm
to an order arbitrary and dependable
as the ABC's. Instead, blackboards

embellished with unsteady
y's are where
the windows used to be.

The sky is strung with lightning
like the lines of fighting
kites or tined with royal

racks that leave afterimages

of antlers on our sight.
We cling to each other

in the dead center of the living
room, as if the least space we can displace
is the one zoned for oasis, sensing as much

as seeing the dowsing
sticks above us. And it storms
till the candles form bright

putties in glass saucers, till the messy,
soft-edged dawn comes on
in rebuttal, and a voice disembodied

as God's proclaims the warning
over. There's a welcome
sense of excavation in the full-

frontal rush of morning, the horizon's
hierarchy under calm free-
falls of sun: it's deliverance

at a designated hour, this propriety
of day, this reliable frame
that lets color be

color and light, light.

Terrestrial Magnetism

Stars threatened you into feeling
negligible while susceptible
to connections, I saw many more
than two dippers riddling the sky.

Nights you'd leap down
from stellar atmospheres, wrap yourself
around me like a sari
as the lead guitar took his
solo. For the first time, I felt

singled out. I know you'd agree

that those letters written from faraway
gigs had the suspect sweetness of breath
mints, leaving me to guess what sour
moonlighting they covered,
and that losing you I lost

a language I couldn't stand
to have back, with words for need
obsessive as daylight,
spectra glowing from all directions.

Together would we have fallen
into offices and sweated
under cubed light, would we
at day's end have gotten into better cars
than those we own and found without meaning
to we'd driven ourselves home?

I've spent years since
tracing the vapor formed between storm
and inner windows, sweeping the sky
for a star undigested by the dark, planet
perturbations, under the left breast, a heart.

Traveling Light

Every restaurant boarded up in softwood,
bars strung with tipsy blinkers, smudgefires
against the dusk-
like day: who could have imagined the light
toppling down, song you can see
over all? Or this salt breeze,
vital and teary as a drunken wake.
The kite store's ringed with stunted Christmas
trees like pathetic closed umbrellas.
This is the year we'll trim with shells.
The man who sells them tells us tales
of smuggling, of price wars over apple coral,
fluted clams. His hair branches and his skin

hardens as he speaks: part baobab, part pirate.
His shells — little bandana prints, green turbans —
are lovely, "droll" might be the word,
but tropical, not from Cape Cod.

It was ten years ago this season
my father died, leaving me odd
wisdoms concerning clip joints,
gypsies, toe-room, elocution,
and traveling light. I was 20,
up to my elbows in developer,
acid, fixative: a microfilm
technician with few discernible skills.
What would he have made of this off-season
resort? Though he never lived to see it
I can hear him say, "Don't worry,
Al, if the poetry don't go
I'll buy you your own beauty shop."
Yes, with sickly pink
smells, well-thumbed back issues
of *Hairdo,* and a 3-D religious picture
that flickered between Mary and Jesus,
in tricky light revealing
the Blessed Mother with a beard.
He liked scenery, Kay Frances
movies, and the fights. I guess,
like you, I never really knew him.

On the last visit I ambled to his room
with my dignified mini hiked up
in the back, flashing
unintentional ass to the joyous
orderlies. Befuddled by dripping
liquids, screens yielding twitchy lights
he said, "What are we doing
in this carwash?" Then he thought he remembered
a long ago close call, when a canvas-topped jalopy
broke down in a Saratoga storm.
His hands froze first, then his flesh turned
dense as a snowman's. Only his brain kept
rolling. He knew he had no money.
The troopers took him to a sumptuous
hospital, and his eyes grew wondrous
as he raved and praised

the decor, the meals. "You can't imagine!
When I went to pay, the nurses
said, 'Mr. Fulton, it was a pleasure
to take care of you. There will be no charge.' "
There will be no charge

for the light or the sea's
skillful flippancies with it,
for the moon softening
the scene with its own
peculiar politeness.
After years of plea-bargaining
with a snooty muse, I've landed
here, where there's nothing I dread
doing. Gifts fall into my hands
from unindicted co-conspirators; suddenly
all three Fates shine
their everloving light on me.
I'm free to watch the dunes
take on the chill
color of shells, the sea
threaten and beckon like a roof's edge,
an absentminded thing.
The way the tide rips itself
out sideways, thoughtless as a torn seam.

And people find things here I've heard:
Portuguese dolls, once encased in airy
pink and green crinolines swish in,
their mouths still
red and pouting. Here on the fragile tip
of this peninsula anything could
return. I'm half-prepared
for hostile mermaids, pilot whales, stranded
miscreants clad in moss and furs.
I'm half-prepared to see my father,
to whom the world gave nothing
without struggle, rise up beaming
anyway upon it, as if he never meant
to let it go. Saltboxes appear and disappear

in the slurry fog. Gulls open
against the sky like books
with blank, beautifully demanding pages,

and behind me the stolid ocean
slams itself on earth
as if to say *that's final*
though it isn't. Behind me the ocean
stares down the clouds, the little last remaining
light, as if to remind me of the nothing
I will always have
to fall back on.

TESS GALLAGHER

Gray Eyes

When she speaks it is like coming onto a grave
    at the edge of a woods, softly, so we
        do not enter or wholly
    turn away. Such speech
  is the breath a brush makes through hair,
      opening into time
    after the stroke.

      A tree is bending
but the bird doesn't land.

      One star,
earthbound, reports a multitude of unyielding
    others. It
      cannot help its   falling   falling
into the dull brown earth of someone's back yard,
    where, in daylight, a hand reaches
in front of the mower and tosses it, dead stone,
      aside. We who saw it fall

are still crashing with light into the housetops,
    tracing in the mind that missing
      trajectory, rainbow of darkness
    where we were—children
murmuring—"There, over there!"—while the houses
    slept and slept on.

Years later she is still nesting on the light
    of that plundered moment, her black hair
      frozen to her head with yearning,
    saying, "Father, I am a colder green
      where the mower cut a swath
        and I lay down
    and the birds that have no use for song
      passed over me
    like a shovel-fall."

She closed her eyes. It was early morning. Daybreak.
    Some bees

were dying on my wing—humming
so you could hardly hear.

Black Silk

She was cleaning—there is always
that to do—when she found,
at the top of the closet, his old
silk vest. She called me
to look at it, unrolling it carefully
like something live
might fall out. Then we spread it
on the kitchen table and smoothed
the wrinkles down, making our hands
heavy until its shape against Formica
came back and the little tips
that would have pointed to his pockets
lay flat. The buttons were all there.
I held my arms out and she
looped the wide armholes over
them. "That's one thing I never
wanted to be," she said, "a man."
I went into the bathroom to see
how I looked in the sheen and
sadness. Wind chimes
off-key in the alcove. Then her
crying so I stood back in the sink-light
where the porcelain had been staring. Time
to go to her, I thought, with that
other mind, and stood still.

Candle, Lamp & Firefly

How can I think what thoughts
to have of you with a mind so unready?
What I remember most: you did not want
to go. Then choice slipped from you
like snow from the mountain, so death

could graze you over with the sweet
muzzles of the deer moving up from
the valleys, pausing to stare
down and back toward the town. But you
did not gaze back. Like a cut rose
on the fifth day, you bowed
into yourself and we watched the shell-
shaped petals drop in clumps, then,
like wine, deepen into the white cloth.

What have you written here on my sleep
with flesh so sure I have no choice
but to stare back when your face and
gestures follow me into daylight?
Your arms, too weak at your death
for embracing, closed around me and held,
and such a tenderness was mixed there
with longing that I asked, "Is it good
where you are?"

We echoed a long time in the kiss
that was drinking me—*daughter, daughter,*
daughter—until I was gone as when a sun
drops over the rim of an ocean, gone
yet still there. Then the dampness,
the chill of your body pulled from me
into that space the condemned
look back to after parting.

Between sleep and death
I carry no proof that we met, no proof
but to tell what even I must call dream
and gently dismiss. So does
a bird dismiss one tree for another
and carries each time the flight between
like a thing never done.
And what is proof then, but some trance
to kill the birds? And what are dreams
when the eyes open on similar worlds
and you are dead in my living?

Death Of The Horses By Fire

We have seen a house in the sleeping town
stand still for a fire and the others,
where their windows knew it,
clothed in the remnants of a dream
happening outside them. We have seen
the one door aflame in the many windows,
the steady procession of the houses
trembling in heat-light, their well-tended
yards, the trellis of cabbage roses scrawled
against the porch—flickering white, whiter
where a darkness breathes back.

How many nights the houses have burned through
to morning. We stood in our blankets
like a tribe made to witness
what a god could do.

We saw the house built again in daylight
and children coming from it
as what a house restores to itself in rooms
so bright they do not forget, even
when the father, when the mother
dies. "Kitchen of your childhoods!" we shout
at the old men alive on the benches
in the square. Their good, black eyes
glitter back at us, a star-fall
of homecomings.

Only when the horses began to burn
in the funnel of light hurrying in one place
on the prairie did we begin to suspect
our houses, to doubt at our meals
and pleasures. We gathered on the ridge
above the horses, above the blue smoke
of the grasses, and they whirled in the close
circle of the death that came to them, rippling in
like a deep moon to its water. With
the hills in all directions
they stood in the last of their skies
and called to each other to save them.

The Hug

A woman is reading a poem on the street
and another woman stops to listen. We stop too,
with our arms around each other. The poem
is being read and listened to out here
in the open. Behind us
no one is entering or leaving the houses.

Suddenly a hug comes over me and I'm
giving it to you, like a variable star shooting light
off to make itself comfortable, then
subsiding. I finish but keep on holding
you. A man walks up to us and we know he hasn't
come out of nowhere, but if he could, he
would have. He looks homeless because of how
he needs. "Can I have one of those?" he asks you,
and I feel you nod. I'm surprised,
surprised you don't tell him how
it is—that I'm yours, only
yours, etc., exclusive as a nose to
its face. Love—that's what we're talking about, love
that nabs you with "for me
only" and holds on.

So I walk over to him and put my
arms around him and try to
hug him like I mean it. He's got an overcoat on
so thick I can't feel
him past it. I'm starting the hug
and thinking, "How big a hug is this supposed to be?
How long shall I hold this hug?" Already
we could be eternal, his arms falling over my
shoulders, my hands not
meeting behind his back, he is so big!

I put my head into his chest and snuggle
in. I lean into him. I lean my blood and my wishes
into him. He stands for it. This is his
and he's starting to give it back so well I know he's
getting it. This hug. So truly, so tenderly
we stop having arms and I don't know if
my lover has walked away or what, or
if the woman is still reading the poem, or the houses—
what about them?—the houses.

Clearly, a little permission is a dangerous thing.
But when you hug someone you want it
to be a masterpiece of connection, the way the button
on his coat will leave the imprint of
a planet in my cheek
when I walk away. When I try to find some place
to go back to.

Bird—Window—Flying

If we had been given names to love
each other by, I would take this one
from you, bird flying all day
in my woodhouse. The door
is open as when you came
to it, into it, as space between branches, "Never
trust doors," you tell the window,
the small of your body flung
against the white bay.

At dusk when I walked in
with my armload of green alder
I could see the memory of light
shining water through your wings. You
were gray with it. The window
had aged you with promises.
I thought the boats, the gulls
should have stilled you
by now. When I cupped

my hands in their shadows, warm
over the heartwings, I saw the skin
of light between my fingers
haloed and glowing. Three steps I
took with you, for
you, three light years traveling
to your sky, beak
and claw of you, the soft burr of flight
at my fingerbones.

If I take a lover for every tree, I

will not have again such an opening as
when you flew from me.
I have gone in to build my fire. All
the walls, all the
wings of my house are burning. The flames
of me, the long hair
unbraiding.

ALBERT GOLDBARTH

A Window Seat

*. . . how carefully the Renaissance masters designed up to the limit of the frame,
the rectangle being accepted and emphasized in the design. The Baroque painters,
on the other hand, endeavor to suggest or even to force upon the spectator, the
supposed continuation of the imagined picture space beyond and behind the
frame . . . "TAKE ME!"*

. . . At which time I close my Roger Fry, successfully
seduced by an in-flight movie. I know it, or
of it, from reviews: this actress flung in a sexy x
on the bed, her peignoir making smoky open wings,
died 5 days into production. Everybody talking to her
talks to empty air she's later spliced, lithe, lusciously,
into. When an actor lusts for her, she's someone out
of the world of this room he's in, and out of the room

of this world now completely. Below, while I fly
to a string of small-town readings, my wife is marking
her sister's early death's first anniversary, at the side
of the freshly flowered-over grave in Waco. I know she'll be
speaking, softly and with an intimate, strict attention,
as if Emily were just beyond some pane of light too
blinding for sight's going through, though with the easy motes of
this life's constant motion in it, and permeable. Words

of simple catching-up—this has happened, that—to someone so
far into the shine of mica, the scales of weathering, time
outdistances news. I eke my slide-up panel open and
"below" becomes the lovely abstract cataracting greens
and sorghum-reds of cultivation—now Pollack, now
Mondrian—or the sharp, if doll-sized, blueprints of communities
long-buried but clear from the air as rows of post-pits,
darker ditch-grass, chalky discs. The Nazca

lines in south Peru cross miles of dun-tone desert, make enormous
geometry-winged birds, fish, even a monkey, for the high eye
of a jetliner or a god, for that eye only (Pan-American highway
workers bulldozed smackdab through those shapes and
never saw them). A hummingbird 100 yards requires that
distance the way this actress—also slight in "real life" but

larger as an image, peignoir tremblingly, exotically (almost
congruently with the bird) spread wide—requires

time outside her time, before we see her acting
interacting with the living cast. So Morgan will set her few
considered flowers down, and simply say, "I've missed
you, Em." She'll weep a little. Of course—her sister a figure
that's reached the vanishing point. But that's the point
exactly where matters of faith take over from matters of paint
—and Morgan's eyes will blur, and Emily speak back,
genuine, tender. So it is that there's a universe outside this

poem this poem's aware of, flush against it, crowded and
extraneous: Squid are folded over a clothesline. Cops
are staking out Le Go Go where the mastectomized dancer is
storing the coke in her foam breast. Someone's dissertation is so
many aphids pushing up so much nutritional goop, per day, per colony.
From a back pew, someone sees the plaster Christ let real blood
and writhe. The perfect planetarium is the night sky
under a goose's wing: small dependable domed dark. All

that, and more, while in this poem (and out of it) I
slide my groundview closed; return half-dozing to the gravity
of movieland body for body; fidget; land—it's no
flat study now but people, wheels, meals, deals, dimensional and
rubbing at the skin. In my motel tonight, from
this height, open beardtrim scissors leave a pterodactyl
fossil in damp and rust on the sink. Some light has come
from the moon to fall on the Roger Fry. The book,

the window, have me thinking Vermeer: inevitably
his picture is a room, the room is filled with the spilling
of thick Delft light through a window, giving pewter that special
white richness of milk, and cloth the depth of landscape,
light from somewhere unknowable glowing off the simple
frames the maps are in, the mirrors, the family portraits.
Soon I'll phone and Morgan say Emily said
she's ok, disembodied now (to us), at home on her own plane.

The Numbering at Bethlehem

He was, he tells his grandson, a grandson
himself. He'd got a red-and-white bone fish hook with his
name on it, inscribed by a peddler who knew such things, and he was
fishing "chust like ve are now, troo a liddle hole in d'ice" but
then a catfish big about as a soldier's boot
with whiskers like broomstraws, gulped bait
hook and all and waggled clean away. Another time . . . The
boy's not listening. He's lost inside
the coalseam streaks in the living fillet of a half-gutted perch
in their basket. It's cold, tomorrow may be colder. His breath
is small and white and leaves his body not unlike, he
thinks, evisceration. His body is small. His whole vignette
—the creel mother weaved, the two poles propped and crossed
like sloppy heraldry, his grandfather muttering
history and dribble—is small in Breughel's
composition of rhythmic smallnesses.
                                        If the title is Biblical,
still this is a 16th-century Flemish village and all
its huff and clutter is true to the shape of that
specific time and place.
An innkeep's offals-boy is sawing his knife
through the deepest hoses and breads
in the throat of a hog; it's stunned and even
so, he needs to keep one knee in its ribs; obligingly,
a serving-girl is here with her long-handled pan for the branch
of blood jutting out. They hear the carpenters Breughel's
lifted dimly into farther ground (this winter
air will carry sound with the thwang of a metal bannister).
There are four, applied to a framework. It's a function
of how far they are that stylization makes them smooth black
silhouettes of tools themselves: an adze, a hatchet.
One arm of the Y-support is sleeved in snow so rich it
seems less fallen from the sky, and more to have risen
like cream from the common white on the ground. Deliverers
drag an ice-sledge over the lake. Two girls, with sticks, propel
themselves on dinner platters. Others have skates. Three chickens
pecking snow could be a homily on faith in a providence
greater than winter's thinness, if anyone noticed.
Nobody notices.
                Nearly 200 figures, and nobody sees
what we see, in administrative
overview: receding wheels

lead the eye discursively into perspective: cart ones,
wagon ones, loose ones left to whiten in ice like ghosts
of wheels, wheels as tall as a man and dwindling
with the men as plane gives way to plane, down distance.
So they make a wreath,
three barrel mouths, and a scatter of baskets
units of a pattern. Nobody notices,
either, the woman on a donkey—just a bent head really,
tented in a voluminous cloak of blue. Why
should they? Everybody has his own white
bellows of breath to contend with.
                                        "Und voomen—
you tink your Grandpapa is so old alvays he nefer
made sniksnak vit voomen?" By the shine in his eye
you'd think that here was salty revelation to make
the white breath of its telling shine, like a new-used ivory
prosthetic in a seraglio. Maybe it does. But the boy's still
worlds away, is living now in a contemplation of bubbles
on the underside of the thinnest ice, like winter grapes
in a rich bunch. In a way it's a pity. His grandfather's
breaths, like anyone's, are nothing so much as a true cast
of the insides of a man; to the extent that this implies the oldest
wholeness of the family is on display, it is. It
disappears, though, unattended, in the air. "Yah, two
goot vives here, hah, but den I go fight, you know?, for kings
in lants so far avay. Vhen I return . . ."
And soforth. We don't see it either, really. This man
and his grandson are an inch or two outside
the frame of the painting, and whatever half-mile or so of
pewter-, delft-, and lime-green lake-ice that this means.
We see, immediately
                        and instead, what almost everybody
sees and clusters hotly about, if not
by curiosity then by proclamation: census-takers,
one in a nearly-regal coat of fox and weasel, number
this village (the reference is to Bethlehem,
of course, and so their particular,
secret interest is in Jews, just,
or about to be, born). This off-center
hub of the general turning of action is in the near left corner,
saying its early New Testament story in loud
concentration of earth-reds. Wasn't that the text
the priest read every year around Christmas?: Herod,
Judas, Calvary, redemption . . . What was it he said . . . Perhaps

the few, far, detail-less churchgoers
will know in a moment, stamping loaves of old snow
off their leggings, then assembling themselves
like sacks of goods on the long hard pews. To them,
we assume, this isn't the horizontal level of least detail
at all: somebody's stubble picks up purpled light
through the stained glass wound of a martyr, so looks
like velvet nap; a baby's drool, by virtue
of that same slash and its pouring, is a mother's loveliest
jewel as it rests in a clutter of cheap brass trinkets;
someone's hoe left in the anteroom, someone's stoatskin mittens . . .
So another time, with its network of information, is in
the lineaments of this ordinary day in 1566, a few nights'
ride from Brussels. And if that's distractive
referential layering
for us, no wonder no one plaiting osiers for the seat
of a much rewickered backyard bench, or piling handwidth brick
on brick in a hod, or shooing a dramatic captain of rats
from its exploratory swagger through the bagged beets,
sees
        the man who leads the donkey from another story
into this one, is hungry
and his woman in the blue cloak seems to be holding herself
as if she, too, were a tent,
a tent of flesh, and an ember inside is keeping her
warm despite the weather. For that matter,
no one sees the way the rounded banks of snow are hard-edged
crystal adhering to crystal, over and over, until they gently
blend; or how the snow is paint
that's snow; or how the dough-white fresh-washed puffy cap
of the serving-girl holding the blood-pan is an agency by
which the mounds of snow in their lateral vanishing
are repeated, here, in smaller but
similar form. ". . .Vhen I return, yes? I go
fishing, chust like dis." What was it he said? Yes,
let's just rest and fish now, not try so demandingly
hard to see. "Und you know vhat I catch? Dis is, oh,
yah, so many years later." Let's just sit and listen
lazily,
        these few blue allegorical December days
B.C. What was it he said
about our lives? *They fit* About our deaths?
into a grand design. As a boy ,
you believed it. One boy's

back in the thick of his grandfather's story again. "Some
damn pretty fish
wit' my hook, wit' my red-and-white bone hook in his botty!"
They fit into a grand design.

Vestigial

1. Appendix, Coccyx, Pineal Eye

Yes: that fingery fraction of a rabbit's commodious
sack, for the slow incorporating of cellulose: is
with us. The slinky bone-links of a tail have fused like flutes
into a panpipes: and are with us. And the lizard's
third, glazed eye is, like a whole yolk, folded
deep in the dough of our brains: and is awake there when
its outer brothers drowse. And there are some of us with
the tent-flap vestige of vaginal lips around the standard
penis; with three-teated breasts . . . Or the One and a
Halfs: with parasite baby-"brother" or -"sister" bodies
dangling partway out: Laloo the Hindu: arms,
waist, buttocks, legs "and perfect nails on the feet" extending forever
from his chest like a child burrowing in him, the head already
whispering to his lungs; it could pee and get hard. And
saying "freak" of them can't naysay what the gill and apehair
stages of the womb mean: everybody's wagged the tag-end of a fish
in the motherly waters. Do we know it, do we dream
the dreams of penguin, ostrich, rhea, kiwi, cassowary,
moa, rail, kakapo: all, birds for which flying's
a pair of muscley nubbins itching the living flesh.

2. The Adventures of John Dee

Not that an omelet of ostrich eggs intensifies
our own ties to the psyche of that African bird. Or
would he have thought exactly that?—John Dee,
astrologer and mage to the court of Elizabeth, himself
the wide-eyed vestige of an older world where poesie
and scientific method were a single creature romping
under planets, seraphs, meteor showers, ghosts. He
conjured ghosts. The Prince of Portugal ate ostrich eggs and
gave the shells to study: they were painted with the travel

86

of the heavenly spheres as agreeably authored by God and
telescope observation. Newton was around the corner.
Dee created a series of ten enormous "moonlight
towers," flashing war news for the Emperor Rudolph all
the way to Prague. And when the last faint light was
understood, and then slipped off its mirror, what did Dee think
in a darkened room of scrolls and crystals? Aubrey was around
the corner, scrutinizing megaliths. This final moment
Stonehenge still might be the footstools giants left. Dee
lifted a dinosaur bone. It might be Noah's, he thought, this
trace of a time when stature matched faith and accomplishment.

3. Big Bang

Ooohing over Stonehenge—over skew-silhouetted
Egyptian gods, or Hopi sand mandalas—finally
recognizes not what's different but what's essentially
us in them. And so we flock to Laloo and his atavistic cohorts,
Alligator Lady, Monkey Boy, to see their fairground skins containing
ordinary life. They wink and sip their scotch. They marry. When
The Human Frog and Mule Woman wed, Sabine the Serpent Girl was
maid of honor—then godmother seven times. They only made the same
attempt as anyone you know, to be the wheel Plato says
we all were in the days when man and woman formed a single-bodied
being rolling breezily over the world. I think that's why
at night, some nights, we see the stars in their terrible solitude
and systems of attachment: as a sign for what our lives are:
smithereens on fire, having been exploded from our wholeness
and our source. That may be accurate cosmology or not. I
only know I've walked the darkness wanting more than any
Stonehenge to align with something bright. And then the lunar
dole of remnant sunlight touched me—here: an x between
the shoulderblades, those made-for-raising things. They stirred. Not
wings, no. More like the fossils of wings.

BARRY GOLDENSOHN

Love And Work: Apple Picking

This is not our real work. We do it
badly. Lots drop. We begin too late—
tense after coming home from work.
It is nearly dark and the wet October wind
numbs my hands as I grapple the sharp bark
along the boughs to reach after the hard
apples that reflect the last light
longer than anything else — green moons,
red moons, swelling with light against the leaves.
Always the impossible twist over my head
and backwards, to the ripest at the top,
the branches' end, my legs wrapped tight
around the tree. You are shivering—
even in this dim light I can see—
as you catch the apples I toss around you,
off balance. I am the Lord of Self-Misrule
up here, fumbling the delicate fruit with ill aim,
swollen hands, making a fool of myself,
hating the work. I would rather climb—
you stand with your skirt lifted, limbs dark,
though your raised face is bright — into you.

War And Peace

From the memiors of Lt. Freedburg,
a Jewish officer in the Army of the Czar

I was a scout and messenger. A shell
burst and I lost my horse, my gun, and came to
sunk in thick alders that bent under me
like an old couch—unhurt, and nearly choked
by the strap of the leather pouch around my throat
I crawled out into the dusk, losing all
my boyhood faster than I could grasp
in that odd, calm and gentle fog. Much seemed
to have gone by, galloped by, and I walked

through the bombarded woods. Half the oaks
with their small early spring leaves,
had fallen and it smelled like a dead city
burnt out and left behind. I found
and lost the path that led to a spot on the river
too swift to cross on foot. Our cavalry
appeared with an old colonel who had turned
their rout into an orderly retreat.

He hung back, dismounted, and we talked
as, high on their horses, they filed across to safety.
Nearing dark, a mist rose from the river.
His face, immobile, shone in the cold
like oiled jade—slabs of soft stone
you could mark with your fingernail: flat cheeks,
a broad nose and high forehead. He looked
like Gerasim, our old servant, with his irony
and discipline, but ready to enter
some durable peace. One of the Chosen People—
I could not fail, could not let myself,
and was concerned with this only, he
with something else that I have struggled since then
to grasp. Was he one of the *lamed vov,*
the holy ones disguised, even from themselves,
scattered through the world who save us with wonders?

His horse had wandered off. He whistled
and it charged up from the river, dumb and eager.
A Golem. Could he have made two that way?
He gave me the horse and I protested faintly.
Then he ordered me and I stopped my protest.
I was young, and too full of urgency
with front line messages. He was firm,
that was all, and he leaned back on a hummock
of tall grass as I mounted and plunged through
the river and came up dry on the other side.
I galloped after the troops but kept him with me:
he is the figure that beckons and disappears
as I re-enact that ending, saving both
him and myself, two on one horse,
or me, or him, flying above the river
with a confident breast-stroke through the air.
I accepted his gift without question
as something due to me. Now he is buried

inside me, the city of the dead that endows
the city of the living with its gods.

The Garrotted Man *(by Goya)*

As if fixed by a long habit of thought
his mouth is turned down, one eye
half open, dreamy. Like the posture
I love, seated and leaning back,
legs stretched out when I am most
at ease with myself, my friends.
His is the moment of rest of the passionate man
who dreams he is superior to the rest.
The collar and the rope are like
insignias of a religious order,
Franciscan, Carmelite. A cross is jammed
in his clasped hands—they are tied
and rest gently on his lap.
His body seems as well accorded
as his soul—the shoulders fallen
in easy repose. Only the feet tell:
this is the terminal scene we struggle
to look at, the difficult knowledge, intimate
stranglehold, death at home in the body.
His toes are spread, curled, rigid
in a splay of agony—his whole
body's last lashing out for air.
If they could loosen! and loosen here
my clenched mind from its dead stare.

The Dream As Calculation

Mug for the camera with your hand on the door.
Your widest smile. Take that again with the head inclined
toward the door. That's it. Then break down the door
and let the horses in. Surprise Mamá, Papá.
How well planned, this dream, shot and cut
and reshot. You with your film-maker friend

with a gift for small details, like two horses, delicious!
His curly head bent over the brick counter, his fat
fingers drumming on a book, while you, at each twist
in the scheme turn to the camera and smirk. And the nervous
flanks of the horses are twitching, swaying their heads
from side to side and flicking them up, lining
and realigning their thick bodies for the charge.
Move the camera in and shape their charge. Control
of this dream, the horses, even the whorish charm
of that opening smile gives you power against the laws.
Move the horses out, then in, then burn away the film.

No Word

"O word, thou word, that I lack." *(Moses and Aaron)*

The warden with his armed guards stalls
in the dull green hall, circles and retreats.
They question us in groups of two and three
and leave us standing about—no need now
to return to the old cells. A conviction
moved into place like a glacial boulder
known to everyone at once, all over,
that one of us is God. No one seems to know
if it is him or her that has received the word
or is the word. Each thinks
It might be me, and suffers in ignorance
of their hidden nature, knows that all suffer
and that suffering is an old sign.
One man, slack pants, dark stains,
white moustache, says to everyone young,
"If they must kill someone, let it be me."
But there is no threat now. The guards are kind.
They will not be trapped again killing a God.
I cannot write without embarrassment
about myself, and I see this in others.
What is hidden makes us modest. Our hopes
leave us too close to every shameful wish
we have for ourselves, and the greed that yells out
our names among the constellations, yells
at us, makes us clasp our hands on our knees

and speak bent downward into them to hide
our eyes. We have stopped dreaming of release
from this prison. Any quiet thing
might be a sign of something else.
The four women laugh among themselves
at jokes they keep from me. The pregnant one
stays alone and laughs at a private joke.
Her breasts shake. Her laugh a breathless hiss.
I fear for her mind. We try to believe
in some coherence, even drunken, wild.
Our questioner, a young lawyer from the city,
now wears her soft suit unbuttoned, and throws
her arms around me in confusion and cries.
Each of us in our cells wants to be loved
for the right reason, and that too is hidden.

LORRIE GOLDENSOHN

Changing The Tire

That you came back, that your plans
were altered by the car —
the spare tire propped against the frame,
the tool kit lying on the damp ground
where we both bent down, and I pretended to help
by handing you things, your hands
moving with their slow security,
tightening the lugnuts —
and we could talk a little longer,
each tasting the other's surprising presence:
between the raising and the lowering
of that familiar metal body, the jack put away,
the wrench, and you came back to the house,
and washed your hands,
more words; another kiss, and then
there was nothing more to do:
but watch as you drove away.

Real Estate

Forward, in disguised laterals, in a broken
plummet across what still remains
the hilled horizon — your foot
urges the falling car
on the downslope, prods it again
to labor on the rise:
we are driving home.

Pepper and bone, the barns slip past;
to our right and to our left
the same old cows that the strong sun
presses into olive meadows, at rest
with their flanks on these flanks . . . .

At every dip in the journey
what greets me is me:

my old and mottled self
come as a ghost that must be welcomed.

Over the crossing that marks old argument —
getting out of the car
I threw myself onto the bank, crying very hard,
snow burning my face and hands —

where you gave me such deep hurt.
That my arm was powerless to rise against you:
as it wanted to, as it wished to return
a blow for a blow.

Last spring I hardly noticed
when we drove past the same spot,
it was all so long ago;
glad and forgetful, your strongly-worded face
joined me behind the moving glass:

while outside, freshly ploughed,
the damp soft April ground
sat there like cooked meat;
in that blank and humid air
both of us hearing the wet, tunneling
whistle of the meadowlark . . . .

Old time like a load of gravel
spilling over back roads,
and memory by intrusive memory, washed away.
Nothing keeps, not even pain;

as the hills continue to signal
their partial ascent,
and in the large blue lung overhead,
damning and treacherous, white spots
re-seed the dissolute core —

the road below.
And the car still fleeing over it.

The Trees, And What They Raise

Is the mind the glass of the body?
a clear nothing
through which the flesh is permitted to peer?
When the body dies, the mind —
When the body dies the mind could be still awake;
reading in bed with the night-light on,
under the snow-cover.
All the leaves go someplace.
In Amherst the empty branches of the trees
are still flung upward:
as if they wanted something.
As if they misunderstood.
And the sunlight itself is full of questions,
as if the blue sky were a surface of cloth,
soft, and full of entities,
and spanning the trees, the empty branches, one
holding a nugget of leaf —

Where do things go when they die,
you ask.
These words that turn into themselves.
Then no one.

The Plains Of Heaven

I am in Heaven.
Look how the sun stays risen — a barn
raised by a team of horses and then forgotten,
abandoned in its blue field.
Below it, an odorless grass
grows thickly, white and cool,
mobs of flowers, pale too, and without texture —
and inwoven among them, clumps of people
stand newly in albino dress,
old tears on their cheeks,
and mouthing a soft, dubbed speech,
eyelids like envelopes steamed open
in that huge, unmerciful light.

Terms

If I could do this, I would,
make sure that I who gave you life,
have you back off, re-enter it
on my terms, oh on my terms,
because I love you:

you crouch and quiver in the kitchen
waiting for the blow of words to subside.
Your careful voice keeping guard
over the sudden flash of your wild
improvisation—the verbal stash
by which I know you as my own.

Black rope of hair
twisting down your back. I move
past you to open the icebox door,
and brush my hand
against your cheek.

Not mine. Nor mine
the softness of your face,
with tears that wet my fingers
when I reach to touch it—
body I love, both of us

terrified—in the rocking chair
up in the attic apartment,
the slow, peaceful sucking
that brought us to this.

JORIE GRAHAM

Evening Prayer

Someone has cut the grass. Someone has cut your tall
    new grass, the sweetness
smears a wild raw dress onto the air, and she
is rising, turning now,
                 in sun, in wind, and she

is free . . . . Walking home
I saw the shadow of a bird, like a heart, like a scythe.
I saw the shadow-wings cross through a wall.

The vacant-lot weeds, too, swayed there. And thistles,
    pods. Terrible
silky wall, abandoned warehouse, thigh . . . .
And the elms, burnt now, were young
all over it, and the wind

in its fatigue . . . .
              But the bird, fistful of time and sinew, blue,
dragged down over the cinderblock by light, lawed down and
brushstroked down—how he went through, went
    abstract,
clean. Not hungry there and not afraid. Thou shalt

dash it to pieces, then, Hand-in-the-light, this potter's
    vessel, vast atomic
girl, shall clean it further, further, spill
    the hollow from her, know her?

Sundial

Today I found myself in the failing light looking in
through some lit windows.
Outside in the trees the rain had ceased.
A few white flowerheads
blazed in the poverty
as if italicised where everything faded to rumor
and blur. As if they were dreaming an unimaginable

quickness.
And somewhere the leaves
clicked and shuddered shut.
And rainbits like hooftaps.
And darknesses roosting,
and everything trussed back into its shadow but me
looking in
at the ground floor dormitory windows,
scores and poster queens and slamming
doors . . . What is it,
when the light in its migration will not take me,
I'm looking for?
Here are god's hot-rod angels in the neon light
gliding from room to room
on dreams
of style. What is it I'm looking for where the lozenge of their light
cuts over the lawn
and does not tremble,
and will not move, at all,
but to go out?
I watch them, in their high harmonies,
being-born still in their ears,
in their rented rooms, in their starry rehearsal.
This is the loneliest place I know.
Is there a way to
not get hurt?
In Barcelona once when I was listening
at the corrida father said to always
sit in the sun, the poverty, said to
always choose so
later on. Over his voice
the wrens were bickering
in the burnt-out evergreens,
drumming their heads, dreaming of moss . . .
Is this to sit unburied, father,
eyeing the shade of flawless desires?
Is this to sit where you cast your stain, your animal,
into the glare?
Is this the right
place, where you can feel your waiting,
its tiny black feet,
crawling all over you, borrowing
your back, your
shoulders now

to cross? Oh let them lean on me to cross,
the long files of minutes in their exhausted exodus. Not
in the expensive shade, you said, with the shop-
owners, the band and the judges' three
embroidered handkerchiefs still hanging now
over their gilded bannister.

The Sacrament of Gravity

To go with the horses over this hill and down into the shadowy
draw, their signature
just where they lean on the earth,
just where they leave it . . . .

To go their way through here, the easy way or
natural,
falling as much as crossing,
blind with going,

saddled by light . . . .
To go by the heart of that other machine, the raw
downslope,
my body the unfound pathway finding itself,

down, where the shut dark of the body threads the open dark
of the world, through leanings, through grasses, true way
past stone, to go
as the slope gives, the incline

banks, the light
dictates, to go by
imbalance,
where movement is vision,

where flesh can subtract and divide and the descent
is its knowledge, what it weaves
of the failures,
this way and that, the drop and the light, to traverse

by the meaningless accuracy
the meanest water knows

over the face of this hill, letting matter
fail me and save me,

a sum of weight and weightlessness,

a law among the laws.

Prayer

   (Penelope)

Fabric I must keep mended. Rend
you must not open. Not for the love, the vertigo. There is
       no *in*.

O weaving, Master-
piece: birdcry and eggshell, truthfulness, hurry,

the light thicker today, or not, the trees dripping with

pollen, wind, a name a neighbor calls

I do not recognize, the ruts in the dirt the wind
is fingering, the wild broom pushing out the daffodils
       across the mad
hillsides this year.

And knotweed. And forget-me-nots. And the promise
of rain that never comes . . .

against thy nakedness, against

confusion, this dress, this holy daily thing I weave awaiting
       indeed the return
of a marriage,
              a wholeness of bits and untorn

halves.

                    *

Though it is, too, the unweaving, simultaneously,
of that grave

                    purposeless
prose, cellwork to its blunt end

rushing, plunging, blind as the packs of horses
the ranchers herd
                    into the emptiness
past the edge of the cliff. O cells what does it matter

that your designs are jubilant, intelligent,

when you fly back-first onto the canyon rock?

                    *

But she waits, she waits, weaving a brainsick gratitude, unweaving
                              the night airs.

The flowers come up
                    right through the rock. What is it

they respect, driving out the sage,
a frenzy of oblivion,

coming up in the draws noone ever crosses,
because of the wind, because of the runoff?

                    *

Only the human needs to unweave. Only the human
is waiting. The flowers I pick in the fields are yellow,
gold, citrine, amethyst, the yellow flowers
I pick in the noonfields I rip right down to the
root, angry. Who are they for, I want to know,
the mad unseen fields, the ferocity of a thousand
yellows sprung up among the rocks in the yellows of
        air and light and no vision?
Once there was nothing on this hillside.
Once there was a temple, or so the stones say.
Once there was a river.
                    Is it further? Is it

                    *

further, this body,

in its nakedness

now? What does it want she thinks picking the flowers

stalk and root. Still they scribble in the wind these
                                                    flowertips,

a grace, bending all one way. And later,

in a vase, bending
                    the way mercy dictates
                                            they bend.

San Xavier Du Bac/ For Jon

(Tucson, Az.)

Inside, beneath the desert sky, beneath the radar
range, the bombers simulating
getaway, the saint, in his blue wedding dress, is married
to eternal sleep. Someone

keeps propping up his head—fresh pillows
are arranged. The terminal have speared
miniature silver legs and hearts
and words

onto the sleeping clothes. The light here
will not clean itself
again. It has arrived. Over the miles
of desert it was headed only

here, breath of this perfect marriage—bones and delay,
bones and embroidery . . . . The child in line
before me leans his head on the saint's sleeping
lap. The passage

from the personal
is everything. The passage into other hands.
Midday, beyond the heavy doors, is razoring
into the miles

of dust . . . . The passage into
other hands, into another's
hurry, greater
pain. I light a candle. As if I could. I leave

a bill here, quick, among the pile, green ashes, wishes,
I leave a note among the ripped and scribbled . . .
But all I burn with is the noonlight, acidlight,
outside, how mean

it is, how it would own me outright, now, and how I
would be, in its fingers,
better owned. Noonlight playing the graves, the shards, and us
making our way among them,

noonlight starching the dusty wind
around the splintering wooden crosses loved ones
have painted dayglow green
or pink, whole companies

bodying forth around that phosphorescent bonework till the wind
suddenly dies. How do I pull myself
up from these blistering
hands? up from their idleness, up from their

flawless dusty math? Above
the incandescent jets do figure-eights deep up into the sky,
      a crown
they place where the air things, a shimmering
infinity,

then drop deadweight, in pairs, perfectly matched,
remembering the curve, the rib,
of this their earth
barely in time.

Lightsplinters flood their backs as they slow terribly
along her flank and drop their landing gear, losing
the grace, fleshing back into
parts—2 tons of

hardware, bolts, wingflaps,
a piece of armor with a mind within,

mind making choices, fingering
levers, cutting this way and that over the minutes over

the blazing runway of oblivion.

LINDA GREGG

Marriage And Midsummer's Night

It has been a long time now
since I stood in our dark room looking
across the court at my husband in her apartment.
Watched them make love.
She was perhaps more beautiful
from where I stood than to him.
I can say it now: She was like a vase
lit the way milky glass is lighted.
He looked more beautiful there
than I remember him the times
he entered my bed with the light behind.
It has been three years since I sat
at the open window, my legs over the edge
and the knife close like a discarded idea.
Looked up at the Danish night,
that pale, pale sky where the birds that fly
at dawn flew on those days all night long,
black with the light behind. They were caught
by their instincts, unable to end their flight.

The Copperhead

Almost blind he takes the soft dying
into the muscle-hole of his haunting.
The huge jaws eyeing, the raised head sliding
back and forth, judging the exact place of his killing.
He does not know his burden. He is not so smart.
He does not know his feelings. He only knows
his sliding and the changing of his hunger.
He waits. He sleeps. He looks but does not know his
seeing. He only knows the smallness of a moving.
He does not see the fear of the trapping.
He only sees the moving. He does not feel the caution.
He does not question. He only feels the flexing
and rearing of his wanting. He goes forward
where he is eyeing and knows the fastness

of his mouthing. He does not see the quickness collapsing.
He does not see at all what he has done. He only feels
the newness of his insides. The soft thing moving.
He does not see the moving. He is busy coaxing
and dreaming and feeling the softness moving in him.
The inside of him feels like another world.
He takes the soft thing and coaxes it
away from his small knowing. He would turn in and follow,
hunt it deep within the dark hall of his fading knowing
but he cannot. He knows that.
That he cannot go deep within his body for the finding
of the knowing. So he slows and lets go. And finds
with his eyes a moving. A small moving that he knows.

At The Gate In The Middle Of My Life

I had come prepared to answer questions,
because it said there would be questions.
I could have danced or sung. Could have loved.
But it wanted intelligence. Now it asks
what can be understood but not explained
and I have nothing with me. I take off
my shoes and say this is a plate of food.
I say the wind is going the wrong way.
Say here is my face emerging into clear light
that misses the sea we departed from to join you.
Take off my jacket and say this is a goat alone.
It embraces me, weeping human tears. Dances
sadly three times around. Then three times more.

White Light

Waiting in the place where the cicadas turn the silence
into something silver. Hot light on the rocks.
Laurel down by the spring. Holding myself still.
Doing one thing at a time. Drink water, burn paper,
wash floor. The sun makes me lower my eyes to see
when I am outdoors. Wind turns the leaves

hour after hour. View of water far below.
Town far below by the water.
Sky beyond the next island.
Loneliness goes out as far as I can see.

What They Ate What They Wore

We see the dog running
and it excites us dimly
as if our lives were important.
The living dog and not
the idea of having one.
Like when my mind sees them
building that great wall
through China and I wonder
where they slept. Huts
with reed roofs or caves in stone.
And what they thought it meant.
I was telling an old farmer
who gave me a ride last month
I might have a job picking apples.
Be sure to wear gloves, he said.
The apples are very cold in the morning.

Winter Birds

Tell me a riddle, I said, that has no answer.
That will hold us to each other fast
and forever, like the dumb things
which cannot grow, that do not change us.
That let us stay here together.
What makes a web of the winter? you answered.
What are the trees of the dead?
What wind blows through all that
as the moon begins her ending, her ending?
you sang. And we danced in the cow-vacant night.
Dancing and singing until our hearts grew fat.

DANIEL HALPERN

Señor Excellent

I was taken there as a child,
the old Farmer's Market on Fairfax.

Spectacular displays of fruit blossomed
everywhere you looked, and men in white

behind glass made candy, their giant vats
of chocolate bubbled like the La Brea tar pits.

And there was always something to eat,
regardless of which way you turned.

But it was the stop in front of Señor Excellent
that was the important event at Farmer's Market.

His vocabulary was limited to one shrill catcall,
a few opening bars of a song and a number of *hellos,* varying

in intensity and pitch. What I remember now
is not what Señor Excellent said, but the wisdom

and irony in the eyes of that myna bird.
We stood around whistling and clicking

and one of us would inevitably try out a few words
of endearment. Have you ever listened carefully

to what people say to talking birds
when they think they are alone? Señor Excellent

just looked at us, his expression one of agony
and disgust. I can picture him

resting on his mauled stick, calmly breathing
and watching us—picking at something

under his wing, going down for a seed, lifting
himself back up with his corn-candy beak—

and I know that his was a life not so different,
witnessing the utterances of the human race.

To A Friend Shot On A Mexican Bus

for Don

He's one of the hard talkers,
hitchhiker, runner,
cold-water swimmer.
He walks Broadway
after the bars have closed
whistling at those willing
to commit harm,
can ignore the tremendous
rush of left-over fish
in the street-trash
of Oriental restaurants.
He has fought the wars
he could have
and writes overly long letters
that break down upon themselves.
If we talk about him
over a few drinks
we remember the cadence
of his walk,
the arguments he had
with each of us
and his lack of relatives.
He's the one who lost an eye
looking for the club of a pre-bop jazzman
in a 1940s Kansas City
backstreet off Troost Avenue,
he's the man on the Mexican bus
shot for insulting the dust,
the friend who called at no-man's hour
to say he needed a friendly voice.
Where were the women
to take him in at night,
the family—
where are we,

the days so entangled these many years
later?
Haven't we
understood this far?
We've hung back,
which was the right thing to do.
We won't insult the dust and die,
we won't die
during the moments
we believe ourselves
beyond the cycles of nature.
We won't die insulting the dust.

Summer Nights

for my mother

You took me to see your friend, a youngish man
    who lived in an iron lung and spoke
through a machine that made his voice
    sound underwater, his head propped
in such a way that I imagined it was
    unattached to what there was of his body.
In the summer of 1952 I lay awake
    in the hot, endless nights
with cars drifting listlessly
    down Chandler Boulevard, their lights
sliding the walls of my room and moving off

    into the desperately calm summer air.
On those nights I thought of your childhood,
    how the doctors wrapped your poor legs
with wool and tar, your mother bathing you
    through the plagued Chicago summer—
the smell of wet wool still makes you sick.
    In the night, as I awaited the morning
that could find my thin body motionless and locked,
    I listened with sentimental care
to my sister crying softly to herself

    in dream, you and your father talking

in a muffled way in your bedroom,
　　the low, barely discernible static
of his transistor radio.
　　It was as if in those airless rooms
there was no hope of surviving the night,
　　that everything was endless and dark,
with sleep coming only with the lights
　　of cars, the final victory of their lulling,
sure movement, drifting steadily awhile
　　on the walls of my room, and passing on.

Walking In The 15th Century

There are angels on the road from San Sepulcro
to Conterchi, and olive trees;
there are grapevines that bring forth
the Umbrian wine Piero drinks
before he goes back
to his pregnant Madonna and the women
attending her. She too will travel this road,
but long after we've gone.

The 15th century sun is up and to us
it seems *youthful*. It seems *uncomplicated*.
There are angels on the road,
or perhaps they remind of us angels
we've seen on the old canvases
500 years later. The air
this time of the year feels strict,
the leaves, late autumn, fugacious.

Sometimes, if the distance is not too great,
it is possible for the unborn
to walk with us. Perhaps they are the angels.
Piero might have experienced his Madonna's child,
destined through his art to remain
in utero forever, in this way.
My daughter and I continue along the road,
the wind travels with us.

Piero will have to hurry along to catch us

before we reach the spectral hilltown
and the little chapel a kilometer beyond it
that awaits his Madonna.
It must be there when I arrive
with the mother of our unborn child
to pay the caretaker the few hundred lira
for a look.

The Summer Rentals

for my father

Today we went to see the summer rentals
that belong to Mrs. Marian Forster.
Her house, up the road from the Camden marina
was off to the left, placed on the bay
across from the Curtis Island lighthouse.

She was a talker, with a quick, momentary smile—
you would have likened it to a jab,
but would have liked her handsome good looks.
I thought of you because she had just married
a man she knew in Los Angeles thirty years ago

who was built like you, tall and thin, elegant
in his dark suit and tie. A European with your face,
had you lived long enough, and your good humor
that lived in the eyes. His name was Harry.
Over proper drinks we talked summer rentals

with Mrs. Forster, or Mrs. Someone Else now—
we weren't given Harry's last name.
It was clear from the way he watched her
he was in love for the first time,
or still in love with his first love.

Talking to him was like talking to you.
Although I don't think we spoke of anything
in particular, it was like the talk we had
tossing a ball back and forth outside our house,
or walking down Van Nuys Boulevard.

Mrs. Forster liked us—we were "an interesting couple."
She took Jeanne's face in her hands
and asked me, "Is this a summer thing?"
Mrs. Forster, working the world of possibility,
never lost the spirit of romance.

She showed us, with delicate speed, "the small house,"
in which we could hear the sounds of the bay—
but not as well as in her house, she explained.
The stove in our kitchen had only four burners
and used electric heat, on which she refused to cook,

hers being a Garland with six gas burners
and a salamander, suitable for her style of living.
She told us the guests who lived on her property
had keys to every door, but as we grew silent,
followed with a confirmation that she of all people

believed in the importance of privacy.
I wonder what you would have thought.
Certainly you would have voted against renting,
in spite of being charmed by Mrs. Forster
and her property's flawless situation on the water.

We returned to her house and the women wandered off
to look at other rooms, pieces of furniture,
photographs of the second wedding and of her first husband,
who remained one rarely referred to in that house.
Harry and I talked a bit about his work in California,

his new life with Mrs. Forster, and he even explained
that when Mr. Forster died he had arrived to take her
"out of the woods." I knew he was Swedish
by the quick intake of breath that occurred when I said
something he agreed with. His sidelong glance and smile

presented the one context we could share.
It seemed to me, as we talked, that he knew
I was talking to you.
It was his eyes that allowed me to imagine asking
the two or three things I've wanted to ask you.

For some reason, as we left, knowing it would be impossible to return,
I remembered the first room I rented, against your better judgment,

as well as the room where I last saw you. I shook Harry's hand.
It was large and dry and surprisingly strong. As strong,
I returned the handshake you taught me as a boy.

Hand, Eye

Here is the salt in the shaker,
and there is the pink of the sunset.
No, here is the salt and rice
I put in the glass shaker
to keep the grains from clotting,
and there, across the electrical wires,
is the sky which contains
a drop of color that is spreading.
Or, here is the salt
(the salt *is* here — and the rice),
there is the sky (or sunset).
Here is white, here is
bone-white and star-white.
There is the shrimp of the sky
curled in the basket of wires.
Here is inside (warm).
Over there is outside (winter).
Here, naturally, is my hand,
what it can hold (salt
inside its window).
Here is nearby, hand, salt, rice, white,
what can be held.
No, looking up, here is the pink blur,
the other hand (not mine),
the huge cupped hand
showing its dark blue wires.
The salt is suddenly pink.
Later, not. Like my hand. Like here.

Leading To Your Hands

The blue Chinese carpet
in the hotel lobby
was the only place
I really wanted to make love.
In the *lobby?* (Your round, literal eyes.)

Not the carpet: the cobalt dragon,
his worsted cloud. Not the palms,
not the room or the clerk standing there,
asking for the first night
in advance if we didn't mind.

In the bar the female vocalist
had ash in her voice,
the Twenties in flint and drizzle.
Not an original voice, but Gershwin
died young again in her throat:
            the man I love,
            the man I love.

Our room smelled of hot showers,
vague damage. We made love there.
We slept. I heard you moan.
You said I spoke.
We're getting to know each other
was the complexion
you put on these things.

Then the walking, the city of slants.
The sidewalks were tall ladders.
We're tourists, you said, so we walk.
Also, we held hands.

In Chinatown we ate black noodles
and were insulted by the waiter
which we decided meant
he likes you, he really likes you.

On the cable car
you put your arm
around my shoulder.
It wasn't gorgeous or reassuring,
any of the things it might have been.
This was weight, burden ending
in the pitiless bloom of your hand.
I'm often depressed, you said, meaning
this is intimacy, the treasure
handed over, the soul tendered.
Others might say *I love you,*
but you wanted to give something

personal, something that sinks in.

It looked like this:
your arm across my shoulder,
a man touching a woman on a cable car,
casual affection, maybe long marriage,
unconscious gesture, tourism.
Wrist, knuckle,
the soft pads of the palm,
moony nails,
the straight-edge of each finger.

That's the life of desire.
But intimacy is this passing
back and forth of bitter news,
stale bulletins, accrued unhappiness,
the family's old gold.
What I wanted (I started this)
was your body. Forever, but
don't laugh.
Breathed fire was the idea,
wild animals, passion
I'd heard about or imagined.
But forget that, forget
the long story I was planning.
As usual, I oversimplified,
even though there was that good omen
we found together in the library:
the city directory from 1900
with our grandfathers' names
on the same page,
both marked Laborer.

Blue Bottle

The blue-black flare at the bottom
of the red tulip. Inside,
the sticks of sex are alert and wet.
The eye of the penis
and its first glistening drop.
That's what happened

last night—not night
but the pink moment of dusk
when every eye, even the sky's,
sees clearly through the pastel motes
of daylight
into the navy steel of night.

Remember that cheap perfume
they used to sell in the dime store
next to the orange face powder?
Evening in Paris.
It came in a blue bottle
with a silver cap shaped like a star.
That's the blue I mean.
I twirled off the star
and smelled what was in there.
Sex was in there.
I drew that blue, bruised fragrance
deep into my nostrils.
I was at the cosmetic counter of T. G. Grant's
and my cousin had just explained
that the man puts *his* on *hers*
and "they have to line their breasts up too."
I wasn't afraid, no matter
how odd it was.
I drew in that heavy blue smell.

Much later I was afraid,
for many years I was afraid with you.
But last night
I looked at the small, sleepy
eye in the intelligent stalk.
The blue light was caught there.
I recognized it.
You I recognized.
I said, blunt as that eye and as innocent,
Your penis smells like the rest of you.
Star opened, flesh opened.
Night and the body
which are blue bottles
opened and opened.
It was the first day of spring,
the tulips which had been aloof
bent out of themselves,
blue night exposed.

from "Resort"

VII

August's dense astronomy fits itself, all stars,
    into the sky's black observatory.
Nothing is solitary up there, nothing is a moon.
    Lying flat on a boulder at the side of the Lake,
I am one edge of things, the sky the other.
    The stars take shallow breaths and burn.

Heaven can't sit still all year: tonight
    the motionless dots dart with electronic brevity
between the fixed white stones of the other stars.
    Are they dying? They betray themselves, shift
their moon-colored light,three inches, three light-years.
    Maybe luck exists, maybe I will betray myself;
a declaration of the changing heart could flare, fade, leave things
    looking harmless after all, just as these

Glancing minnows of the summer sky do: a star
    spurts and disappears. Death without loss.
I keep wanting something big to happen, but painlessly.
    I'd cheat any way I could, if I knew how.
But the random light of change, casual, soundless,
    happens and happens. Everything is remote,

Even my back against this rock is anonymous, all bone,
    although bodies have sloping curves meaning touch me.
The damp strokes of the shooting stars splash, send
    a rain that never arrives. I'm safe in contemplation,
no thorns in the white torn petals above,
    no thoughts, only memories.
Something happened a long time ago—
    What was it? Who made me so happy I was full of stars?

It is my father, standing by me again on the screened porch
    (easy tonight to flare delicately to his side,
the motivation of years is swift as these stars).
    It is raining, Dad, all those St. Paul summer nights.
The street is a stone floor, we agree, beneath a cathedral vault
    of elms, sooty from night and our idea of religion.

A moment ago we were in the living room, Mother was reading
    herself into her furious Irish elegy (Parnell is dead, dead).

Peter was placing a decal on the lacquered wing of a model plane,
    his tweezer poised, a passion for small, sane moves.
They are behind us still, wavering in the skim-milk glow of the Magnavox
    while we are drawn, strange moths, away from the light
of the wet fire of rain. How we love the thirsty communication
    of clumps of dirt and heavy air, you and I, you and I.

Your hands are in your pockets. I'm next to you, girlish
    and electric, all my talk talk talk. You're silent
enough for both of us, a man who grows roses for a living, wearing
    the mouse-smile of a listener though not necessarily listening
to me: some joke from 1937 you never quite got, some
    greenhouse crop to worry. I chatter, am distant as a star,

Which is how you love me, though sometimes you put
    your hand on my shoulder, a gesture
so affectionate it is unwilled, unaware of itself:
    I am unlikely but yours.
We are animals and have caught the scent of rain.
    Or we are even more subtle, we are roses
and lift our burdened heads on the tender necks;
    we see the first random dash come carelessly down,

A splayed particle of the night sky, tentative and large,
    less targeted than the rapid fire that follows,
the plain rain that puts on a show,
    a fast dance, I tell you.
Doesn't the rain look just like ballerinas, Dad?
    (I'm all for metaphor.)
The ricochet of rain on the black street makes
    little tulle skirts (I'm telling you) with tiny legs on point.

Can't you, can't you see them, the ballerinas? (The strident voice
    of women comes from wanting the world to be lyrical.)
How silent you have always been, waiting for
    something big, not money (though money is a flower,
it opens bright and wide), not the greeting
    of the bank president (you admitted

You were pleased — that suit cost $400, easy),
    not the satisfaction of important work (in the hospital,
after your first heart attack, scared and humble, saying
    if a guy'd been a doctor or *done* something . . .).
What you wait for has no name, though I keep insisting:
    Doesn't the rain look like ballerinas?

Every wet summer night we stand here, every night I gush
        my metaphor, every time you say

The true word, patient integrity of eyesight:
        No, you say, it doesn't look like ballerinas.
Not bothering to argue, just saying
        No, most fatherly of words, saying No
so that it can be dark and raining — just raining,
        so that somebody around here is telling the truth.

So that twenty years later I lie on my back alone
        and say *alone,* so that I regard the stars
saying nothing more complicated than *stars.*
        You didn't just grow roses, you sold them —
such an unlikely thing to do with a rose.
        Is that what honesty is, knowing the soul of the world is economic?
Then, Dad, what is freedom? Your hand is on my shoulder,
        the night is slivered with stars.

I'm supposed to say something,
        that's why I'm here.
I get scared if things get too simple:
        The safety of ornamentation is what I trust.
But maybe that's what you meant: don't describe things,
        just call them by their names: star, rain, rose.

ROBERT HASS

Calm

1.

September sun, a little fog in the mornings. No sanctified
terror. At night Luke says, 'How do you connect a *b* to an
a in cursive?' He is bent to the task with such absorption
that he doesn't notice the Scarlatti on the stereo which he
would, in other circumstances, turn off. He has said that
chamber music sounds to him worried. I go out and look at
the early stars. They glow faintly; faintly the mountain
is washed in the color of sunset, at this season a faded
scarlet like the petals of the bougainvillaea which is also
fading. A power saw, somewhere in the neighborhood, is en-
acting someone's idea of more pleasure, an extra room or
a redwood tub. It hums and stops, hums and stops.

2.

In the dream there was a face saying no. Not with words.
Brow furrow, crow's feet, lip curl: no, it is forbidden
to you, no. But it was featureless, you could put your
hand through it and feel cold on the other side. It was
not the father-face saying no among the torsos and
the pillars of aluminium nor the mother face weeping at
the gate that guards rage; it was not even the idiot face
of the obedient brother tacking his list of a hundred and
seventy-five reasons why not on the greenhouse door. This
face spits on archetypes, spits on caves, rainbows, the
little human luxury of historical explanation. The meadow,
you remember the meadow? And the air in June which held the
scent of it as the woman in religious iconography holds the
broken son? You can go into that meadow, the light routed
by a brilliant tenderness of green, a cool v carved by a
muskrat in the blue-gray distance of the pond, black-eyed
susans everywhere. You can go there.

The Apple Trees at Olema

They were walking in the woods along the coast
and in a grassy meadow, wasting, they came upon
two old neglected apple trees. Moss thickened
every bough and the wood of the limbs looked rotten
but the trees were wild with blossom and a green fire
of small new leaves flickered even on the deadest branches.
Blue-eyes, cranes-bills, and little dutchmen
flecked the meadow and an intricate, leopard-spotted
leaf-green flower whose name they didn't know.
Trout-lily, he said; she said, adder's-tongue.
She is shaken by the raw, white, back-lit flaring
of the apple blossoms. He is exultant
as if something he knew were verified
and looks to her to mirror his response.
If it is afternoon, a thin moon of my own dismay
fades like a scar in the sky to the east of them.
He could be knocking wildly at a closed door
in a dream. She thinks, meanwhile, that moss
resembles seaweed drying lightly on a dock.
Torn flesh, it was the repetitive torn flesh
of appetite in the cold white blossoms
that had startled her. Now it seems tender
and where she was repelled, she takes the measure
of the trees and lets them in. But he no longer
has the apple trees. This is as sad or happy
as the tide, going in or coming out, at sunset.
The light catching in the spray that spumes up
on the reef is the color of the lesser finch
they notice now flashing dull gold in the light
above the field. They admire the bird together.
It draws them closer and they start to walk again.
A small boy wanders corridors of a hotel that way.
Behind one door, a maid. Behind another one, a man
in striped pajamas shaving. He holds the number
of his room close to the center of his mind
gravely and delicately, as if it were the key,
and then he wanders among strangers all he wants.

Paschal Lamb

Well, David said—it was snowing outside and his voice
contained many registers of anger, disgust, and wounded
justice—I think it's fucking crazy. I'm not going to be
a sacrificial lamb.

In Greece sometimes, when she walked on the road above the
sea back to her house from the little village in the dark,
a friend told me, and the sky seemed immense, the moon ter-
ribly bright, she wondered if her life would be a fit gift.

And there is that poor heifer in the poem by Keats, all
decked out in ribbons and flowers, no terror in the eyes,
no uncontrollable slobber of mucus at the muzzle, since
she doesn't understand the festivities.

And David, after he had quit academic life, actually bought
a ranch in Kentucky near a town named Pleasureville and began
to raise sheep. When we visited that summer, and the night
was shrill with crickets and the heat did not let up, we sat
talking for a long time after dinner and he told again the
story about his first teaching job and the Vice President.

When he bought the place, he continued his subscriptions to
the *Guardian* and the *Workers' Vanguard,* but they piled up
in a corner unread. He had a mortgage to pay. He didn't
know anything about raising animals for slaughter, and so
he read the *American Sheepman,* he said, with an intensity
he had never even approximated when he was reading political
theory for his Ph.D. orals.

The Vice-President of the United States, after his term in
office, accepted a position as lecturer in political science
at a small college in his home district where David had just
taken his first job. The dean brought Hubert Humphrey around
to introduce him to the faculty. When they came to David's
office, the Vice-President, expensively dressed, immensely
hearty, extended his hand and David did not feel he could
take it because he believed the man was a war criminal and,
not knowing any other way to avoid the awkwardness, he said
so, which was the beginning of his losing the job at that
college.

But that was the dean's doing. The Vice-President started
to cry. He had the hurt look in his eyes, David said,
of a kicked dog with a long, unblemished record of
loyalty and affection, this man who had publicly defended,
had *praised* the terror bombing of villages full of peasants.
He seemed unimaginably empty of inner life if he could be
hurt rather than affronted by a young man making a stiffly
moral gesture in front of two men his father's age. David
said he had never looked at another human being with such
icy, wondering detachment.

And so, in the high-ceilinged kitchen, the air drenched with
the odor of clover, we remembered Vic Doyno in the snow in
Buffalo, in the days when the war went on continuously like
a nightmare in our waking and sleeping hours.

Vic had come to work flushed with excitement at an idea he
had had in the middle of the night. He had figured out how
to end the war. It was a simple plan. Everyone in the coun-
try—in the world, certainly a lot of Swedish and English
students would go along—who was opposed to the war would
simply cut off the little finger on the left hand and send
it to the president. Imagine: they would arrive slowly at
first, the act of two or three maniacs; but the news would
hit the papers and the next day there would be a few more.
And the day after that more. And then on the fourth day
there would be thousands. And on the fifth day clinics
would be set up—organized by medical students in Mad-
ison, San Francisco, Stockholm, Paris—to deal with the
surgical process safely and on a massive scale. And on
the sixth day the war would stop. And the day after that
the helicopters at Bien Hoa would sit on the airfields in
silence like squads of disciplined mosquitoes, and peasants,
worried and curious because peasants are always worried and
curious, would stare up into the unfamiliar silence of a
blue, cirrus-drifted sky. And years later, we would know
each other by those missing fingers. An aging
Japanese businessman minus a little finger on his left
hand would notice the similarly mutilated hand of his cab
driver in Chicago and they would exchange a fleeting, unspo-
ken nod of fellowship.

And it could happen. All we had to do to make it happen—
Vic had said, while the water for tea hissed on the hot

plate in David's chilly office and the snow came down thick
as cotton batting—was cut off our little fingers right
now, take them down to the department secretary and have
her put them in the mail.

Churchyard

Somerset Maugham said a professional was someone who could
do his best work when he didn't particularly feel like it.
There was a picture of him in the paper, a face lined deeply
and morally like Auden's, an old embittered tortoise, the
corners of the mouth turned down resolutely to express the
idea that everything in life is small change. And what he
said when he died: I'm all through, the clever young men
don't write essays about me. In the fleshly world, the red
tulip in garden sunlight is almost touched by shadow and be-
gins to close up. Someone asked me yesterday: are deer mono-
gamous? I thought of something I had read. When deer in the
British Isles were forced to live in the open because of
heavy foresting, it stunted them. The red deer who lived in
the Scotch highlands a thousand years ago was a third larger
than the present animal. This morning walking into the vil-
lage to pick up the car, I thought of a roof where I have
slept in the summer in New York, pigeons in the early morning
sailing up Fifth Avenue and silence in which you imagine the
empty canyons the light hasn't reached yet. I was standing
on the high street in Shelford Village, outside the fussy
little tea-shop, and I thought a poem with the quick, lice-
ridden pigeons in it might end: this is a dawn song in Man-
hattan. I hurried home to write it and, as I passed the
churchyard, school was letting out. Luke was walking toward
me, smiling. He thought I had come to meet him. That was
when I remembered the car, when he was walking toward me
through the spring flowers and the eighteenth-century grave-
stones, his arms full of school drawings he hoped not to
drop in the mud.

Novella

A woman who, as a thirteen-year-old girl, develops a
friendship with a blind painter, a painter who is going
blind. She is Catholic, lives in the country. He rents a
cabin from her father and she walks through the woods—
redwood, sword fern, sorrell—to visit him. He speaks to
her as an equal and shows her his work. He has begun to
sculpt but still paints, relying on texture and the memory
of color. He also keeps English biscuits in a tin and gives
her one each visit. She would like more but he never gives
her more. When he undresses her, she sometimes watches him,
watches his hands which are thick and square, or his left
eye with a small cloud like grey phlegm on the retina. But
usually not. Usually she thinks of the path to his house,
whether deer had eaten the tops of the fiddleheads, why they
don't eat the peppermint saprophytes sprouting along the
creek; or she visualizes the approach to the cabin, its large
windows, the fuschias in front of it where Anna's humming-
birds always hover with dirty green plumage and jewelled
throats. Sometimes she thinks about her dream, the one in
which her mother wakes up with no hands. The cabin smells
of oil paint, but also of pine. The painter's touch is sex-
ual and not sexual, as she herself is. From time to time
she remembers this interval in the fall and winter of the
ninth grade. By spring the painter had moved. By summer
her period had started. And after that her memory blurred,
speeding up. One of her girlfriends frenchkissed a boy on
a Friday night in the third row from the back at the Tamal-
pais theater. The other betrayed her and the universe by
beginning to hang out with the popular girls whose fathers
bought them cars. When the memory of that time came to her,
it was touched by strangeness because it formed no pattern
with the other events in her life. It lay in her memory like
one piece of broken tile, salmon-colored or the deep green
of wet leaves, beautiful in itself but unusable in the design
she was making. Just the other day she remembered it. Her
friends were coming up the road from the beach with a bucket
full of something, smiling and waving to her, shouting some-
thing funny she couldn't make out, and suddenly she was there—
the light flooding through the big windows, the litter of
canvases, a white half-finished torso on the worktable, the
sweet, wheaty odor of biscuits rising from the just-opened
tin.

Santa Lucia II

Pleasure is so hard to remember. It goes
so quick from the mind. That day in third grade,
I thought I heard the teacher say the ones
who finished the assignment could go home.
I had a new yellow rubber raincoat
with a hat, blue galoshes; I put them on,
took my lunchpail and my books and started
for the door. The whole class giggled. Somehow
I had misheard. "Where are *you* going?"
the teacher said. The kids all roared. I froze.
In yellow rubber like a bathtub toy.
That memory comes when I call, vivid,
large and embarassing like the helpless
doglike fidelity of my affections,
and I flush each time. But the famous night
we first made love, I think I remember
stars, that the moon was watery and pale.

It always circles back to being seen.
Psyche in the dark, Psyche in the daylight
counting seed. We go to the place where words
aren't and we die, suffer resurrection
two by two. Some men sleep, some read, some
want chocolate in the middle of the night.
They look at you adoring and you wonder
what it is they think they see. Themselves
transformed, adored. Oh, it makes me tired
and it doesn't work. On the floor in the sunlight
he looked sweet. Laughing, hair tangled, he said
I was all he wanted. If he were all I
wanted, he'd be life. I saw from the window
Mrs. Piombo in the backyard, planting phlox
in her immaculate parable of a garden.
She wears her black sweater under the cypress
in the sun. Life fits her like a glove,
she doesn't seem to think it's very much.

Near Big Sur lighthouse, morning, dunes
of white sand the eelgrass holds in place.
I saw at a distance what looked like feet
lifted in the air. I was on the reef,

128

I thought I was alone in all the silence,
poking anemones, watching turban snails
slide across the brown kelp in tidal pools.
And then I saw them. It was all I saw—
a pair of ankles, lifted, tentative.
They twitched like eyelids, like a nerve jumping
in the soft flesh of the arm. My crotch throbbed
and my throat went dry. Absurd. Pico Blanco
in the distance and the summer heat steady
as a hand. I wanted to be touched
and didn't want to want it. And by whom?
The sea foamed easily around the rocks
like the pathos of every summer. In the pools

anemomes, cream-colored, little womb-mouths,
oldest animal with its one job to do
I carry as a mystery inside
or else it carries me around it, petals
to its stamen. And then I heard her cry.
Sharp, brief, a gull's hunger bleeding off the wind.
A sound like anguish. Driving up the coast—
succulents ablaze on the embankments,
morning glory on the freeway roadcuts
where the rifles crackled at the army base—
I thought that life was hunger moving and
that hunger was a form of suffering.
The drive from the country to the city
was the distance from solitude to wanting,
or to union, or to something else—the city
with its hills and ill-lit streets, a vast
dull throb of light, dimming the night sky.

What a funny place to center longing,
in a stranger. All I have to do is reach
down once and touch his cheek and the long fall
from paradise begins. The dream in which
I'm stuck and father comes to help but then
takes off his mask, the one in which shit, oozing
from a wound, forms delicate rosettes, the dream
in which my book is finished and my shoulders
start to sprout a pelt of hair, or the woman
in the sari, prone, covered with menstrual
blood, her arms raised in supplication.

We take that into the dark. Sex is peace
because it's so specific. And metaphors:
live milk, blonde hills, blood singing,
hilarity that comes and goes like rain,
you got me coffee, I'll get you your book,
something to sleep beside, with, against.

The morning light comes up, and their voices
through the wall, the matter-of-fact chatter
of the child dawdling at breakfast, a clink
of spoons. It's in small tasks the mirrors
disappear, the old woman already
gone shopping. Her apricot, pruned yesterday,
is bare. To be used up like that. Psyche
punished for her candle in the dark.
Oil painting is a form of ownership.
The essay writer who was here last year,
at someone's party, a heavy man with glasses,
Persian cat. Art since the Renaissance
is ownership. I should get down to work.
You and the task—the third that makes a circle
is the imagined end. You notice rhythms
washing over you, opening and closing,
they are the world, inside you, and you work.

WILLIAM HATHAWAY

Still Life

Three yellow wasps belly crawl by slow feel
over boulders of black ripe cherries
in a blue china bowl. Their bands stripe
even blacker against the sun color
as they crouch to split skin, curl down
to the lavish gore. That sugary pulp
blazes crimson, royal purple and pink—
all bright as a brass horn's highnote.

I've jammed wet brushes under many eaves,
but wasps let me be. My stink is right
or wrong, I guess. But I don't go stabbing
them with rolled papers or coffee cans
either, when they do their buzz-bounce dance
off walls and window panes. I can peer close
to see their feelers stroke, so very slow,
as they suck. Because I fidgeted for years

in chalky rooms and twirled home, light after
yellow light, smashed on the brain-busting Grace
of a girl's smell still on my clothes, I can
half-doze this instant into hours. My voice
once stormed all night like candy-colored lights
kids bang off the walls to help their minds race
wild. It's luck to smell good or bad, to still
be here with a brain jam-packed with old noise

and color. So still now sleeping in soft folds,
dark wrinkles where each yellow thought creeps
feeling the way slow, sure and alone.

The Iceball

Mittens tucked fat in my armpit,
I packed it harder and harder to ice
in bare hands. My outraged blood

blazed rosepetal-pink through the skin
of my palms. This one I meant
to throw with all my might
at Larry Darrah's head when they charged.
Anonymous in the arcing blizzard
of snowballs, this one would speed
deadly true to knock his god damn eye
out of his ugly face. Because Darrah
was a cruel prick, that was my scheme.

This bomb was too beautiful: ball-
bearing round, smoother than a crystal
globe, of heft so perfect my arm *knew*
it could not miss, but could not let it go.
I cached it in a niche of our snowfort
to juggle it home in my bare hands
so red yarn from my mittens would not
fuzz it up. O, it was too good for Darrah!
This iceball transcended craft to hold
its own absolute light—a fierce sparkle
too pure for any enemy I knew.

When I took it from the freezer
on the big scorcher in late July
one side had flattened and rough frost
furred its once-slick curves.
The clear glisten had clouded to milky
dun; it had shrunk and smelled
like stale food. Yes, it was interesting
to see it sweat so fast into a cold
puddle on hot cement, how geometric
crystals clung and clarified
in their final blaze. But in those coils
below my stomach where things turn
really disgusting I felt regret—
a miser's loss clogging the pipes.

Ah, that Larry Darrah. He walked ram-
rod straight, like a coke bottle
filled his poop-chute. He chewed
tobacco just to spit it on my pants
and he washed my face with snow
many times, in front of lots of girls.
Teachers loved him and said he was

likely to be elected president one day.
The day I did not knock his damn eye
out was the first time I let this country
down.

Why That's Bob Hope

The comedian, holding a chunk of flaming shale.
If only *Der Bingle* could see him now! He looked
so puffed and sleepy in that Texaco hard-hat,
I could've popped a fuse. Well, like the oil,

here today and gone today. In *my* good old days
Hope was on Sullivan's 'shew' so often us kids
dropped TV for longhair sex and smoking weeds.
What a mistake! But now we're past our wild phase

and Bob's back with this burning rock, funny
for a change. No, no old quips now about Dean's double
vision, Phyllis Diller's breasts or Sinatra's aging treble.
He says if we all squeeze the rock together real money

will drip out. We'll live real good and still afford a war
where he'll bust our boys guts on tour in El Salvador.

This Tree

said the little plaque in sober brass,
"replacing the beloved 'Stump'
is a gift from the Class
of 1977." Clearly a playful crowd,
and the tree is a ginkgo, coy fans
all aflutter, already heliotroping
hard to the east. Stump hell,
I remember that old elm,
stemming higher than slate roofs
to open wide to the sky full
of God. Before they all

got dutched. Well, to this tree
someone had tethered a half-grown
spaniel bitch with vinyl clothes-
line and gone off, to class
I guess. The black pool
on gray asphalt, thick drool
roping from her sweating tongue,
mirrored a ghostly flit
of shadows from those waving
leaves. Far away her steady bark,
like a handsaw's cry as it comes
and goes through cheap pine,
or that hammer we hear
wedging air with an anger
without heat, annoyed me.
For small dogs disgust me,
yet to let loose one so young
to lose herself would be
as cruel as to tie her in the sun.
I didn't think hard
for anyone before I retied
her in some scanty locust shade.
I was sweating and panting
and probably blushing all red
and stupid, holding the styrofoam
plate of water like a choir boy
and it still sloshed anyway
on the stairs and worn tiles
before the doors of a "Job Fair"
where the kids were all three-
pieced and talcumed, holding
big brown portfolios
and getting the hell away
from my spill and red face
and knee-worn corduroy smelling
of loss and sick dog.
But I thought two small thoughts
watching the puppy shlup-shlup
it up. My dad was born (1909)
the year the chestnuts died.
Cow that is, not horse. The ones
you can eat. Also how very much
I'd like to beat the shit
out of the smug prick or princess

who left this dog tied to that tree
in the full heat of this sun.
Because, I guess after all these
trees and stumps, which I never
thought to love, I'm still
not civil. In fact, probably
only lethargy and technical
boneheadedness keeps me
from mounting the famous clocktower's
winding stairs with a trombone
case full of grief. Ah hell,
I won't hurt anyone; it's just
a little hard here in this future
with its new trees and the sun
so bright my eyes water. I'll
tell you though: take all the trees,
I'll never love a god damn stump.

You Had To Know Her

For a long time she listened to the sound
of Leo waving his arms. Then as she listened
she began listening to a few carefully chosen
other things and gradually she called these sentences.
Soon she was seeing what it seemed others were not seeing
that these ones were a lot like talking and talking was sounding
like thinking and if one could be thinking it why should one be doing.
So she stopped listening
and did what Leo was not doing with his thinking.

I'm sorry. There is no other way to describe
it. I'm describing what cannot be described
because she said it all when she said it.

Once you spent all day Christmas taking
apart and putting together a puzzle
from Formosa. Your headache was special,
had nuance that night and your tantrum
was misunderstood. Over-tired and over-
excited they said, but you had just learned
the best moments would never be enough.

Miss Stein not interested in your problem.

Let's not get confused; like Mallarme
you had to know her beautiful voice, her jig-
saw salon: that museum for the talking.
She loves your worry, your tender buttons,
half your words; she just don't like your
story. "I very recently met a man who said,
how do you do. A splendid story." she said.

O.K., goodbye.

EDWARD HIRSCH

I Need Help

For all the insomniacs in the world
I want to build a new kind of machine
For flying out of the body at night.
This will win peace prizes, I know it,
But I can't do it myself; I'm exhausted,
I need help from the inventors.

I admit I'm desperate, I know
That the legs in my legs are trembling
And the skeleton wants out of my body
Because the night of the rock has fallen.
I want someone to lower a huge pulley
And hoist it back over the mountain

Because I can't do it alone. It is
So dark out here that I'm staggering
Down the street like a drunk or a cripple,
I'm almost a hunchback from trying to hold up
The sky by myself. The clouds are enormous
And I need strength from the weight lifters.

How many nights can I go on like this
Without a single light from the sky: no moon,
No stars, not even one dingy street lamp?
I want to hold a rummage sale for the clouds
And send up flashlights, matchbooks, kerosene,
And old lanterns. I need bright, fiery donations.

And how many nights can I go on walking
Through the garden like a ghost listening
To flowers gasping in the dirt—small mouths
Gulping for air like tiny black asthmatics
Fighting their bodies, eating the wind?
I need the green thumbs of a gardener.

And I need help from the judges. Tonight
I want to court-martial the dark faces
That flare up under the heavy grasses—
So many blank moons, so many dead mouths

Holding their breath in the shallow ground,
Almost breathing. I have no idea why

My own face is never among them, but
I want to stop blaming myself for this,
I want to hear the hard gavel in my chest
Pounding the verdict, "Not guilty as charged,"
But I can't do this alone, I need help
From the serious men in black robes.

And because I can't lift the enormous weight
Of this enormous night from my shoulders
I need help from the six pallbearers of sleep
Who rise out of the slow, vacant shadows
To hoist the body into an empty coffin.
I need their help to fly out of myself.

Indian Summer

It must have been a night like this one,
Cool and transparent and somehow even-tempered,
Sitting on the friendly wooden porch of someone's
Summer house in mid-October in the country

That my father, home from the Korean War
And still in uniform, wearing a pilot's bars
And carrying a pilot's stark memories (still
Fingering a parachute in the back of his mind)

Jumped from the front steps where he'd been sitting
And held a sweating gin and tonic in the air
Like a newly-won trophy, and flushed and smiled
Into the eyes of a strangely willing camera.

It must have been winning to see him again
Safely home at the close of a vague war
That was too far away to imagine clearly,
A little guarded and shy, but keenly present,

Tall and solid and actual as ever, and anyway
Smiling past the camera at his high-school sweetheart

(Now his wife, mother of his two small children)
Surrounded by friends on a calm midwestern night.

It must have been so soothing to have him back
That no one studied him closely, no one noticed
That there was something askew, something
Dark and puzzling in his eyes, something deeply

Reluctant staring into the narrow, clear-eyed
Lens of the camera. I've imagined it all—
And tonight, so many light-years afterwards,
Looking intently at a torn photograph

Of that young soldier, my distant first father,
Home from a war that he never once mentioned,
I can foresee the long winter of arguments
Ahead. The hard seasons of their divorce,

The furious battles in court, and beyond that,
The unexpected fire, the successive bankruptcies,
The flight to California with a crisp new bankroll,
The move to Arizona with a brand new family.

Tonight the past seems as sharp and inevitable
As the moment in Indian Summer when you glance up
From a photograph album and discover the fireflies
Pulsing in the woods in front of the house

And the stars blackening in a thicket of clouds . . .
Yes, it must have been a night like this one
When my mother glanced over her husband's head
Into a cluster of trees emerging behind him

And heard the wind scraping against the branches
Like the *strop strop* of a razor on rawhide,
And saw the full moon rising between the clouds
And shattering into hundreds of glassy fragments.

Commuters

It's that vague feeling of panic
That sweeps over you
Stepping out of the #7 train
At dusk, thinking, *This isn't me*
Crossing the platform with the other
Commuters in the worried half-light
Of evening, *that must be*

Someone else with a newspaper
Rolled tightly under his arm
Crossing the stiff, iron tracks
Behind the train, thinking, *This
Can't be me* stepping over the tracks
With the other commuters, slowly crossing
The parking lot at the deepest
Moment of the day, wishing

That I were someone else, wishing
I were anyone else but a man
Looking out at himself as if
From a great distance, through water,
Turning the key in his car, starting
His car and swinging it out of the lot,

Watching himself grinding uphill
In a slow fog, climbing past the other
Cars parked on the side of the road,
The cars which seem terribly empty
And strange,
            and suddenly thinking
With a new wave of nausea
This isn't me sitting in this car
Feeling as if I were about to drown

In the blue air, *that must be*
Someone else driving home to his
Wife and children on an ordinary day
which ends, like other days,
With a man buckled into a steel box,
Steering himself home and trying
Not to panic

happily sheltered from a sudden rainfall.
But later when I saw the bag lady
sprawled out on a steaming vent for warmth
I remembered how Clare had moved on, crippled
by tiny bits of gravel lodged in his shoes,
and how he tried to escape from the wind
by lying down in an open dyke bottom
but was soaked through clear to his bones;
how he came to the heavy wooden doors
of the Wild Ram Public House hours later,
and gazed longingly at the brightly-lit windows,
and had no money, and passed on. Whoever
has stood alone in the night's deep shadows
listening to laughter coming from a well-lit house
will know that John Clare's loneliness was unbending.
And whoever has felt that same unbending loneliness
will also know what an old woman felt today
as she followed an obedient path between the huge
green garbage cans behind Kroger's Super-Market
and the small silver ones behind Clarence's grocery.

I began this day by following a bag lady
in honor of John Clare but suddenly, tonight,
I was reading "The Journey Out of Essex, 1841,"
in honor of the unknown bag lady.
I had witnessed a single day in her life
and was trying hard not to judge myself
and judging myself anyway.
I remember how she stooped to rub her foot;
how she smiled a small toothful grin
when she discovered a half-eaten apple;
how she talked on endlessly to herself
and fell asleep leaning against a broken wall
in an abandoned wooden shed on Second Avenue.
Tonight when I lie down in the dark
in my own bed, I want to remember
that John Clare was so desperately hungry
after three days and nights without food
that he knelt down, as if in prayer,
and ate the soft grass of the earth,
and thought it tasted like fresh bread,
and judged no one, not even himself,
and slept peacefully again, like a child.

In the last moments of nightfall
When the trees and the red-brick houses
Seem to float under green water
And the streets fill up with sea lights.

Three Journeys

Whoever has followed the bag lady
on her terrible journey past Food-Lane's Super-Market,
and Maze's Records, and The Little Flowering Barbershop
on the southeast corner of Woodward and Euclid
will know what it meant for John Clare
to walk eighty miles across pocked and jutted
roads to Northborough, hungry, shy of strangers,
"foot foundered and broken down" after escaping
from the High Beech Asylum near Epping Forest.
And whoever has followed the bag lady
on her studious round of littered stairwells
and dead-end alleys, and watched her combing
the blue and white city garbage cans for empties,
and admired the way that she can always pick out
the single plate earring and one Canadian dime
from a million splinters of glass in a phone booth
will know how John Clare must have looked
as he tried to follow the route that a gypsy
had pointed out for him, scaling the high
palings that stood in his way, bruising
his feet on the small stones, stooping
to admire the pileworts and cowslips, scorning
the self-centered cuckoos but knowing the sweet
kinship of a landrail hiding in the hedgerows.

I began this morning by standing
in front of the New World Church's ruined storefront;
I was listening to the bag lady and a pimply-
faced old drunk trading secrets with the vent man,
and remembering how a gentleman on horseback
had mistaken John Clare for a broken down haymaker
and tossed him a penny for a half-pint of beer.
I remembered how grateful he was to stand
elbow to elbow in the Old Plough Public House

Dawn Walk

Some nights when you're asleep
Deep under the covers, far away,
Slowly curling yourself back
Into a childhood no one
Living will ever remember
Now that your parents touch hands
Under the ground
As they always did upstairs
In the master bedroom, only more
Distant now, deaf to the nightmares,
The small cries that no longer
Startle you awake but still
Terrify me so that
I do get up, some nights, restless
And anxious to walk through
The first trembling blue light
Of dawn in a calm snowfall.
It's soothing to see the houses
Asleep in their own large bodies,
The dreamless fences, the courtyards
Unscarred by human footprints,
The huge clock folding its hands
In the forehead of the skyscraper
Looming downtown. In the park
The benches are layered in
White, the statue out of history
Is an outline of blue snow. Cars,
Too, are rimmed and motionless
Under a thin blanket smoothed down
By the smooth maternal palm
Of the wind. So thanks to the
Blue morning, to the blue spirit
Of winter, to the soothing blue gift
Of powdered snow! And soon
A few scattered lights come on
In the houses, a motor coughs
And starts up in the distance, smoke
Raises its arms over the chimneys.
Soon the trees suck in the darkness
And breathe out the light
While black drapes open in silence.
And as I turn home where

I know you are already awake,
Wandering slowly through the house
Searching for me, I can suddenly
Hear my own footsteps crunching
The simple astonishing news
That we are here,
Yes, we are still here.

T. R. HUMMER

Empty Backstreet In A Small Southern Town

The daughter who has never been here
Will make the connection. It will not be time
For the vine-grip of morning-glory,
It will be the rain-silvered winter
You never hear much about, February,

And wind will blow raw down
The left side of a street the locals call
Main Street, Niggertown.
She will come here alone, dark-skinned
For a white girl, pitiful

In her unbelief. From the first
House she comes to, the unpainted tin-roofed
Wrack-frame shack, she will hear
Nothing, no hymn-singing mother-voice, no left-
Over cottonfield harmonica, no ghost

Of a pot-bellied white-eyed child
Squealing from a doorway. She would swear
On the whole street there is nobody
Home. This is not what she came here for,
This is not the story

She wanted: no: there will be nothing
To keep her rust-colored
Hair from blowing loose, nothing to hold
Back the blood-poisoning
Bite of this unexpected

Wind. In her grimace she will look
So much like her mother
It would break your heart if you had one,
If you could know her
Unspoken history of abandonment: but the sun

Will slap its ice-white
Presence on the blacktop,
And nobody will come to explain,

No mammy and no pistol-sagging cop,
Nobody will come to say what

Any of this means, or could ever mean,
In the unfolding human
Heresy of pain.

–for Jodi Baker

The Sun

Something is happening in the garden. The woman leans
Over ragged rosebushes raggedly trained
On a low wood fence. Her breasts, in the flower-embroidered
Linen of her halter top, reveal

A plumb-bob's sensitivity to gravity, the deep
Crease between them a hard right angle to the crease
Her bending crimps in the off-white plane of her belly.
She reaches. She touches the buds' reddening tips.

You think I think this is Eden, don't you? I don't.
I think this is sex. I lie
On the lounge chair, balance my Budweiser bottle
Right-angled on this belly that years of beer

Would leaven and lift like yeast
If I ever gave up the old war against excess of flesh,
And I watch her. I think this is good. I think
Something is happening. It comes to me

With the irreducible momentum of the involuntary:
Late afternoon, a summer Saturday:
I am lying on my bed, where sun
Through a window throws its hard-edged light:

I am having the first conscious sexual fantasy
In my memory: there is a stage, far away:
I am sitting, perhaps, in a balcony,
Or maybe I am simply hovering in the air,

High up, and distant from the action:
Onstage, a tiny woman takes
Her clothes off, piece by indistinct piece.
That's all. It's unrealized and conventionally abstract

As anyone's painful first poem, but for now it's enough:
I am nine years old, and I suddenly know a secret
Knotted connection between mind and body:
The center of the sunlight's hot rectangle

And my solar plexus coincide, squaring the circle,
And just below that geometry, my hard-on makes a chafed
Right angle: penis, ghost finger that will not answer
Directly to orders, as hands do, has answered:

And to what? To the image of breasts, however
Unclear: to the naked image of the woman
Moving in her faraway dance, removing
Only what stands between us most superficially,

Bending, when it's over and nothing else matters,
In a deep ironic bow. This is my first knowing. I lift
My beer bottle, look through it, and see her refracted
At two removes: from my far seat

In the balcony, or the place where I hang
In the air like an angel: and from here in the hot
Back yard where I lie in the sun turning red,
Where everything is happening, where you bend

And let me imagine the line between your breasts
Abstractly extended to intersect the belly-crimp
Exactly at your navel, crossing the two
Planes and four corners of the world at the arc

Of the solar plexus, the thousand-petaled lotus,
The rose that unfolds in summer when the sun
Touches it there, at noon, in the garden,
Whatever name you want to give it,

Whatever you know it by: uncontrollably risen.

The Second Story

And we may well heave a sigh of relief at the thought
that it is nevertheless vouchsafed to a few to salvage
without effort from the whirlpool of their own feelings
the deepest truths, towards which the rest of us have to
find our way through tormenting uncertainty and with
restless groping.

—Freud

On the other side of the arc-light-level window
Hung at the top of that slope of Victorian porch,
Someone believes in the laying on of hands,

Or some two believe, and the woman of them sings
Her hymn. It comes down to me where I stand unashamed
To listen, unashamed to be here under these morning stars

Where they do not know I am, where no one should be.
This is the life in the body, certainty, uncertainty:
I am here, and if they knew they would not be

What I imagine so easily, the woman a darkness
In the shadow the man above her casts, starlight and arclight
From the window by the bed eclipsing his face from her,

Her legs lifted around him in that delicate poise
Of the almost-come, so when he lowers
His invisible mouth that could be any man's

And takes her breast, her knees stiffen in the same
Upward motion that suddenly and beautifully breaks
This contralto out of her, as the freed light strikes

Her face: that, or some familiar variation. But if they knew
Another darkened body stood on the innocent
Corner of two sidewalks below them, listening,

What would they be? I ask myself and know:
Up there in that bedroom I can almost see
With its various reproductions—armoire, nightstand, vanity,

Surrounding its crucially refinished bed—
They would, if they could suddenly know me, stop

148

Their singular motion in the paralyzed reflex of fear,

Afraid, God help me, of nothing, of me,
A human stranger. So knowledge is fear.
I look up at the house spreading its white facade

Streetlight-struck in the blackness of this summer morning,
Five a.m., Vermont, windless and cloudless,
And I see, I want to tell myself simply,

A house, but I know it is no house
I ever lived in. These are the second homes
Of the rich, on a street of stained glass and cupolas

And high balconies where a cliched lover might declaim
Wherefore? and the answer rise *What light?*
And where lawns of tame maples yield

That storied Vermont sweetness: sap.
I have come here insomniac, waked by a dream
Not frightening, but strange in its inexplicable

And boring complications, the way the mind is,
And I remember the old joke: *The rich
Are not like us,* it goes, to which the answer is

The only one possible: *Right, they have more
Money.* I imagine those two up there, after,
Smoking identical Turkish cigarettes while he tells her

The details of an obscure incident from his childhood.
She nods in the dark and explains. After all,
Her Ph.D. is Viennese and psychological

And ought to do her some good in what she likes
To call her *private life.*
Yes, it is good to lie in the dark and breathe

That alien smoke through bruised lips, good to imagine
The love lives of distant and exotic peoples
In inner-city Detroit or Mississippi

And how, unexamined and mentally unhealthy,
They must hurt each other. And yes, it is good

To stand on the sidewalk hearing it go on and on,

That utterly unknowable woman transcendentally moaning
Out of a life I can only pretend to imagine,
And which I tell myself I could cause

To come to a crashing *coitus interruptus* by a single
Shouted word. Any word would do: *me*
I could yell, or *here,* or *Detroit,* or *dysfunction,*

It would all be the same word: *fear.*
So words are fear, as long as they let us know
Someone is out there, someone is close by, present

Any mysterious in a body that has a familiar shape
But no known face. This is the life
In the body, what we know of each other, the nothing

Names tell us: this is the song
Of the woman touched by the man she thinks
She knows or loves or her life

Would be nothing without
Touching in rooms so dark nobody can say
Who anybody really is, where nobody has

Words songlike enough to touch
The reason I am out here, afraid
Of whoever is up there, lifted

In their Victorian construct
Over the world they speak to without knowing,
Moaning down their wordless and irrefutable explanations,

Giving hands and tongue to name me
Their human groping, making
What even the most petrified among us certainly

Could agree to call *love,* could say
Is good. But now her low voice rises
Toward a classic soprano. I feel its pure

Shudder low in my spine as she tells me
What I translate roughly as *My God*

Someone is doing something right:

And I know I have missed my chance, they are beyond me,
Too far gone for any word
I could shout ever to bring them down.

This is the rapture, these are the sinless
Raised beyond the reach of any voice
Of mine. This is salvation, I am forgiven

My fear and my dreams: I am foretold,
In this flesh that holds me, wherefore
What light (it is the east) grows suddenly unashamed

On the other side of trees that are only
Eclipses of themselves, thrown hard on the edge
Of this world's unearnable laying on of richness.

MARK JARMAN

Cavafy in Redondo

Our ruins run back to memory.
Stucco palaces, pleasure bungalows, the honeycomb
of the beachcombers' cluster of rentals—
I remember them, filings in sand
pricking up at the magnet of nostalgia,
a sigh of dusty filaments. Our ruins
wear the as-yet-unruined like coral crowns.
Night life blows through the boardwalk's
conch-shell coils of neon, skirting the water.
This was never—Ask my parents—a great city.
It had its charm, like a clear tidal shallows,
silted-in now, poldered, substantial, solid,
set for the jellying quake everyone expects.

I walked these streets one night with a new lover,
an as-yet-to-be lover—it took a whole night
of persuasion. I had been gone a year,
and walked as sea mist compounded the dew.
My legs ached by the time bed was agreed to.
How sentimental it was, to flatter, listen,
cajole, make little whining endearments,
plodding ritualistically among landmarks,
sandy shrines in alleys, the black meccas
of plate glass windows fronting the beach
where white froth reflected in the night.
I kept that ache, not love's, after we parted.

We did not part to history with its glosses;
we were not even footnotes. Our ruins
will bear out no epics or histories here,
footprints compounded of dew and fog
and under them, maybe a rusty antique
that, boiled in acids, will tell a tale.
After all, ships passed, broke up on the point.
Mainly, the beach eroded in great ridges
until ground cover belted it back. A pleasure dome
was dismantled, certain fashions
of dress and of love. History builds to last,
crumbles to last, shakes off its dust

under the delicate excavating brush—to last.

Built above the beach was a colossus,
humped and strutted and roaring with many voices.
Winds chased through it screeching and then
it stood silent. People flocked to it, entered it,
and though not lost, screamed as if tortured.
I am joking. There was a roller coaster
of some note and no small size. Where did it go?
Ah, yes, lost in the coral make-up
of that teetering lover who walked beside me,
tired of my harangue, the persuasive underlove
that wanted to rise to the lips, those lips
colored by fuming street lamps.

Young, my parents drove out from a distant city,
through tawny hills medallioned with oak.
I have seen their worn postcards of the town,
a tide pool of neighborhoods mantled around
by semi-wilderness and orange groves.
Missiles came to squat above our house
on a benchmarked hill, turned obsolete,
and floated away on flatbeds, ruptured patios in their places.
We, too, left that house that heard,
in every lath and windowpane, the industry of phosphorus,
grinding out the waves in the late darkness.
My parents—all of us—have come and gone and left
no ghosts here, and that is our good fortune,
to give it all to the ocean, the troubled sleeper.

By-blows

They wake like opening sea anemones,
although none turns into a flower—
wake with their dew, a salt clamminess
on gritty skin, under the pier.
Above them, boards thump, panels unlock,
food machines cough. The gaunt morning moon
(Why should they look?) turns blue in the jowl.
From the surf I would watch them climb
the nubbled walk to the library park—

watch the sun accept if not bless them
as they rose, hung over on cough syrup
or pop wine—where bladed cacti filled
with sprinkler water, and certain benches
were somewhat safe. Told to move on,
there was the library, the nook tables
and pillowing books, and after a decent interval
the discreet voice that spoke.

What did my father tell me? About that one
who whirled to face a soaped window
as we passed on the bare avenue?
They blow into town, beg money, blow out again.
But you know the rest of it.
They taste sand every morning, wake
in flannel grayed with their sweat,
touch the tide's cold hem, and smell the sunrise.
Planting their fingertips, they can tell
a story as roundabout as any medieval allegory,
with their damp gunpowder stubble,
their drain-waste of hair,
their air of illegitimate princes
double-crossed by sires and stars.
What we see looking at them is what they see
looking away—the otherness of the moon,
which we feel no urge to correct.

The Supremes

In Ball's Market after surfing till noon,
we stand in wet trunks, shivering
as icing dissolves off our sweet rolls
inside the heat-blued counter oven,
when they appear on his portable TV,
riding a float of chiffon as frothy
as the peeling curl of a wave.
The parade M.C. talks up their hits
and their new houses outside of Detroit
and old Ball clicks his tongue.
Gloved up to their elbows, their hands raised
toward us palm out, they sing,

"Stop! In the Name of Love" and don't stop
but slip into the lower foreground.

Every day of a summer can turn,
from one moment, into a single day.
I saw Diana Ross in her first film
play a brief scene by the Pacific—
and that was the summer it brought back.
Mornings we paddled out, the waves
would be little more than embellishments:
lathwork and spun glass,
gray-green with cold, but flawless.
When the sun burned through the light fog,
they would warm and swell,
wind-scaled and ragged,
and radios up and down the beach
would burst on with her voice.

She must remember that summer
somewhat differently, and so must the two
who sang with her in long matching gowns,
standing a step back on her left and right,
as the camera tracked them
into our eyes in Ball's Market.
But what could we know, tanned white boys,
wiping sugar and salt from our mouths
and leaning forward to feel their song?
Not much, except to feel it
ravel us up like a wave
in the silk of white water,
simply, sweetly, repeatedly,
and just as quickly let go.

We didn't stop either, which is how
we vanished, too, parting like spray—
Ball's Market, my friends and I.
Dredgers ruined the waves,
those continuous dawn perfections,
and Ball sold high to the high rises
cresting over them. His flight out of L.A.,
heading for Vegas, would have banked
above the wavering lines of surf.
He may have seen them. I have,
leaving again for points north and east,

glancing down as the plane turns.
From that height they still look frail and frozen,
full of simple sweetness and repetition.

To the Reader

Today, having turned 83,
I turn back in my coma.
I see my last moment awake, erect.
Sun fills the empty piazza
crenelated by shadows of towers.
There is the first step of the flight
to the blank-faced duomo
and a sound of Sunday mumbling
amplified by open doors.
If I step forward, I am here
jangled, drifting, and stilled,
with a flashback of ambulance bells,
a huddle of nursing nuns,
faint Italian farewells.
So I step back and find
the reversal ironically clear,
dustless, rhythmical.
My clothes, difficult
all those years of old age,
turn smooth, slipping on thoughtlessly
like my own face in the mirror
and my wife's appearing beside it.
We have our whole past ahead of us.
Our children reattach
and like us grow younger
but more rapidly. They shrink
back to their births.
What is it like to lose them so?
Affection intensifies
inversely to their departures.
Soon so small, they hide
within their baby blankets.
Then birth is reversed.
My wife swallows
their pain and hers

and that pain and affection are gone
and we continue.
I understand the room-building
of marriage now,
as if the baroque could be picked apart,
broken arches rejoined,
rounded and then uninvented.
As we built we could separate,
work all day out of thought
of each other. Finally,
we are alone in one room;
the sexual sweetness is almost too much.
Then she vanishes.
How quick was our courtship.
How brief adolescent loneliness
that had seemed endless.
My childhood knots up again,
all of its strings and entwinings
just as enigmatic,
emboweled with codes, insinuations,
untying one by one.
Flat characters who are siblings
zip off like meteors.
Then, parents. I see four hands
knitting this carefully
to make a clear thing—

> But reader, within the hill
> of this city where I am dying
> are vaults of an ancient people.
> They undermine the city.
> A framework of steel
> has been built for support.
> Water flooding the vaults
> rusts the steel, more is added.
> The I-beams bristle
> inside the hollow crown.
> The city stands on its brittle base,
> a wall sinks, a tile courtyard cracks.
> We have reached a steady state
> of support and collapse
> like the human face—

not this ball of entanglements.

They gather me up.
And I am lost.
And it is not to death.

DENIS JOHNSON

Travelling

When I was waiting for a haircut at Joe's
the man in the chair said, "Hey, do you know
Tony? Lives right up the hill from me?" and Joe
said, "Sure. Sure I know Tony. How long Tony
live up the hill from you?" The man said, "He been living
there about fifteen years I guess it must be." "Been living
there about fifteen years, huh?" Joe said. "Yeah,
right up the hill from me. And you know what? Funniest thing,
the guy's dif! Dif!" "Dif?" said Joe. "Yah! Dif! And I been
saying hello to the guy every day just about fifteen years."
"That so," Joe said. The man in the chair said, "Yeah!
Funniest thing! He must have good eyesight though,
because when I says hello, he says, 'Hi!' "
"What do you know," Joe said. Outside above the harbor,
clouds were moving freely over the sun's face,
and the shifting illumination in the place
made it seem we were travelling. "Dif,
huh?" Joe said, and the man
said, "Yah! Dif!" "Well well," Joe said.
The man remarked, "He must have pretty good eyesight:
because he talks to you when he can't even hear you."
"How about that," Joe said.
"He can't hear a word you're saying," the man said.
"How about that," Joe said. The man
in the chair said, "He can't hear a word of nothing."

Movie Within A Movie

In August the steamy saliva of the streets of the sea
habitation we make our summer in,
the horizonless noons of asphalt,
the deadened strollers and the melting beach,
the lunatic carolers toward daybreak —
they all give fire to my new wife's vision:
she sees me to the bone. In August I disgust her.

And her crazy mixed-up child, who eats with his mouth open
talking senselessly about androids, who comes
to me as I gaze out on the harbor wanting
nothing but peace, and says he hates me,
who draws pages full of gnarled organs and tortured
spirits in an afterworld —
but it is not an afterworld, it is this world —
how I fear them for knowing all about me!

I walk the lanes of this heartless village
with my head down, forsaking permanently
the people of the Town Council, of the ice-cream cone, of the out-of-state
        plate,
and the pink, pig eyes
of the demon of their every folly;
because to say that their faces are troubled,
like mine, is to fail: their faces
are stupid, their faces are berserk, but their faces
are not troubled.
Yet by the Metro
I find a hundred others just like me,
who move across a boiling sunset
to reach the fantastic darkness of a theater
where Paramount Pictures presents
An Officer and a Gentleman.

I am not embarrassed by the tears
streaming over my face as I leave the theater.
I go to the movies as I'd go to the dawn,
and the triumphs there, the things that are brought to light,
the large, sad lives of people not so different
from me, their stories heard
through a tumbler held to the ear
and seen through a gauze of falling sand —
these are my triumphs; I am brought to light.

At home the two of them are asleep.
They can never know who I've been, who I am —
I, an officer and a gentleman, make
some tea and I am not hated.
Now in the famous
movie starring all of us
the themes of an evening commence:
the black gerbils scrape their wheel,

160

the foghorns call themselves back
out of the fog, the homosexuals
in the quaint hotel sing happy birthday around a piano —
but nothing can disturb my wife and child,
for now they are in another world.

The Rockefeller Collection of Primitive Art

Softer my neighbor rocks his lover through the human night,
softly and softly, so as not to tell the walls,
the walls the friends of the spinster. But I'm only a spinster,
I'm not a virgin. I have made love. I have known desire.

I followed desire through the museums.
We seemed to float along sculptures,
along the clicking ascent
of numerals in the guards' hands. Brave works
by great masters were all around us.

And then we came out of a tunnel into one of those restaurants
where the natural light was so unnatural
as to make heavenly even our fingernails and each radish.
I saw everyone's skull beneath the skin,
I saw sorrow painting its way out of the faces,
someone was telling a lie and I could taste it,
and I heard the criminal tear-fall,
saw the dog
who dances with his shirt rolled up to his nipples,
the spider . . .

Why are their mouths small tight circles,
the figures of Africa, New Guinea, New Zealand,
why are their mouths astonished kisses beneath drugged eyes,
why is the eye of the cantaloupe expressionless
but its skin rippling with terror,
and out beyond Coney Island in the breathless waste
of Atlantia, why
does the water move when it is already there?
My neighbor's bedsprings struggle
— soon she will begin to scream —

I think of them always
travelling through space,
riding their bed so
softly it staves the world through the air

of my room — it is their right,
because we freely admit how powerful the sight is,
we say that eyes stab and glances rake,
but it is not the sight
that lets us taste the salt on someone's shoulder in the night,
the musk of fear in the morning,
the savor of falling in the falling
elevators in the buildings or rock,
it is the dark that lets us it is the dark. If
I can imagine them then
why can't I imagine this?

In Palo Alto

Every day I have to learn more about shame
from the people in old photographs
in second-hand stores, and from the people
in the photographic studies of damage and grief,
where the light assails a window and the figure's back
is all we see — or from the very faces
we never witness in these pictures, several of whom
I passed today in their windows, some hesitant,
some completely committed to worthlessness —
or even from my own face, handed up suddenly by the car's
mirror or a glass door. When I was waiting
for a bus, the man beside me
showed me a picture of a naked youth
with an erection, and the loneliness
in his face as he held this photograph
was like a light waking me from the dead.
I was more ashamed of it than I was of my own
a few days later — just tonight, in fact —
when solitude visited me on a residential street
where I stopped and waited for a woman to pass
again across her unshaded window, so that
I could see her naked.

As I stood there teaching
the night what I knew about this sort of thing,
a figure with the light coming from in front
while the axioms of the world one by one disowned me,
a private and hopeless figure, probably,
somebody simply not worth the trouble of hating,
it occurred to me it was better to be like this
than to be forced to look at a picture of it
happening to someone else. I walked on.
When I got back to the streets of noises and routines,
the places full of cries of one kind or another,
the motels of experience, a fool in every room,

all the people I've been talking about were there.
And we told one another we ought to be ashamed.

The Veil

When the tide lay under the clouds
of an afternoon and gave them back to themselves
oilier a little and filled with anonymous boats,
I used to sit and drink at the very edge of it,
where light passed through the liquids in the glasses
and threw itself on the white drapes
of the tables, resting there like clarity
itself, you might think,
right where you could put a hand to it.
As drink gave way to drink, the slow
unfathomable voices of luncheon made
a window of ultra-violet light in the mind,
through which one at last saw the skeleton
of everything, stripped of any sense or consequence,
freed of geography and absolutely devoid
of charm; and in this originating
brightness you might see
somebody putting a napkin against his lips
or placing a blazing credit card on a plastic tray
and you'd know. You would know goddamn it. And never be able to say.

RICHARD KATROVAS

The Mystic Pig

On the balcony of *La Fitte in Exile,*
on the corner of Bourbon and Dumaine,
at the intersection of the Merciful
Embrace and the Middle Finger, where Hope's punk,
Desire, taps his cane along the cracked sidewalk,
where I, awed, disgusted, yet wholly
reconciled must pass each night never daring
to gaze up, the Boys of Summer are doing
the Mystic Pig. It seems they are not always
gentle with one another. It seems they
are forever beating their wings yet never
taking off. In this city, where the mauve
resonance of a summer dusk is just
another flag announcing predilection,
these sons have found sanctuary. They will
go forth upon the packed avenues, seeking
love while shunning the rhetoric of love;
for they have learned to live in a new
language and it is terminal:

Blue flag right hip pocket—*I shall cradle*
you for an hour and fill you up with your
father's shadow.

Brown flag left hip pocket—*I shall humble*
myself before you and receive your darkest
blessing.

Red flag right hip pocket—*I shall salute you*
as you sing your anthem of remorse . . .

So the passions of men for men are beautifully
reduced, refined, bathed in the blood of the Mystic Pig.

How shall I go forth among these angels,
an interloper to their world,
to them a charter member
of the Brotherhood of Mother Fuckers?

164

I'll go quietly,
gazing neither up nor down
nor left nor right,
keeping their joy, their pain,
their mysterious nobility
on the slow-burning periphery.

Star Boys

All the tough dudes
are whistling in the dark.
Wildman Bob's in Chino.
Dirty Dave's doing time
in his daddy's garage.
Wolf's a woman.
Lizard's got nobody.
Now we all know nothing
really happens, boys.
Things just get perpetrated.
Besides, the sun's a pain
when you're tripping
on what's gone down
and I'd rather stick
my finger in the cool moon.
I'd rather sit and watch
purple curls of smoke
flatten on the ceiling
in the blacklite
chew on salted scallions
pop a couple beers
and think a white wall
till fog comes in early morning
and I can go outside
walk down to the pier
and listen to the birds
and water. But I can't
wait. The stars
are whistling lips
of the dead arranged
in a great tattoo and if
we could back up, boys,

I mean, right out of the universe,
we'd see it's just an anchor,
a naked body, a pierced Heart.

Blues' Body

The souls of drunks bob in the rafters
and a keen, grey glow shimmers the counter.

Fished-faced old man stirs me a cool one
out of what is left of night.

He spins the rocks glass into the air
to glaze it with Pernod, then pours my seventh Sazarac.

Only now, in this light, at this time,
in these states of Louisiana and Inertia

will Blues' body show itself:
Creole hermaphrodite decked in denim and chiffon.

From the electric-blue dawn she enters,
trolling her wrap over the parquetry.

The bartender rolls his somnolent eyes,
sees, blinks slowly, and turns to the well.

Layering six liqueurs
over a spoon-lip into a double-shot jigger

he says nothing. She turns the *Pousse l'amour*
in the lamp-light and is satisfied

then closes her eyes and sips, pinky erect,
the Secret of Life etched on her broad bicep:

Momma love Daddy
but he be dead.

Our Island

Our father's ship
has entered the mist.
His charmed cargo
will grow precious in the hold
but will never spoil,
salted, as it is, by tears.
He's charted a course
for the birthmark
you have on your back,
I in miniature on my forearm.
Once, dripping from the shower,
laughing, drunk and steaming
in the cold motel room,
he stretched the blue-veined skin
of his scrotum into a map
and showed us the same marking.
I wish him safe passage.
I hope you do, too, Theresa Rene.
I wish him safe passage
from this world of banks and prisons
so he may haul his cargo of outrageous needs
into his own blood and search always
for our island. May he be a hero
unto himself and may you
never forget,
that though I do not know
the woman you've become
you were my first lover
lying upside down next to me
so we could tickle each other's feet.
Come here, turn over, I'd whisper,
and in the dirty light from street lamps
illuminating our room,
I traced with my best finger
over and over
the coastline of your island
till you slept.

Bloomfield, Inc.

My little ones pull
from the ground, hands
cupping their faces like petals,
like shields. Thus they go
wandering, not so blindly
as aimlessly, under several stars
bumping, turning, robed
in gauze-white gowns.
That is my dream.
In this life, rooted
in the mercy of the State,
they are the flowers of the Commonwealth.
Peroxide, urine, Betadine, Unisalve:
the several scents comprising
a single scent that will not wash
from my skin. The coins
I am given to care for them
are diminished in their eyes.
I look into their eyes.
What do they see in my eyes?
Nothing gauche as pity.
I cannot wipe their asses,
lift them in and out of bed
and pity them.
Not for minimum wage.
Harry, seventeen,
sixty-four-pound quadraplegic
my *Mr. Nonsequitur,* what do you *mean*
I'm a bad angel in God's air force?
What do you *mean* I ain't seen
pussy since pussy seen me?
When I pull the morning shift
I lift you from the sheets—
your eyes still closed, your
gorged penis pointing to Heaven—
Little friend, when you die
I won't weep. I won't even
get drunk. I'll drive
real fast on Rt. 29
and if a full moon's up
I'll cut the lights. Home,
I'll read John Clare's

168

"I Am" and later on
burst out laughing in the dark.
Harry, some of us are real slow.
Some of us will never get it.
Now, I gather what I can and cannot
hold. The earth's burnt fingers
I hold to my lips and coo into them.
My dreams are prophylactic, small, and soiled.
In one there is a door I kick and kick.
My arms spilling flowers from the field.
Richard, I say, *Richard, let me in.*

SYDNEY LEA

A Natural Shame

The moon's small aura pins
the shadow of the sleeping children's
hobbyhorse down, black comic
monster, flat to the floor.
And I, inept at prayer,
clutching the bedclothes, I picture
wreck, gun, epidemic.
Tabloid headlines figure
in the elm tree's leaves. Unmoored,
a shingle flaps into air.
Snapped from sleep so short
it only dried the throat
by a phrase: "A natural shame . . . ."
As if in her long career
nature had ever known shame —
this sentence, out of the country
junkyard that is the mind
untended, wakes me to sentry
duty. Unsettled by wind,
my old dog clicks along
the halls in disrepair.
Their ancestors' cells among
the bloodways of the babies
conspire, too soon, too soon.
The will would impose its stasis,
but in every pictured scene
I envision a moving thing:
bicycle tire spinning,
glucose bottle dripping
like heartbreak, murderer fleeing,
solid realist, Earth, unfurling
into romantic flight,
ink going white.

After Labor Day

Your son is seven years dead.
"But it seems," I said, seeing your face
buckle in mid-conversation
as over the fields came winging the trebles
of children at holiday play—
I said, "But it seems like yesterday."

"No," you said,
"Like today."

In the first of the black fall drizzles,
in a morning when world's-end seems to hover
too near, the early fallen
leaves slick on the highway as blood,
the yellow ball had spun to a halt
on the white line:
your small child scurried there like an ignorant vole . . .

It is the time of year
when hawks rush down the pass where you live,
but the heat last weekend held them
northward. So grounded, we talked like voluble schoolkids
inside, instead.   —Or I did.
You lost in thought, dark brows arched
like the wings of birds at travel,
or soaring to hide, or seek.

At home, I recall your eagle visage, how now
and then it falls
just so. In the change, in the first cold autumn rain,
I play at identification.
I imagine how Redtail, Cooper's,
Roughleg, Little Blue Darter,
and the odd outsider —Swainson's, say—
now pass you by,
as at home in my study I watch
two scruffy starlings on a wire outside
fronting what they seem to have
no choice but to front
till one peels off, is sucked it seems into woods, and through
the glass I yet can hear him.
His croaks come this way, as if the other

were the one who had vanished, not he.

Just so lost children imagine
their parents are lost, not they.
"Where did you go?" they chirp, as if we hadn't been
shrieking, searching.
Or as if our terror had been a game.

It's the season of the mushroom all of a sudden.
Closed though my window is,
over the vapors and trees I also hear
the doubled scream of a kestrel.

You heard, these seven years have heard, the swish
of tandem tires through puddles,
the last gasps
of airbrakes, screams.
And loud as unthinkable detonation
—or so at least in dreams it seems—
the impact:

every outside sound raced clear to you.
But walls and panes cut short your shouts
from inside the house,
as if *you* were the small boy
to whom the remote roar
of the world was suddenly apparent,
yet whose voice was as in dreams
unheard or worse: irrelevant.

In the lulls, by way of compensation,
I talked the holiday away.
Talked and talked and
talked and talked
and catalogued the game:
I called attention
to early Goldeneyes out on the marsh;
to the way in later light
—like cheap raincoats— the feather's colors
on the backs of seaducks would change and change;
and, higher, to the cloud that would mean this greater change,
swooping against the yellow ball of the sun.

As if through a shield of thin glass,

there was the further drone of the bomber whereby,
you said, "One day the world will be lost,"

and the bitter joke, I understood,
be on those of us who all these seasons
have played at discourse.
"Where did you go?"
So the world will ask.

To the Summer Sweethearts

The easiness of August night:
a fall of meteors,
moths jewel my house

across the lane, I float
in the fire-pond, in the light-
riffled fire-pond. Cattails puff
their buoyant seed. The tadpoles
have absorbed their tails:
they hum and pause and hum.

Innocent, I ask you in.

The egg-rich mayflies dip and rise,
dimple the surface, die.
The silver guppies sip them.

Come sit, at least, composite
(eyes of Margot, Susie's hair,
the even smile of Sarah),
there on the bank.
You've seen the evil-looking turtles,
but sweetheart they never bite.

There. There.
Let's have a look at you.

Listen to the Whip-Poor-Will,
Chuck-Will's-Widow,
Nightjar.

The Return: Intensive Care

—for David Field

I felt for the button . . .
There's a circle of perpetual occultation
at the depressed pole
within which stars never rise,
and at the elevated one, one of apparition
from which they never fall.
I used these facts
to figure the limits of my situation
—mine? or was it yours?—
as again I came back.

Where was I? . . .
I thumbed the button for your floor.
It lit.
Suddenly, I thought,
everywhere there are circles,
as in some new weather or fashion:
the breasts both of a young farmgirl
and, sadder, of a fat old orderly
riding up beside me;
the elevator's orbicular lampbulbs;

and, the color of linen,
each drop of snow the night before,
big and round as a saucer —
a night such as we persist in
calling a freak, though it isn't
anything more than the cycling back of things
too cursedly familiar.
Yes, though it was spring,
though it was April,
the moon had worn a great wet halo.

Signifying what?
Why look up
the facts on charts?
How often in history
has everything happened!
The nurse again wheeled away
your tray with its apple, untouched,

174

and two dark plums
which precisely matched,
in color and conformation,

the raccoon rounds
of valor and of exhaustion
through which your eyes peered,
brighter, still, than any planet.
O *Jesus Jesus Jesus Jesus!*
inwardly I cried,
to me the word
recurring like any old habit.
Poor stately Jew, forgive the helplessness
that enforced my genteel outward mode

as you lay there,
my small talk Yankee palaver
of mercilessness in Mother Nature —
buds in remission,
pathetic birds
spiraling up from the sheeted roads
as if —I surmised— nothing now remained
but vertical migration.
I dropped my eyes. All else, anything
that I might have been moved to say,

anything that might have reached to the heart
of what we may or may not be
here on earth
to do or serve, dismayed
and frightened me.
I couldn't speak
of anything beyond the trivial,
by horror of risk held back,
by horror of saying something
even more banal.

You were on morphine.
You who for the length of this evil illness
had never complained
but had made for yourself a figure
—*Look to the light,*
or *Don't try to cling . . .*
Shy of prayer,

desperate with my own feckless
impulse to speech, at length I hung
as if in mid-air

as the dark outside
began again its round.
All so cursedly dignified!
At length, in the distilled absence of sound,
I recalled my *why why why why why!*
at the death of my small terrier.
What a petty thing to remember!
And yet perhaps those yelps
when I was so young
were the only eloquence possible.

As was perhaps the gentle rejoinder
(she had seen more than I)
of my mother's mother:
Revelation helps.
There in the hospital,
lacking for words to tender,
I had recourse to fashion.
Forgive me, I nattered;
then left, once more pushing the button;
then lifted my eyes,

searching a sign of perpetuation.
Would it do any good to tell you that I cried?
There were stars, or there were none,
from wherever it was I stood.
There was, or there wasn't, a moon.

LARRY LEVIS

The Poet at Seventeen

My youth? I hear it mostly in the long, volleying
Echoes of billiards in the pool halls where
I spent it all, extravagantly, believing
My delicate touch on a cue would last for years.

Outside the vineyards vanished under rain,
And the orchards held still or seemed to hold their breath
When the men I worked with, pruning trees, sang
Their lost songs: *Amapola; La Paloma;*

Jalisco, No Te Rajes — the corny tunes
Their sons would just as soon forget, at recess,
Where they lounged apart in small groups of their own.
Still, even when they laughed, they laughed in Spanish.

I hated high school then, & on weekends drove
A tractor through the widowed fields. It was so boring
I memorized poems above the engine's monotone:
Sometimes whole days slipped past without my noticing,

And birds of all kinds flew in front of me then.
I learned to tell them apart by their empty squabblings,
The subtlest change in plumage, or the inflection
Of a call. And why not admit it? I was happy

Then. I believed in no one. I had the kind
Of solitude the world usually allows
Only to kings & criminals who are extinct,
Who disdain this world, & who rot, corrupt & shallow

As fields I disced. I turned up the same gray
Earth for years. Still, the land made a glum raisin
Each autumn, & made that little hell of days —
The vines must have seemed like cages to the Mexicans,

Who were paid seven cents a tray for the grapes
They picked. It was hot inside the vines, & spiders
Strummed their webs: Black Widow; Daddy Long Legs.
The vine canes whipped our faces. None of us cared.

A life like that? It seemed to go on forever —
Reading poems in school, then driving a stuttering tractor
Warm afternoons, then billiards on blue October
Nights. The thick stars. But mostly now I remember

The trees, wearing their mysterious yellow sullenness
Like party dresses. And parties I didn't attend.
And then the first ice hung like spider lattices,
Or the embroideries of Great Aunt No One,

And then the first dark entering the trees —
And inside, the adults with their cocktails before dinner,
The way they always seemed afraid of something,
And sat so rigidly, although the land was theirs.

Adolescence

Our babysitter lives across from the Dodge Street cemetery,
And behind her broad, untroubled face.
Her sons play touch football all afternoon
Among the graves of clerks & Norwegian settlers.
At night, these huge trees, rooted in such quiet,
Arch over the tombstones as if in exultation,
As if they inhaled starlight.
Their limbs reach
Toward each other & their roots must touch the dead.

When I was fifteen,
There was a girl who loved me; who I did not love, & she
Died, that year, of spinal meningitis. By then she
Had already left home, & was working in a carnival —
One of those booths where you are supposed
To toss a dime onto a small dish. Finally,
In Laredo, Texas, someone anonymous, & too late, bought her
A bus ticket back . . . .
Her father, a gambler & horse dealer, wept
Openly the day she was buried. I remember looking off
In embarrassment at the woods behind his house.
The woods were gray, vagrant, the color of smoke
Or sky. I remember thinking then that
If I had loved her, or even slept with her once,

She might still be alive.
And if, instead, we had gone away together
On two bay horses that farted when they began to gallop,
And if, later, we had let them
Graze at their leisure on the small tufts of spring grass
In those woods, & if the disintegrating print of the ferns
Was a lullaby there against the dry stones & the trunks
Of fallen trees, then maybe nothing would have happened . . . .
There are times, hiking with my wife past
Abandoned orchards of freckled apples & patches of sunlight
In New Hampshire, or holding her closely against me at night
Until she sleeps, when nothing else matters, when
The trees shine without meaning more than they are, in moonlight,
And when it seems possible to disappear wholly into someone
Else, as into a wish on a birthday, the candles trembling . . . .

Maybe nothing would have happened, but I heard that
Her father died, a year later, in a Sierra lumber camp.
He had been drinking steadily all week,
And was dealing cards
When the muscle of his own heart
Kicked him back into his chair so hard its wood snapped.
He must have thought there was something
Suddenly very young inside his body,
If he had time to think . . . .
And if death is an adolescent, closing his eyes to the music
On the radio of that passing car,
I think he does not know his own strength.
If I stand here long enough in this stillness I can feel
His silence involve, somehow, the silence of these trees,
The sky, the little squawking toy my son lost
When it slipped into the river today . . . .
Today, I am thirty-four years old. I know
That horse dealer with a limp loved his plain & crazy daughter.
I know, also, that it did no good.
Soon, the snows will come again, & cover that place
Where he sat at a wobbling card table underneath
A Ponderosa pine, & cover
Even the three cards he dropped there, three silent diamonds,
And cover everything in the Sierras, & make my meaning plain.

Winter Stars

My father once broke a man's hand
Over the exhaust pipe of a John Deere tractor. The man,
Rubén Vásquez, wanted to kill his own father
With a sharpened fruit knife, & he held
The curved tip of it, lightly, between his first
Two fingers, so it could slash
Horizontally, & with surprising grace,
Across a throat. It was like a glinting beak in a hand,
And, for a moment, the light held still
On those vines. When it was over,
My father simply went in & ate lunch, & then, as always,
Lay alone in the dark, listening to music.
He never mentioned it.

I never understood how anyone could risk his life,
Then listen to Vivaldi.

Sometimes, I go out into this yard at night,
And stare through the wet branches of an oak
In winter, & realize I am looking at the stars
Again. A thin haze of them, shining
And persisting.

It used to make me feel lighter, looking up at them.
In California, that light was closer.
In a California no one will ever see again,
My father is beginning to die. Something
Inside him is slowly taking back
Every word it ever gave him.
Now, if we try to talk, I watch my father
Search for a lost syllable as if it might
Solve everything, & though he can't remember, now,
The word for it, he is ashamed . . . .
If you can think of the mind as a place continually
Visited, a whole city placed behind
The eyes, & shining, I can imagine, now, its end —
As when the lights go off, one by one,
In a hotel at night, until at last
All of the travelers will be asleep, or until
Even the thin glow from the lobby is a kind
Of sleep; & while the woman behind the desk
Is applying more lacquer to her nails,

180

You can almost believe that the elevator,
As it ascends, must open upon starlight.

I stand out on the street, & do not go in.
That was our agreement, at my birth.

And for years I believed
That what went unsaid between us became empty,
And pure, like starlight, & it persisted.
I got it all wrong.
I wound up believing in words the way a scientist
Believes in carbon, after death.

Tonight, I'm talking to you, father, although
It is quiet here in the Midwest, where a small wind,
The size of a wrist, wakes the cold again —
Which may be all that's left of you & me.

When I left home at seventeen, I left for good.

That pale haze of stars goes on & on,
Like laughter that has found a final, silent shape
On a black sky. It means everything
It cannot say. Look, it's empty out there, & cold.
Cold enough to reconcile
Even a father, even a son.

Family Romance

> "Dressed to die . . . "
> —Dylan Thomas

Sister once of weeds & a dark water that held still
In ditches reflecting the odd,
Abstaining clouds that passed, & kept
Their own counsel, we
Were different, we kept our own counsel.
Outside the tool shed in the noon heat, while our father
Ground some piece of metal
That would finally fit, with grease & an hour of pushing,
The needs of the mysterious Ford tractor,
We argued out, in adolescence,

Whole systems of mathematics, ethics,
And finally agreed that *altruism,*
Whose long vowel sounded like the pigeons,
Roosting stupidly & about to be shot
In the barn, was impossible
If one was born a Catholic. The Swedish
Lutherans, whom the nuns called
"statue smashers," the Japanese on
Neighboring farms, were, we guessed,
A little better off . . . .
When I was twelve, I used to stare at weeds
Along the road, at the way they kept trembling
Long after a car had passed;
Or at gnats in families hovering over
Some rotting peaches, & wonder why it was
I had been born a human.
Why not a weed, or a gnat?
Why not a horse, or a spider? And why an American?
I did not think that anything could choose me
To be a Larry Levis before there even *was*
A Larry Levis. It was strange, but not strange enough
To warrant some design.
                              On the outside,
The barn, with flaking paint, was still off-white.
Inside, it was always dark, all the way up
To the rafters where the pigeons moaned,
I later thought, as if in sexual complaint,
Or sexual abandon; I never found out which.
When I walked in with a twelve gauge & started shooting,
They fell, like gray fruit, at my feet —
Fat, thumping things that grew quieter
When their eyelids, a softer gray, closed,
Part of the way, at least,
And their friends or lovers flew out a kind of skylight
Cut for loading hay.
I don't know, exactly, what happened then.
Except my sister moved to Switzerland.
My brother got a job
With Colgate-Palmolive.
He was selling soap in Lodi, California.
Later, in his car, & dressed
To die, or live again, forever,
I drove to my first wedding.
I smelled the stale boutonniere in my lapel,

A deceased young flower.
I wondered how my brother's Buick
Could go so fast, &,
Still questioning, or catching, a last time,
And old chill from childhood,
I thought: why me, why her, & knew it wouldn't last.

Sensationalism

In Josef Koudelka's photograph, untitled & with no date
Given to help us with history, a man wearing
Dark clothes is squatting, his right hand raised slightly,
As if in explanation, & because he is talking,
Seriously now, to a horse that would be white except
For its markings — the darkness around its eyes, muzzle,
Legs & tail, by which it is, technically, a gray, or a dapple gray,
With a streak of pure white like heavy cream on its rump.
There is a wall behind them both, which, like most walls, has
No ideas, & nothing to make us feel comfortable . . . .
After a while, because I know so little, &
Because the muted sunlight on that wall will not change,
I begin to believe that the man's wife & children
Were shot & thrown into a ditch a week before this picture
Was taken, that this is still Czechoslovakia, & that there is
The beginning of spring in the air. That is why
The man is talking, & as clearly as he can, to a horse.
He is trying to explain these things,
While the horse, gray as those days at the end
Of winter, when days seem lost in thought, is, after all,
Only a horse. No doubt the man knows people he could talk to:
The bars are open by now, but he has chosen
To confide in this gelding, as he once did to his own small
Children, who could not, finally, understand him any better.
This afternoon, in the middle of his life & in the middle
Of this war, a man is trying to stay sane.
To stay sane he must keep talking to a horse, its blinders
On & a rough snaffle bit still in its mouth, wearing
Away the corners of its mouth, with one ear cocked forward to listen,
While the other ear tilts backward slightly, inattentive,
As if suddenly catching a music behind it. Of course,
I have to admit I have made all of this up, & that

It could be wrong to make up anything. Perhaps the man is perfectly
Happy. Perhaps Koudelka arranged all of this
And then took the picture as a way of saying
Goodbye to everyone who saw it, & perhaps Josef Koudelka was
Only two years old when the Nazis invaded Prague.
I do not wish to interfere, Reader, with your solitude —
So different from my own. In fact, I would take back everything
I've said here, if that would make you feel any better,
Unless even that retraction would amount to a milder way
Of interfering; & a way by which you might suspect me
Of some subtlety. Or mistake me for someone else, someone
Not disinterested enough in what you might think
Of this. Of the photograph. Of me.
Once, I was in love with a woman, & when I looked at her
My face altered & took on the shape of her face,
Made thin by alcohol, sorrowing, brave. And though
There was a kind of pain in her face, I felt no pain
When this happened to mine, when the bones
Of my own face seemed to change. But even this
Did not do us any good, &, one day,
She went mad, waking in tears she mistook for blood,
And feeling little else except for this concern about bleeding
Without pain. I drove her to the hospital, & then,
After a few days, she told me she had another lover . . . . So,
Walking up the street where it had been raining earlier,
Past the darkening glass of each shop window to the hotel,
I felt a sensation of peace flood my body, as if to cleanse it,
And thought it was because I had been told the truth . . . But, you see,
Even that happiness became a lie, & even that was taken
From me, finally, as all lies are . . . . Later,
I realized that maybe I felt strong that night only
Because she was sick, for other reasons, & in that place.
And so began my long convalescence, & simple adulthood.
I never felt that way again, when I looked at anyone else;
I never felt my face change into any other face.
It is a difficult thing to do, & so maybe
It is just as well. That man, for instance. He was a *saboteur.*
He ended up talking to a horse, & hearing, on the street
Outside that alley, the Nazis celebrating, singing, even.
If he went mad beside that wall, I think his last question
Was whether they shot his wife & children before they threw them
Into the ditch, or after. For some reason, it mattered once,
If only to him. And before he turned into paper.

ROBERT LONG

First Day of Spring

My shoes are in their firing squad position
In the closet. My dog's dead,
But if he were here, he'd be snoring on the floor.
Accidents will happen. If you make them happen,
So much the worse. Yet

Everything goes by so quickly! The first stanza's
Already as ancient as any high-school history,
And sudden absences like those leave sudden holes.
When I got cracked in the nose with a baseball bat
Playing grammar school softball,

I saw angels, Lyndon B. Johnson, and doctors
For the next three years, until my nose
Stopped bleeding and started breathing again.
You could say my nose went on a strike.
Now it veers toward Portugal

No matter where I'm headed. I'm talking
About my generation, or re-generation.
I saw my best hand-patched jeans
Hit the heap, then reappear, miraculously,
On angels walking down Main Street.

Burning Out

I shot pool in a bar last night,
With a pal. Someone was playing the piano badly:
Show tunes, mostly. The room was filled
With smoke from the fireplace, cigarettes, pot.
There was a complex curtain in the air.

I told my friend I hated to see him drinking so much,
Hanging out with self-destructive people,
Running up tabs and running out of rope.
We're old friends, since high school.
He sank the seven. I chalked up.

Lying on my stomach in bed, at seventeen,
After a tab of four-way sunshine,
I knew that all energy emanates from the solar plexus.
I'd seen the sun, a miraculous red pill,
On the wall. I loved everything, anything was special.

Once, I talked someone down from a bad trip.
He said everything was on fire; I told him he was right.
We sat there watching the rain come down.
I knew this other kid, a good athlete,
Who jumped out a window when he was twenty.

The last time I saw him, his eyes were like
Two cigarette burns. We drove around
Until we were both sick to death with the whole thing.
I told him to call me that night, after work:
We could talk. But he didn't.

This is me talking my head off,
Saying I grew up, where did you go?
This is me talking to you in a metallic voice,
Through tin cans on string, across backyards with blue wash flapping,
Saying I loved you, saying goodbye.

Chelsea

I'm comfortable here, on 50 mg. of Librium,
Two hundred bucks in my pocket
And a new job just a week away.
I can walk the streets in a calm haze,
My blood pressure down to where I'm almost human,
Make countless pay-phone calls from street corners:
Buzzing, they go by in near-neon trails,
People, people like me, headed for black bean soup,
For screams in alleyways, for the homey click
Of the front door's closing, heading home
Past all those faces you know you've seen before:
Like a rear-screen projection in an old movie,
The actors pacing a treadmill or pretending to steer,
And the same '56 Dodge weaving in the background.

It's like walking into a room
And suddenly realizing you've had sex with everyone there
At least once, watching your friends' lives
Tangling as you all grow somewhat older,
Somehow more resolute. Bookshelves grow, too,
And you notice your handwriting becoming more matter-of-fact.
It's as if all that comic smartness we glided through in youth
Were somehow desperate. And now we come to terms
With the sidewalk's coruscating glamor,
The rows of dull but neat garbage cans,
Each with its own painted number,
The poodles and patrol cars, the moon rising high,
Like aspirin, over Eighth Avenue.

I get some cigarettes on a corner,
Catch my reflection in the glass. I'm neatly tranquilized,
And strangely happy just to walk out near the traffic,
Consider the asphalt intersections where kids lean on lamp posts
              and fire alarms,
Where a man is shutting the iron gate on his ochre divans,
Where the beautiful taxis whizz and honk,
Clanking over sewer covers and smashing beer cans.
And windows light, one by one, like comic strip inspirations,
And me, here, on your streetcorner,
In my second-favorite neighborhood in the world,
My index finger in the hole marked "9,"
Ready for anything, finally, and finally ready.

Somewhere on the Coast of Maine

I think I like it here, I mean I think
There's something attractive about the ocean's way
Of insinuating itself into anyone's life,
As if salt air could solve anything, as if
That watery presence insured a special kind of luck,

Some new variety of insurance:
Like walking out onto the street and knowing
That a bus will come by to take you up- or down-
Or cross-town. All you need is ninety cents
And a half-decent haircut. I like

The way the sun comes down, here:
It's kind of sweet, and calm: orange
And aquamarine over all that field, that green stretch
Of quiet, despite everything. Here's what I'm talking about:
The way you dragged me all over the island

Your parents own, that kind of curious enthusiasm;
Let's keep this on hold, this anyone
Who's close to you. But I don't want to veer
Away from things. Listen,
I love Maine as much as the next guy,

Maybe moreso. There's nothing like mussels
Fresh-scrubbed, cooked in a little white wine, and there's nothing
Like the 7 a.m. view from my window, of the sun
Shining bravely over New England, and everyone:
Your parents, your sister and two nephews,

Sitting downstairs, scrambling eggs, brewing coffee,
Thinking only of breakfast, or extensions of breakfast:
Say, that time I made a complicated pasta
Which served as lunch, the next day. I like pasta.
I *love* pasta. Don't you? Lately, I've become fond

Of movies starring Rod Taylor, movies
From the late sixties: limousines, diplomats from Australia.
But back to Maine: It was swell.
I'm glad we went. Someday
I'll drop you a postcard describing exactly how swell it was,

But I don't think you're ready for it, quite yet.
Such indecision—where, when, why—
Leads to a kind of illumination; by crossing off
Obvious possibilities on the List of What One Does,
One can't help but be steered, somewhat like a drunken tourist,

In the direction of novelty. The snow that came
When we wanted it to snow. Encounters
With hostile men in gun shops: I almost bought it,
That beautiful 30.06 we ran into. Those guys
Were real nice; they nearly blew off our heads

For breathing, but what the heck. It comes
With the territory. I had this friend who wrote mysteries

For a living, but he died. The last thing he told me
Was to keep things "light." I've never
Been able to understand exactly what he meant by that—

I mean, I actually think about these things—

But such advice seems appropriate,
Here in Friendship, Maine, where we had
Two or three games of pool (I lost)
And a few beers, where we cruised the wet highway
Endlessly: the slow slope of hills,

The mystery of landscape turning gray-blue at dusk,
Where I loved you, for better or for worse,
Ex post facto, purely confidential,
In the little white Honda, wishing
We were somewhere else.

Debts

Things disappear:
The glove lost in snow, pens,
Books loaned and never returned,
Virginity, your dog

Who had to be put to sleep
Because he wouldn't do it himself.
They say rules are to be broken,
But if you break one

They come knocking on the door
Right in the middle
Of a game of Parcheesi,
Or dinner, or your life.

The car's stupid grin
Lights up the driveway all night long,
And another, different dog
Twitches at the foot of the bed,

But you're still there, in the dark,
Thinking about the phone bill,
Watching the end of your cigarette:
The Incredible Glowing Skull.

THOMAS LUX

Barn Fire

It starts, somehow, in the hot damp
and soon the lit bales
throb in the hayloft. The tails

of mice quake in the dust,
the bins of grain, the mangers stuffed
with clover, the barrels of oats
shivering individually in their pale

husks — animate and inanimate: they know
with the first whiff in the dark.
And we knew, or should have: that day
the calendar refused its nail

on the wall and the crab apples hurling
themselves to the ground . . . Only moments
and the flames like a blue fist curl

all around the black. There is some
small blaring from the calves, and the cows'
nostrils flare only once
more, or twice, above the dead dry

metal troughs . . . . No more fat tongues worrying
the salt licks, no more heady smells
of deep green from silos rising now

like huge twin chimneys above all this.
With the lofts full there is no stopping
nor even getting close: it will rage

until dawn and beyond, — and the horses,
because they know they are safe there,
and horses run back into the barn.

Pedestrian

Tottering and elastic, middle name of Groan,
ramfeezled after a hard night
at the corpse-polishing plant, slope-
shouldered, a half loaf
of bread, even his hair tired, famished,
fingering the diminished beans
in his pocket—you meet him.
On a thousand streetcorners you meet him
emerging from the subway, emerging
from your own chest—this sight's shrill
metallic vapors pass into you.
His fear is of being broken,
of becoming *too* dexterous in stripping
the last few shoelaces of meat
from a chicken's carcass, of being moved by nothing
short of the Fall of Rome, of being stooped
in the cranium over some loss he's forgotten
the anniversary of . . . You meet him,
know his defeat, though proper
and inevitable, is not yours, although yours also
is proper and inevitable: so many defeats
queer and insignificant (as illustration:
the first time you lay awake all night
waiting for dawn—and were disappointed), so many
no-hope exhaustions hidden,
their gaze dully glazed inward. —And yet we all
fix our binoculars on the horizon's hazy fear-heaps,
and cruise towards them, fat sails
forward . . . You meet him on the corners,
in bus stations, on the blind avenues
leading neither in
nor out of Hell, you meet him
and with him you walk.

Night Above The Town

In the glassed-in jazz club acres above
flat streets spoking distant ovals
I think of: Foster Grandparents. Because,

so many stories below, isolated,
oxygen-starved on asphalt, is a blue
and white Foster Grandparent's bus. The tunes
up here are dumb and loud
so I look down
to what I can see: I think
it would be good
to have a foster grandparent, I'll apply
and plead a need for wisdom
and brownies. —Grandma, pinched one,
I need your tin-tasting sharp calm,
come back both grouchy
and smart; Grandfather, distanced,
disinherit me, pass again your cool palms
along the flats of my head . . . . I'll apply
tomorrow—if there's a bus
then there's an office
and *slam!*: what I'm back to is bad
music, the xylophonist seems to be beating
mice to death, there's a foul
pelican sax and the smell
of youth's pleasant sex and sweat and all
their hundreds of feet on the floor
and fists keeping time
on the tables . . . Grandmother. Grandfather.

Graveyard By The Sea

I wonder if they sleep better here
so close to the elemental pentameter
of the sea which comes in incessantly?
Just a few square acres of sand
studded mainly with thick posts
as if the coffins beneath were boats
tied fast to prevent further drift.
I half stumble around one pre-dawn,
just a dog following the footprints
of another dog with me, and stop

before one particular grave: a cross
inlaid with large splinters of mirror.

Whoever lies here is distinguished,
certainly, but I wonder—why mirrors?
For signaling? Who? No, they're embedded
in the stone and so can't be flicked
to reflect the sun or moonlight.
Is the sleeper here unusually vain
and the glass set for those times of dark
ascensions — to smooth the death gown,

to apply a little lipstick to the white
worms of the lips? No again. I think
they're for me and the ones who come,
like me, at this hour, in this half-light.
The ones who come half-drunk, half-wild,
and wholly in fear — so we may gaze
into the ghosts of our own faces,
and be touched by this chill of all
chills, — and then go home, alive,
to sleep the sleep of the awake.

It's The Little Towns I Like

It's the little towns I like
with their little mills making ratchets
and stanchions, elastic web,
spindles, you
name it. I like them in New England,
America, particularly—providing
bad jobs good enough to live on, to live in
families even: kindergarten,
church suppers, beach umbrellas . . . The towns
are real, so fragile in their loneliness
a flood could come along
(and floods have) and cut them in two,
in half. There is no mayor,
the town council's not prepared
for this, three of the four policemen
are stranded on their roofs . . . and it doesn't stop
raining. The mountain
is so thick with water parts of it just slide
down on the heifers—soggy, suicidal—

in the pastures below. It rains, it rains
in these towns and, because
there's no other way, your father gets in a rowboat
so he can go to work.

Empty Pitchforks

There was poverty before money.

There was debtor's prison before inmates,
there was hunger pre-fossil,

there was pain before a nervous system
to convey it to the brain, there existed

poverty before intelligence, or accountants,
before narration, there was bankruptcy aswirl

in nowhere, it was palpable
where nothing was palpable, there was repossession

in the gasses forming so many billion,
there was poverty—it had a tongue—in cooling

ash, in marl, and coming loam,
thirst in the few strands of hay slipping

between a pitchfork's wide tines,
in the reptile, and the first birds,

poverty aloof and no mystery like God
its maker, there was surely want

in one steamed and sagging onion,
there was poverty in the shard of bread

sopped in the final drop of gravy
you snatched from your brother's mouth . . . .

MORTON MARCUS

Tongue

Tongue,
       wild meat rose
surrounded by carrion breath;
tongue,
       our one wing struggling
for flight, wing in the head
that the body grips
and won't let fly;
             tongue
that hisses, tongue that sings,
tongue that flops, that flaps,
that stabs inside its cage;
that articulates gasps and cries
or those long passages of breath
that would escape without hope
or chance of salvation;
              tongue, tongue,
if there's one thing in the body
that defines us, it's you.
You are the wild flame
that leaps from the hearth;
and from a campfire at night—
as though the face that owned you
were the earth's chapped skin—,
from a campfire surrounded
by charred stones,
you jump at the stars
and then fall back.

When God boomed, "Let there be light!"
it was his tongue, fat and purplish red
and longer than ten billion miles,
that leaped through the dark
to make clear what he had said.

That is why old women marvel
at each new word a child exclaims:
the mouth cracks open as if the head
were an egg, and tentative yet impudent
the tiny pink wingtip thrusts into the light.

196

Swan Song

Maurice Kantrowich
died August 29, 1968

cold black soup

because I am an old man
they serve me this:
it swirls through the spaces
where my teeth should be
like the shadows of buildings
on a sunny morning

my tongue whips one way
then the other
a weather vane in a storm
whose directions I followed
until I woke this morning
to find my legs were crutches

two hands lay before me
weighted with air
I cannot lift them
to wipe my mouth:
either they are not mine
or I have finally been chosen

to hold up the world

Tuba

a flaming tuba
blazes on the boulevard

the flames are wings
and the tuba rises

above the city and up
through the sunlight

a brass kite
sailing to the clouds

harrumphing like an uncle
tying his shoelace

who has sprouted wings
that sear through his back

and who finds
he is no longer sitting

by the side of the bed
but flying flying

over bridges and shops
still doubled over

still tightening the laces
while he wheezes and grunts

all along he had known
this would happen

had been waiting
for the day

when he would be flying
waving to the crowds

smiling and nodding
to his astonished friends

but not this way
not bent over

pulling at his shoelace
harrumphing harrumphing

as he disappears
into the mouth of the sun

The Dance

I said, "No!" to my parents and left the house. I said, "No!" to the boss and kept my moustache.

Then I saw *her* standing at a bus stop. I rushed toward her at the bus stop. I rushed toward her in the park. A wind shoved me forward, then tugged me back.

She was thrust toward me, yet withdrawn before we could touch.

My arms streamed outward. Her black hair whirled. It was a frantic dance.

Finally: she clung to me, I clung to her. Around us the air collapsed, then reassembled, and we woke in a room formed by our bodies. A wind surrounded the room.

Now each night we clutch and cling all night in this room. And as the vibrations resonate from us, other rooms surround this one, until a house surrounds us. And, needless to say, a wind surrounds the house.

Above our room, my parents, sitting in a trunk, paddle back and forth across the attic floor. "Don't worry, mother," my father calls, "the outrigger is the safest canoe there is." They are conditioning themselves for the vacation they've saved for all their lives.

We hear them scraping across the ceiling, chanting, "No-no! No-no!" or crooning versions of South Seas love songs that were popular when they were young. Sometimes they rock the trunk from side to side while practicing what I guess must be a variation of the hula.

Below, we buck and cling, although at times, as a novelty, we adjust our rhythms to the scraping sounds above.

Children are shouting in a farther room. Beyond the windows, voices call, cars rumble and roar. Around them all, a wind drones.

"Darling, a neighborhood is grouping up around us," my clinging woman sighs.

I don't reply. But, damn it, I'm beginning to suspect it's more than that.

The Moment For Which There Is No Name

On the sixteenth floor of one of the tall old buildings in the north end of the city, the windows of a vacant apartment look out over the bay. The apartment is empty, the floors and walls bare. There is only a chalked circle on the living room floor. The circle traces the spot where an armchair once stood, an armchair in which an old man regularly sat watching the smokestacks come and go in the harbor in the same way he had watched the swaying forests of masts when he was a boy, years before he became a bookkeeper for one of the city's three tool and die works.

The circle was drawn by the old man's grandson, while the child's parents were supervising the movers.

Tomorrow the new occupants will arrive, and preparatory to moving in they will clean the apartment. In the course of their cleaning, they will erase the chalk.

That is the moment for which there is no name.

The Angel Of Death Is Always With Me

The Angel of Death is always with me —
the hard wild flowers of his teeth,
his body like cigar smoke
swaying through a small town jail.

He is the wind that scrapes through our months,
the train wheels grinding over our syllables.
He is the footstep continually pacing through our chests,
the small wound in the soul,
the meteor puncturing the atmosphere.
And sometimes he is merely a quiet between the start of an act
and its completion,
a silence so loud
it shakes you like a tree.

It is only then you look up from the wars,
from the kisses,

from the signing of the business agreements;
It is only then you observe the dimensions
housed in the air of each day,
each moment;
only then you hear the old caressing the cold rims of their sleep,
hear the middle-aged women in love with their pillows
weeping into the gray expanse of each dawn,
where young men, dozing in alleys,
envision their loneliness to be a beautiful girl
and do not know they are part of a young girl's dream,
as she does not know that she is a dream in the sleep
of middle-aged women and old men,
and that all are contained in a gray wind
that scrapes through our months.

But soon we forget that the dead sleep in buried cities,
that our hearts contain them in ripe vaults.
We forget that beautiful women dry into parchment
and ball players collapse into ash;
that geography wrinkles and smoothes
like the expressions on a face,
and that not even children
can pick the white fruit from the night sky.

And how *could* we laugh while looking at the face
that falls apart like wet tobacco?
How could we wake each morning
to hear the muffled gong beating inside us,
our mouths full of shadows, our rooms filled with a black dust?

Still,
it is humiliating to be born a bottle:
to be filled with air, emptied, filled again;
to be filled with water, emptied, filled again;
and, finally, to be filled with earth.

And yet I am glad that The Angel of Death is always with me:
his footsteps quicken my own,
his silence makes me speak,
his wind freshens the weather of my day.
And it is because of him
I no longer think
that with each beat
my heart

is a planet drowning from within
but an ocean filling for the first time.

MEKEEL MCBRIDE

The Will To Live

On the green lawn of a city park
a sentence of dark insects completes itself:

Believe! Believe!
Above, two Monarchs matter and flash

in this immense summer air.
Small scraps of wing, good weather, a will

to live, they come
from the tenuous country of now

whatever the heart is asking for. Even if I
weren't here

they'd still congratulate the sky
with a fragile disbelief in sorrow. Graceful

as the hands of the deaf
they form a language in air that I understand

almost not at all. Being human
I might say

they kiss and part and kiss again, but
know they're governed by desire

or law or lack of these
beyond me. They fling themselves

against a sky so big
they do not understand it's there. Clouds

fat and ample, grow
fatter still and if the old June maples

stand weighted and without words
it is not from human grief, or any other.

Lessons

1.
Denied: the secret notebook of roots
hidden beneath every step I take,
where earthworms curl
like apostrophes
at the feet of stones,
where the snake dreams, the hedgehog laments
nothing.

These things, even these,
have been denied.

2.
The sky remains empty
like the back room in a museum
closed off by blue velvet ropes.
There are no trees,
only the bent arm of a cactus
scribbled by a sad child
who should have been doing his lessons.

Emptiness opens its little cafe
and does a lively business.

3.
You can't possibly know.
Even drought's bouquet of dead grass remembers
Eden and accepts that loneliness
for what it's worth. My eyes open
to everything
and I can't even locate
the little peasant girl

who wears shoes of daylight and goes
where she needs to, where she wants.

4.
Here, behind the blue cafe, I wait.
The deaf old man reshingling the roof
would somehow know and like me less
if I began to sing.
You can't possibly understand.

The words were diamonds. The words
were amulets the moon dreamed up
on its day off.

Now the curator, in colorless gloves,
pins them to an impersonal heaven of black burlap.

5.
Now you are sitting in a room
somewhere. It is evening. It is a country
untroubled by earthquakes. Darkness
returns quietly from the wedding
although with no keepsake. Evening
and still you have failed to notice
the cocoon, the loom, the black scissors.
And yes, it has already started,

although you do not notice,
the June-bug's dark and ceaseless prayer.

Transmigration

The lingering scripture of bleach
praised itself in each towel and sheet
while insect-starred roses
stitched the red thread of sweet
July into the collars and stiff cuffs
of our well-worn summer clothes.

Coarse rope, tied from elm to elm,
like the thin line of white a child
will sometimes draw for heaven,
held us all bodiless and pure
in that distant air. My mother's pastel dresses,
inhabited by wind, swayed, almost danced
as she danced in the kitchen alone

and the sleeves of my father's weekday shirts
pointed to a day moon, tree stump,
the white wheelbarrow,
as if looking were lesson enough or cure

for the slight ache at the shoulder
where the colorless V of clothespin

kept with soldierly pinches
the float and swell of drying clothes
in place. And so a day might pass, give way
to the setting sun through a backyard tree,
making a foreign lace, a frail brocade
of nightgowns, blouses, handkerchiefs

and wind invaded them with such levity
that I could guess at their escape;
ghost clothes blue in the evening air
like odd birds or aliens migrating slowly
over the trees, a whole tribe
of cloud-grazing nomads. Then one blouse

drops, the white one my mother wore on holidays,
the one with rhinestones at the collar
and the sleeves; each replica gem
silly with star glitter, the gossip of comets.
All of this to be claimed, taken in, submitted
to the hissing oracle of the small flat iron,

then blessed away into the dark kingdoms
of wardrobe and drawer —
like souls who believe nothing
can be lost, nothing dies — waiting
in windless dark, in summer sleep
to be taken out again and worn.

Red Letters

Hot-spit-and-damn of unchartable cargo flashes past
lightning blessed. Bridge shakes, almost shatters
with the passing. Gone, and then it's gone. Train

rumbling and plummeting out of summer air. Honest
in its passage, shakes bones, blooms hair. Seduces
and then stands you up, hopeless, in one long whistle blast,

almost gets you there, getting and getting. Lackawanna
cars swollen with omniscient thunder, coffins, cheap
wine from Hungary. Gives you shot-stained wind,

a lust for the long worthless wheatfields of America.
Makes sealed baggage cars sing out their locked contents:
gladiolus, apple, Aunt So-and-So's black lace-up shoes,

a last letter from death row, nothing but snow
sealed under the silk skins of Maine potatoes. Shamelessly
invades the bedrooms of the unhappily married, inventing

their semi-tropical dreams of parole. Prudence, absent
even in the once-was-blue caboose. Won't be back
with its bereaved sheep grazing in the tiny meadow

of a box car next to the red letters of separated lovers.
Keeps no schedule, keeping nothing, and keeps going,
mad sweetheart to each steadfast tree it passes,

spits its way into the future, dragging with it
tracks and vantage point, sunset and perspective,
marries them all in a black daze of closed horizon

leaving only a slight sigh in the shaken trees, no birth
of storm, just ordinary dusk and the common burden
of having to admit that being witness was enough.

The Going Under Of The Evening Land

> "But it should be quite a sight,
> the going under of the evening land . . .
> And I can tell you, my young friend,
> it is evening. It is very late."
> —Walker Percy
> The Moviegoer

In the evening land, a woman
places fresh bread on a polished table.
She turns on lamps, watching light
make golden maps on table top and parquet floor.

Here, without her knowing,
an interior continent completes itself.
She listens

to the glittery chatter of silverware
released from drawers that smell of Chinese tea.
Crows begin sleep now,
a few stars hidden in their pockets of black silk.
In the evening land
she considers how darkness leans cleanly
into its bright double—

how neither leaves for very long. Outside,
a child plays hide and seek with the rose bush
ghost. Now between light and dark,
the world splits open but only a little—
what is, what could be. And in this time
there are words that no one needs to speak:
                    I woke last night

thinking the bed to be an ocean liner
in touch with Antarctica, something
breaking up, something going under.
Tier on tier, the glittery necklace of the ship
sinking, or the iceberg singing, but I was
safe, I was safc and I
wanted you to know.

HEATHER MCHUGH

The Oven Loves The TV Set

On the refrigerator a gash
of abstract expressionist girl

and on the radio a riff
of rotten sax and on

the mind, the self-help book. We sprawl
all evening, all alone, in the unraised ranch;

our days were spent in no one's company,
incorporated. As for poverty,

we do our best, thanks to a fund
of Christian feeling, and Amelia, the foster child,

who has the rags and seven photogenic
sisters we require

in someone to be saved. Her picture stands
as coffee table objet d'art, and proof

professional Americans have got a heart
to go with all that happy acumen you read about.

We love a million little prettinesses, decency, and ribbons
on the cockapoo. But who will take the time to study

alphabets for hands? Who gives a damn what goes into
a good wheelchair? Who lugs the rice

from its umpteen stores
to the ends of the earth,

to even one dead-end? Not we.
Our constitutional pursuit

is happiness, i.e.
somebody nice, and not

too fat, we can have
for our personal friend.

Down, Down, And Down

After seven months in space, the astronauts
sank back into the blues that blanket earth.
We saw them land, we saw them trundled
from their second home, and then we saw

they couldn't hold a bunch of flowers up;
they couldn't stand, the world had got
so heavy. Now the story they had starred in
wasn't Music of the Spheres, but rather

Newsreels of their New Wheelchairs. So much
for weightlessness as grace. For months
thereafter, none of them could sleep:
they told us down was hard.

*

My first twelve thousand nights on earth
were fine, I always had
a quilt or a religion or a man,
some comforters and dreams, the stars sewn up

along a storyteller's lines. My life was always
looking up; I always had
a little always in my bag. So then
what happened? Just exactly when

was my comedown? Did I get old?
Sooner or later does the future leave
everyone warm-blooded cold? Sometimes I think
that I can think the vacancy away—I tell myself

*

I thought it up, or time is nothing more
than weather, in Marseilles; by then I've used up

maybe thirty of the eight-seven thousand
seconds in a human day, and still

it doesn't help—for time on earth
is not a code, it won't be cracked.
The man I loved is just
as lost as ever

and no hill or hole, no president
or anchorman, has pull enough;
my bluest moons and oceans don't mean
anything to him. He won't come back.

What We Call Living

*

His watch is wicked, going up
without him. Pass your hand
across the blue man's lips and
Q.E.D. We know we breathe

(and quite without our help) but then
we know we know, and so we usually
forget. It's very strange to be alive
but we have not felt awe since we were someone's

kid, and that was once
upon a time. In time
we taught ourselves to find the world
mundane, and all the unknown

unsurprising, like
next Sunday, for example.
God himself
gets bored, God knows.

*

On holidays we like to make
some sugar on a rope, some fallout

in the form of rocks, thanks to
the Science City someone gave

to Junior, Christmas Day.
You learn to etch your name
in the petri dish with pure
bacteria, or in the virgin

snow with piss. I wonder why
we draw the line at skin
for different, at heart for dead?
The EEG goes on all by itself. We used

to sing, and when we did, the air itself
would come alive to us. But then we fell
back into dream, we froze. And all night long
in the drawing room, after the household's fast

asleep, the crystal grows.

The Ghost

I held my breath for years,
for fear of being breathless,
fear of being afraid.
Whenever someone left my bed

I took a deeper one. Addicted
to the flesh, attracted
to the very quick, I thought
I'd never let them go—my child,

my man, a little red. But lately,
in the winter stoneyards, when the still heaps
hold their blue, and a hand is all
wool thumbs, and no one

says hello, or
hello's other half,
and stars, above all, after all,
strike fire from the lapidary slope,

then something rises out of me at last,
my hope and heat, the spirit I had
hidden most. Because we have to give up
everything of love—even the ghost.

The Trouble With In

Enarmoured, here in English, we're
in trouble. If a love is said to be a place
we fall into, then sooner or later they ask
how deep. If time is measured in extent

sooner or later they ask how long. We keep
some comforters inside the box, a heart
inside the chest, but still
it's there the trouble with the dark

accumulates the most. The end
of life is thought to be
a boat to a tropic, good or bad.
The suitor wants to size up

what he's getting into: so he asks
her measurements, and then he has to wonder
what's enough? The best man cannot help him out:
he's given to a cummerbund. In English

boys and girls regard themselves
in the worst half-light—too long,
too little, not enough alike—and who can stand
to be made up for good? and who can face

being adored? I swear there is no frame
that I would keep you in; I didn't love a look
and find you fit it. Every day
your sight was a surprise—you made my taste,

made sense, made eyes. But when you set me up
in high esteem, I was a star that's bound,
in time, to fall. The point's the sorrow
of the song. I loved you to no end

and when you said, So far
I knew the idiom. It meant So long.

Memento Vitae

> *"If money goes, money comes. If money stays,*
> *death stays. Did you ever hear that useful*
> *Urdu proverb?"*
>
> E.M. Forster, *A Passage to India*

Melt the money down and take
denomination's tons
of sangfroid from the coffers.
Let the sold silk ravel from its ropes,
and music flood out of the gold, to undermine
the laws of club and bar.

I mean the way it is the wealthy haul
a shitload in their wake; they're hooked
to weights and measures, hold
long talks with watches, have
much truck with locks. The more

they make, the less is warmable
in pockets or by hand; so hands
are hired. And money-heaters, money-manacles—
the wealthy must get sick of all that
forethought, money being given
more to futures than to presents. Soon to have

insinuates to hold. You marry money,
and you marry cold. So give up goldwasser
and take a slug
of aquavit instead. Let's drink our dearest,
break the glass. Didn't the doctor promise
money comes when money leaves? And don't I love you

out of the question how much? You grew
inside me and were small; you fell in love
and woke up towering. No one can keep us
in a number—baby won't make three, she'll make

a million—love's our moolah, quickened
silver, wing and buck. And there can be no crib

for money in the house, no bank for sperm,
no ergo for a sum. Death comes,
the doctor said, where money stays,
though everywhere the underwriters whisper
do not listen, time
is savable, love pays.

SANDRA MCPHERSON

Conception

I was seeing, as the police
Came again this week, that moment
Of pleasure in your student room
Carefully darkened with serious
Bindings and a pulldown lamp
That left, to patrol beside our love,
Only a glowing woolen peony.
Others' facsimiles of our heat that year
Initiated embryos that today have pressed
Our daughter against the bridge rail
And thrown her schoolbooks off to educate
Commuters' tires, truckers' windshields.
Her Spanish doe's eyes now
Are black with fear and hate.
                          In those days
We were translating a Spanish poem
Almost gory with *rosas,* one we
Finally hid from English because it had
Too many *corazons.* Into that world
We brought a child. Into our house
Old pleasures have brought police.
And as one picks the softest chair
To bundle his hip revolver in,
I remember you were thinner then.
I counted your ribs.
You were starving, nearly, surviving
On corned bear meat
Which you tweezed with chopsticks.
I was fat. You sighted along my thigh
For one last moment when
There would be just two of us.

. . . And we sit now in the wooden chairs,
Pinning as much hope on the officer's badge
As on a star in the blue.

216

Poem Begun In The Haro Strait When I was 28
And Finished When I was 38

Those I vainly wish to meet are like the whales.
I can hear their every breath loud as if near

Across the iris straits. First they exhale
With the bass rasp of a shovel digging a grave.

Then take in before the dorsal fin splits the sea
To cordwood above their head. It is a gasp.

They lift the cover. It has all been headfirst
For them. I love the way they buckle

Their dance-floor, destroy the limp waterlevel
Where, that year, we kept together

Because of the whales' schedule. Since
Those days when I was grateful, there is no one

I have not met, no one I haven't almost touched
While they parade as the whales do.

Those affectionate pods
Blend the space between nations. They believe

In riding buoyant and sunken, rowdy
And unreversed as they plough over

The dashed accident, swim toward the "Go away!"
I only spook at the buoy, the clear-voiced,

So clearly saying, "Go away." Some expert
Makes clear voices for the buoys; but I've had

To torture out my cry, slap together my roar,
My entreaty, expurgate my whimper, my frog, a crack

In my testimony, had to sand my echo smooth
Until I thought it could be heard

With scientific charity. A dialect to say, "Come here,
Come forward; you are in my family of languages."

Only to realize the buoy is not for the whale,
The buoy mines its throat for the boat.

It doesn't know one begging note a grampus has sung.
I should never have tried to love you with the mother tongue.

On Being Told "You Have Stars In Your Eyes"
By A Man Who Denied That 95.6% Of Single-Parent Households
On Welfare In Our State Are Headed By Women

The sage desert: swept in the window by a snow-broom
From the summits left white in April, with no passes.
To be registered alone, not even talking to oneself.
To want a moment's deafness to our language.
Before I'll carry luggage to the room,
To look at the crushed light in the sky;
Through the opened door to see
Those fires of the plain
Two-eyed constellation in the mirror.

Television off, arrange to borrow a language.
Icelandic: it is a strong-toothed language with three-legged words
And hard-shinned sentences. Held in
Janne's dictionary: cool, full of seal-words and fish-terms,
Cliff-caves and tides and hummocks of ice.
It is the size of

The infant-stones
In the narrow-running, tall-elmed Pocatello graveyard:
Their names are Chinese picture-words,
Are Mexican, and Greek (with picture-pictures ovaled there).
All have become American,
All sound American now.
I step carefully, trying not to cross their borders,
While one woman digs, one woman jogs, a sprinkler whirls its drink,
The trees spray air with shade until it's

Night: he was a salesman
Of desks and files.
The man who—like a drawer against a finger—
Gnashed at welfare cheats

218

Was banqueting by now—he had to prize a woman
"Salesclerk of the Year."
He had been kind
About her, she could work the hardest.
She must be some kind of

Word-witch: speaking only a strong, implacid mother tongue.
Not chat: she'd say—
                    We're always cheating
        On some guy, why not on welfare;
            Or are such ogresses imaginary?
        And can the imaginary cheat us much?
She must be some kind of skald-quean, *far-seeing witch*
To wicked women welcome always.

For she will think of the very small, their graves
The size of desk drawers. Dead before words. Lives
The shape of keepsakes, trivia, small writing tools.
I imagine, estimating by these green-glossed,
Unmoving grave-lanes,
Some mothers do get off relief:
For Twins Jeanette and Emma, Infant Joe and Baby Cain—
Perpetual child care.

Red Seeds Opening In The Shade

Laura is my friend, and as I shade my eyes
From squirrel-kicked redwood strings,
As I duck, look down, and see black pods
And kneel studying the seeds,
And as the gardener, Mr. Hernandez, calls to me,
"Have you found what you are looking for?"—
Laura appears by surprise.

I've found what we are looking *at*,
Seeds sticky and glistening like fish eggs.
Hernandez picks them up, our heads tilt back
To hunt for the conceivable tree.
Laura's about to tell me of her arrest.
But doesn't want the gardener
To find more than he was looking for.

So we hold everything to marvel
At the seeds' red roe inside black beetle wings.

This is the Garden of the Women Scholars.
It's also the garden of those who don't know what to think.
We're just women of the garden,
Poor scholars of the seeds,
Who don't know if they'll bear us fish, insects, or trees.
They won't give us children,
They'll be-sister us with ancients,
Roman or Chinese. Hernandez leaves,

And Laura's hands mime the bombing
Of the induction center across the bay
With her paint-hearts. Pericardium
One Baggie, waterbase paint a leftist
Ventricle red—these "weapons" were meant
To remind our whole big government
Of a little significant waste of blood.

This pathway, with its seeds igniting clay
Beside the rush of Strawberry Spring,
Is like a deity's eye view of her dissent.
The Roman Emperor or the Governor of Honan
Can't exile her. And if they could
Her exile would be a seed
Carried on the wind.

With human hearts, Laura fears
A single one bursting.
With these, ripe-full of paint, she trusts
That each one breaking, hitting home,
Begins to sprout where it should.

Helen Todd: My Birthname

They did not come to claim you back,
To make me Helen again. Mother
Watched the dry, hot streets in case they came.
This is how she found a tortoise
Crossing between cars and saved it.

It's how she knew roof-rats raised families
In the palmtree heads. But they didn't come—
It's almost forty years.

I went to them. And now I know
Our name, quiet one. I believe you
Would have stayed in trigonometry and taken up
The harp. Math soothed you; music
Made you bold; and science, completely
Understanding. Wouldn't you have collected,
Curated, in your adolescence, Mother Lode
Pyrites out of pity for their semblance
To gold? And three-leaf clovers to search
For some shy differences between them?

Knowing you myself at last—it seems you'd cut
Death in half and double everlasting life,
Quiet person named as a formality
At birth. I was not born. Only you were.

SUSAN MITCHELL

Once, Driving West Of
Billings, Montana,

I ran into the afterlife.
No fluffy white clouds. Not even stars. Only sky
dark as the inside of a movie theater
at three in the afternoon and getting bigger all the time,
expanding at terrific speed
over the car which was disappearing,
flattening out empty
as the fields on either side.

                      It was impossible to think
under that rain louder than engines.
I turned off the radio to listen, let my head
fill up until every bone
was vibrating—sky.

                  Twice, trees of lightning
broke out of the asphalt. I could smell
the highway burning. Long after, saw blue smoke twirling
behind the eyeballs, lariats
doing fancy rope tricks, jerking silver
dollars out of the air, along with billiard cues, ninepins.

I was starting to feel I could drive forever
when suddenly one of those trees was right in front of me.
Of course, I hit it—
branches shooting stars down the windshield,
poor car shaking like a dazed cow.
I thought this time for sure I was dead
so whatever was on the other side had to be eternity.

Saw sky enormous as nowhere. Kept on driving.

Boone

It might be true
the story that Daniel Boone slept in a cave

222

not far from Rockville, Indiana.
It might even be true that the cave he slept in
was the one I ran into during a downpour.
Striking a match, I saw BOONE
carved into hard rock.
Of course, anyone could have done that.
I could have done it myself.
Once, camping near Rockville, I came on the skeleton
of a dog. It had recovered its cleanliness
from the black soil
the way flowers recover after a rain.
Sometimes I'm afraid of what I'll find, not
animal bones or the arrowheads
that turn up everywhere,
but the skeleton of a man,
someone who listened to the soil
asserting itself day after day until his bones
became tools for digging him deeper.
I've had a stone scraper reach into my hand
like another hand wanting me
to feel my way back to it.
I felt the grass growing westward
starting to pick up speed
like an animal running for the sheer
joy of running,
and I thought of Boone following his traps,
each trap biting deeper
into the green absence of prairie.
I understood
his wanting to keep it for himself,
the space that lay down with him each night,
breathing into his face.
On the prairie night asserts itself like a smell.
One night I heard the prairie talking,
it said *itself, itself* over and over.
I lay there thinking of all the disguises
a body can take: stone, stump, vine, root.
I listened to the wind
turning over in my sleep and I prayed
to be unremembered as the dirt
that cakes the nails of men and women as they work,
humming to themselves softly.

Bread

Slowly the taste of bread rises into my life,
the bread I was given each morning
before I left for school.
Now I reach for the steaming slice,
the loaf I walked on
to keep my shoes shiny and clean.

When a voice tells me to sit down
in the bus with the other fifth graders,
I sit down.
That is the teacher talking.
She is taking us to the place where bread is made.

At night I have dreamed it,
the workers robed in white like nurses,
beads of sweat falling from their foreheads
into enormous vats,
and the teacher warning us
not to fall in. But I know when her back is turned
a child throws itself into a vat,
giving its life to the bread.

When no one is looking, the mothers
mix in their own blood,
the blood a mother hides under one nail
as she lays out her child's clothes,
the little drops you never notice
as she buttons you into your life.

Humbly, I accept the miniature loaf
a woman offers each of us before we leave,
along with a postcard:
a girl holding out a sheaf of wheat tied with red ribbon.
A red kerchief half covers her blond hair.
Her mouth smiles up into mine.

Though I know she's a lie, I keep her
under my pillow.
At night I hear the dull machinery of the wheat
turning through her hair, the squeals
of the mice
as the combine slices into their lives.

Slowly the smell of bread rises
from her hands and with it a draft from the cold room
where someone tries to sleep
before getting up in the dark to go to work
and the TV which is smashed one night and the bruise
starting to show on a woman's cheek
as she sweeps up the broken glass,

the bruise inside the man's fist
as he stands over her,
which opens his hand in the morning
and closes it at night,
which he takes from the bread and the bread from the grain,
which can never be thrashed out
no matter how the bread sings like a fly
in a child's hand
no matter how hard the horse kicks
when it is beaten
no matter how the soil blooms each spring in furrows
of yellow and violet and delicate pink

that dark place under the crust
where the earth
keeps bleeding into my life.

Blackbirds

Because it is windy, a woman
finds her clothesline bare, and without rancor
unpins the light, folding it into her basket.
The light is still wet. So she irons it.
The iron hisses and hums. It knows how to make the best of things.
The woman's hands smell clean. When she shakes them out,
they are voluminous, white.

All night my hands weep in gratitude
for little things. That feet are not shoes.
That blackbirds are eating the raspberries. That parsley
does not taste like bread.

From now on I want to live

only by grace. In other words, not to deserve things.
Without rancor, the light dives down
among the turnips. I eat it with my stew.

Today the woman's hands smell like roots. When she
shakes them out, they are voluminous, green.
All day they shade me
from the sun. The blackbirds have come to sit in them.
Since this morning, the wind has been enough.

A Story

There is a bar I go to when I'm in Chicago
which is like a bar I used to go to when I lived in New York.
There are the same men racing toy cars
at a back table, the money passing so fast
from hand to hand, I never know who's winning, who's losing,
only in the New York bar the racers sport Hawaiian shirts
while in the Chicago bar they wear Confederate caps
with crossed gold rifles pinned to their bands.
Both bars have oversized TV's and bathrooms
you wouldn't want to be caught dead in,
though some have. Once in the New York bar I watched a film
on psychic surgery, and I swear to you
the surgeon waved a plump hand—
the hand hovered like a dove over the patient's back,
and where wings grow out of an angel's shoulders
a liquid jetted, a clear water, as if pain
were something you could see into like a window.
Later, walking home with a friend
who was also a little drunk, I practiced psychic surgery
on our apartment building, passing my hands
back and forth over the bricks.
I don't know what I expected to happen,
maybe I hoped a pure roach anguish would burst forth.
But there was only the smell that rises out of New York City
in August, a perennial urine—dog, cat, human—
the familiar stench of the body returning to itself as alien.
Sometimes, before stopping in at the Chicago bar,
I would either sleep or go for a walk

especially in October when the leaves had turned red.
As they swept past me, I thought of my blood
starting to abandon my body,
taking up residence elsewhere like the birds
gathering in feverish groups on the lawns.
In the Chicago bar there were men who never watched TV
or played the video games, mainly from the Plains tribes they
sat in silence over their whiskey, and looking at them,
I could even hear the IRT as it roared through
the long tunnel between Borough Hall and Wall Street,
the screech of darkness on steel.
And it happened one night that a man,
his hair loose to his shoulders, stood up and pulled
a knife from his boot, and another man
who must have been waiting all his life for this
stood up in silence too, and in seconds
one of them was curled around the knife in his chest
as if it were a mystery he would not reveal to anyone.
Sometimes I think my life is what I keep escaping.
Staring at my hands, I almost expect them to turn
into driftwood, bent and polished by the waves,
my only proof I have just returned from a long journey.
The night Tom Littlebird killed Richard Highwater
with a knife no one knew he carried, not even
during the five years he spent at Stateville,
I thought of men and women who sell their blood for
a drink of sleep in a doorway or for a bus ticket
into a night which is also a long drink to nowhere,
and I thought of the blood I was given
when I was nineteen, one transfusion for each year of my life,
and how I promised myself
if I lived, I would write a poem in honor of blood.
First for my own blood which,
like the letter that begins the alphabet,
is a long cry AAAAH! of relief.
Praise to my own blood which is simple
and accepts almost anything.
And then for the blood that wrestled
all night with my blood
until my veins cramped and the fingers of one hand went rigid.
Praise to the blood that wanted to remain alone,
weeping into its own skin,
so that when it flowed into me, my blood contracted

on the knot in its throat. For you
who raised a rash on my arms
and made my body shiver for days, listen,
whoever you are, this poem is for you.

JACK MYERS

Coming To The Surface

Sometimes you get tired of the dark, the humming,
the shimmering and the echoes of others,
the whole long story that robs you of your life.

So you break into the world
of air and light
just to feel heavy and freezing
which is a good release from thinking
but not a permanent cure.

Once in a while someone plunges by you
with his whole being combed back
into a scream of forgetfulness,
a command.

He's going the other way.

As Long As You're Happy

—in memory of Ruth Myers

I don't know what the Bible says—
my mother who died after being
mercilessly kept alive
by machines at the hospital
looked at the photo of my fiancée
and said, "As long as you're happy . . ."
as if it were the final measure of my reach.

The star through which I shot
my young heart has little value now
except as an occasional reference point,
a piece of cosmic punctuation
some third-rate planet may depend on
to survive.

What I thought was an ethical problem
of existence was just a broken heart.
The woman for whom I have ransomed
my wife and children would like to erase
the past. I would like to gather them all,
please, under one roof, one heart.

About my mother . . .
each day the doctors and machines
said her chances of living
with one more operation
on her overburdened heart
would probably be better.
I thought of reading the Bible then.
It wasn't a question of being happy.

The Diaspora

By what name will they call
the disheveled temple
inside me
except by my name.

In whatever city this is
whoever hears the congregation
of my voices chanting
in a rented room
will be disabled by them.

I keep two immaculate white cats
to restore my memory of tranquility
and I have nailed the people I love
in another life and more and more
the temple is inscribed
in an alphabet of indecipherable
accidents and impressions.

Once I looked up to a God who wore
an expression from a joke
I never quite got. Now I hide my face
in the beauty of my lover

whose cries of pleasure twist shamelessly
like smoke from beneath a door.

She tells her father maybe someday
I'll be famous, but he thinks
it is only in the way
someone has perfected a technique
for decanting a dangerous fluid.

She puts the stone I'm curled inside of
in her mouth and speaks about our future
in which I am the distant blueness
and the blown stars of her breath
are lights along our way. I hold onto her
blinded by promises.

After the many deaths and accomplishments,
each man makes an order of his own.
I think this solitude of rock
is a tiny piece of God's great loneliness
in which birds with strings of sunlight
in their beaks fly through. So, saying my name,
I make an order of my own.

Natural Ice Cream

Sometimes, when I'm tired of your dark beauty,
my right hand grows enormous.
The tunnel of my eye shoots inward
and I can't bear to eat a piece of fruit.

I love you, I love you, I love you
with all my heart, I say
driving the car back and forth
over a pomegranate.
The meter is stuck on red.

And now my brain outweighs me.
Now I'm tired.
After I clean the house
I'm gonna put a bullet through my head.

Later on, we can go out someplace nice
for natural ice cream.

A Manner of Speaking

My wife exclaims, "Qué macho!"
"How mature your penmanship is!"

I said "That is nothing, my bird-like bird,
"but why do you speak to me in Spanish?"

"Oh," she said with her little mouth stuck like a cherry tomato,
reminding me of the times she has called me a jeweler with a salad,

"I was to market today and this stallion of a farmer
took me in his arms and sold me muchas penumbras."

"Qué Dios, Conchita Estrellita Con Quesa," I explained,
"Do you think it is me when I am not at the market?"

She twirled her entire body around twice and said
in her palest voice, "No, Herbert, my life is the trudging bore
"I'm trapped inside of. I would soon evaporate in madness
if it weren't for the efficacious power of your vocabulary."

"That is nothing, my flower-like tulip," I said, asking if
we were now in England and by what fortuitous trick
in my expression had we been transported there.

"Mon chere," she whispered, twisting her waist coquettishly,
reminding me of the sensual syntax of Balzac,

"Zee chauffer took me to a tiny garden on the outskirts
"of zee city—tres magnifique—and there in your name and honor
"praised your incomparable generosity to zee hilt."

"Mon Dieu!" I gasped. "Francois du Monde du Vichyssoise,
"is it me you think I am when I am not in the driver's seat?"

"Ziegfried," she shuddered, "vhen vill you see zee devastating
"power off your mind on me? Your mere presence eez incredible."

"Zat eez noszing, my doe-like fawn," I laughed, to which she laughed,
and then my laughter roiled over hers, and then hers cut under mine,
and then I tried my lower boiling gutterals, and she careened even higher,
and so I could do nothing but enlarge the geography of our bliss
as she set sail and I watched over her to discover, as it were,
the farthest regions of our communal joy.

Do You Know What I Mean?

For the sake of argument
let's say there are three of me:
the one with the bummed-out body,
the one who senses things are going badly,
and the bright one who can't cope. That's me!
Don't get me wrong. It's a family.
For example if #2 has a sexy dream,
#1 may salivate. That leaves 3 free to feel guilty
or write. Only sometimes in the face of authority
1 opens his mouth and 3 slips out "I hate your guts!"
Then 2 tries to get 3 to repent, but isn't smart enough
and then everyone feels like shit and gets a headache.

Do you know what I mean?

2 and 3 are always sniffing each other suspiciously
while 1 sticks a bottle of sour mash in his face.
We know that somewhere some elegant in a grey silk suit
and shiny black shoes reflecting the tip of the Alps
is slowly turning toward his tasty companion
the date 1957 on their green bottle of Pouilly-fuissé.

I did that so #3 would feel better
having said a spot of French.
That means 1 has the green light to celebrate
and 2 can slink around pretending he's French.

Dear God,
I don't believe in you
but #2 is feeling badly today.
He thinks you're out there and you're great.
He can't tell the difference between something small

tearing apart and the sound of something large in the distance
moving far off.

So this is for my brother, #2,
standing here like we're in church.
Sometimes when we're quiet like this
I think we're all the family we've got.

Trying To Name What Doesn't Change

Roselva says the only thing that doesn't change
is train tracks. She's sure of it.
The train changes, or the weeds that grow up spidery
by the side, but not the track.
I've watched one for three years, she says,
and it doesn't curve, doesn't break, doesn't grow.

Peter isn't sure. He saw an abandoned track
near Sabinas, Mexico, and says a track without a train
is a changed track. The metal wasn't shiny anymore.
The wood was split and some of the ties were gone.

Every Tuesday on Morales Street
butchers crack the necks of a hundred hens.
The widow in the tilted house
spices her soup with cinnamon.
Ask her what doesn't change.

Stars explode.
The rose curls up as if there is fire in the petals.
The cat who knew me is buried under the bush.

The train whistle still wails its ancient sound
but when it goes away, shrinking back
from the walls of the brain,
it takes something different with it every time.

With The Greeks

When you dance Greek-style,
you wave a handkerchief,
the foot stomps, a necklace of islands
rises in the blood.
Moving through days,
the shadow of this circle
stays with you.
Outline of a wheeling fish

that says you are less alone
than you like to think.

At the grill, shrimp curl perfectly
on sticks. A sleek woman with a bow-tie
strokes her husband's hand.
What have we in common?
Grandmother spooning honey-puffs
smiles at anyone, Here child, eat,
fortify yourself for the journey
between homes.

Floating heart, who knows
which hand is on which arm?
Whether any story begins or ends
where we say it does,
or goes on like a circle,
common sea between stones and lamps.
In the villages of Greece
windows light up like eyes.
Children carry things in baskets,
a basket sits on a floor.

I heard of an orchard where statues grew up
between the roots of trees. Stones were men,
one trunk had feet. I heard of an island
where snails rose out of the dirt
and saved the people, who were starving.

Tonight there is no ocean
that does not sing. Even sorrow
which we have felt and felt again
in all our lands, has hands.

One Island

When you meet a man who is satisfied with one island,
you want to walk around him, a complete circumference,
to find where his edges are. If there is sand
or reef – you want to see how the trees grow,
trapped in the wind. He shows you the spine

of a sea urchin nested in his foot.
This man whose soul is a boat tied to a single post.
You want to sit with him long enough
to hear the curled shell of your body whistling.

When you say "California" you are a space creature
talking about a star. Nothing grows there.
Here we have mangoes, sea-grapes,
hog-plums spilling ripe across a path.

He could show you where to dive to see caves underwater
but you are not brave enough.
The sky is filled with people like you, halfway coming,
halfway going. A plane lands every day between five and six.
The islanders hear it the minute it leaves the shore.

On cloudless days the mountains of the mainland
are visible in the west.
Grocers write proud lists on blackboards:
American Cheese, Canned Pork.
Inside are men counting pennies, suspenders ordered in 1968.

There's a lot to do here: walk, watch, breathe.
Yesterday the man found a hunk of driftwood
tangled in the swamp. Hired four friends to drag it out.
Today it becomes a woman listening.
The man drops his chisel, turns her so we can see all sides.
We dream of taking her home with us,
placing her away from the wall in a house far from water.
Why? Because she is like one island,
complete in herself, curves connected.
She only lets you go so far.
After that you are taking the chances the pirates took,
the chances you take every day,
when you live in a world that barely knows you,
on a ship that is always pointed somewhere else.

Utila, Honduras, 1980

The House In The Heart

How it is possible to wake this empty
and brew camomile, watching the water
paint itself yellow and the little flowers
float and bob —

The cars swishing past in dark rain
are going somewhere.
This is my favorite story.
The man with a secret jungle growing
in his brain says chocolate
can make him happy.
I would find a bar
heavy as a brick. With almonds.
And lean forward whispering of
the house in the heart,
the one with penny-size rooms,
moth-wing ceilings, cat-lip doors.

This body we thought so important,
it's a porch, that's all.
I know this, but I don't know
what to do about it.

How it is possible to move
through your own kitchen
touching a bamboo strainer curiously:
Whose is this? And know it is
the one you use every tea,
to feel like an envelope
that travels in and out of the world
carrying messages
and yet not remember
a single one of them —

Today I look out the glass
for some confirmation.
The lights will stay on late this morning.
Palm tree fronds were frozen last week,
there is rain in the street.
And the house in the heart cries
no one home, no one home.

Mother Of Nothing

Sister, the stars have no children.
The stars pecking at each night's darkness
above your trailer would shine back at themselves
in its metal, but they are too far away.
The stones lining your path to the goats
know themselves only as speechless, flat,
gray-in-the-sun.
What begins and ends in the self
without continuance in any other.

You who stand at pre-school fences
watching the endless tumble and slide,
who answer the mothers' Which one is yours?
with blotted murmur and turning away
listen. Any lack carried
too close to the heart
grows teeth, nibbles off
corners. I heard one say
she had no talent,
another, no time, and there were many
without beauty all those years,
and all of them shrinking.
What sinks to the bottom of the pond
comes up with new colors, or not at all.

We sank, and there was purple,
voluptuous merging of purple and blue,
a new silence living
in the houses of our bodies.
Those who wanted and never received,
who were born without hands,
who had and then lost; the Turkish mother
after the earthquake
with five silent children lined before her,
the women of Beirut
bearing water to their bombed-out rooms,
the fathers in offices
with framed photographs of children on their desks,
and their own private knowledge
of all the hard words.

And we held trees differently
then, and dried plates differently,
because waiting dulls the senses
and when you are no longer waiting,
something wakes up. My cousin said
It's not children, it's a matter of making
life. And I saw the streets
opening into the future,
cars passing, mothers with car seats,
children waving out the rear window,
keeping count of all who waved back,
and would we lift our hearts and answer them,
and when we did, what would we say?
And the old preposterous stories of nothing
and everything finally equalling one another
returned in the night. And like relatives,
knew where the secret key was hidden.
And like relatives, let themselves in.

The Garden Of Abu Mahmoud

He had lived in Spain
so we stood under a glossy loquat tree
telling of madres y milagros
with clumsy tongues.
It seemed strange in the mouth
of this Arab, but no more so
than everything.
Across his valley the military
settlement gleamed white.
He said, That's where the guns live,
as simply as saying, it needs sun,
a plant needs sun.
He stooped to unsheath an eggplant
from its nest of leaves,
purple shining globe,
and pressed it on me.
I said No, no, I don't want
to take things before they are ripe,
but it was started already,
handfuls of marble-sized peaches,

hard green mish-mish and delicate lilt
of beans. Each pocket swelled
while he breathed mint leaves,
bit the jagged edge.
He said every morning found him here,
before the water boiled on the flame,
he came out to this garden,
dug hands into earth saying I know you
and earth crumbled rich layers
and this result of their knowing —
a hillside in which no inch went unsung.
His enormous onions held light
and the trees so weighted with fruits
he tied the branches up.
And he called it querido, corazon,
all the words of any language
connecting to the deep place
of darkness and seed. He called it
ya habibi in Arabic, my darling tomato,
and it called him governor, king,
and some days he wore no shoes.

West Bank, Israel, 1983

STEVE ORLEN

Paradise

When the bird saw how innocent they were
    It flew toward the garden
In a swallow's perfect curves.
    So luminous, she placed it
In her companion's mouth. They kissed,

    They passed the light between them.
They spoke, and the bird flew out . . . .
    This is the story I tell myself
When I'm most unsure. When I stare
    Out a window at dusk and can't decide.

At times love and at times hate
    Like a phone ringing all night,
Sometimes the truth, sometimes the lie,
    The heart's reasons or the mind's.
Above my room the swallow fascinates

    Even when I feel most sure.
Oh, come back, they must have cried,
    Mouths held open in a perfect
Human singing *O,* the certainties
    Dissolving on their tongues.

How large the sky looks now,
    The swallow's locomotion and obstacle.
Air holds him, makes him graceful,
    Sometimes baffled, a shifting
Helpless light above the garden.

Acts Without Consequence

All one summer I thought about God.
This in the factories, and this at an age
When I'd just as soon have felt like any
Ordinary apprentice machinist, a recently

242

Graduated high school kid no different
From anyone else. Then I began to wonder
What they'd be thinking about—all around us
Din of huge machines, routers and lathes
That cast the high windows with metal dust,

And now and then the random lap of waves came
Off a nearby canal, creating a timeless
Sanctuary baffle. I'd let my mind work
The same thought until the thought broke
When the whistle blew. One time one of the men
Must have sensed the burden of my thoughtfulness
Because he asked a question so generalized
It felt intimate. I don't remember what—where do
The dead live? About love?—but I must have been

Amazed, as I am now by any unexpected, heartfelt,
Endlessly answerable question.
Maybe I felt that slurring in the brain
That happens a split second into an accident. Anyway,
I didn't so much decide to quit
As I drifted into other jobs, then college . . . .
I thought about it just a while ago. Probably,
I was so shy back then God kept me company.
Or God was pure abstraction, seductive, like a mantra.

It hardly matters now. It so happens
The poplars are in leaf. Bordering each yard
The white perennial African daisies, and poppies
Whose languid yellow petals seem to palpitate,
Like flesh. I was out walking.
I glanced up. On a balcony above the avenue
Stood a very old woman dressed in a robe
And slippers. I saw that in the raised circle
Of her arms she held a photo in a frame. Then

She was moving, she was dancing—a waltz,
A box in four—as though she'd heard the call
While ironing and it just fell on her like
Old clothes or spring snow. Cheek to cheek,
Early on a Sunday morning. Who'd have imagined
Ever doing such a thing? And just as suddenly
As she began she stopped and bent her body
Out a little over the neighboring yards,

Rows of houses, trees, flowers in their beds. Sometimes
This world's almost the safest place to be.

Boy Hiding In A Closet

After a while he got used to it,
So when the door opened
And his sister entered
And her body in the mirror
Enlarged the room, he hid
Between the coats and dresses.

Between his sister's body
And the glass, a sourceless
Radiance. He rubbed his eyes,
He couldn't sleep or wake
And who was there to tell him
One from the other. And what
A boy sees so late at night
No one would believe—breasts
Pioneering like sudden daisies
Into air.

            What he'll keep
The way we keep a secret,
First loves, and ghosts,
Their loneliness, our shame,
Her skin which kept the smoothness
Of a pond before the skaters came.

Acts of Grace

1.
Entering any unknown lovely mysterious place,
    Woods or water, and for whatever reason,
Carries you along a slurred amnesiac passage.

It's dark. The bus slows around a curve.
It's always dark when I remember this.
        I'd been traveling alone awhile

From one European country to another.
        Every city looked the same—cathedrals,
Farmers' markets; from any hill the harbors

        Gleamed with a broad and tireless
Contentment. So when the bus stopped
        I entered the woods at the side of the road

And did not care to wonder where I was
        Or what drew me down a path between
The trees so late, unable to distinguish

        One darkness from another. (Have you
Ever looked in a mirror in the dark
        And seen yourself grown older, *other?*

I did, as a child, and could not help but touch
        That terrifying face, which was a skull.)
There was a lake, and in the distance

        A cottage with a single light, a thought
So lonesome I felt myself dissolve.
        Whatever I saw, it went abstract . . . .

Out of such emptiness I would invent a future—
        Husband, friend, poet, prodigal son.
What a lovely foolish luxury of thought!

2.
Have you ever looked in a window at night,
        Out walking when you can't sleep?
The shade is up. Table and chair, a lamp,

        An open book, a half-filled whiskey glass,
Though no one's there. I wrote one poem,
        Willful, and exact. I love a slim woman

In a house in a quiet neighborhood.
        This yard, and small trees I've planted
To resemble other yards, are shapes

I've almost memorized. Wherever I look
The same bright patient stars pause overhead.
    On nights like this I can recite

Names of streets and local flowers;
    I know the seasons by the turning light—
Knowledge to fit in a coffee cup

    Mornings when I watch one lovely
Yellow flower opening to light. There,
    History begins. I cannot see but know

The rising breath of houses, as I pass,
    Is valuable, even as it vanishes. (Once,
At the funeral of a quiet man, I elegized

    The quick familiar motion of his waving hand.)
If there's a light, I stop.
    I look in. Here is what the book says:

Whatever you learn you will forget
    So you might have its glimpse again.
When have I ever felt lonelier? happier?

Bagatelles

My father who forgets that yesterday
    He saw a bird the color of sky not slate,
Who argues with the endless irritation
    Of the elderly, remembers which leg
He broke at soccer, not the year but the sharp
    Blueing bone escaping through his skin.
He phones to tell me the past comes to visit
    When he sits listening in his room alone,
And the simple accumulation of years,
    Like a jigsaw puzzle pieced together
In an afternoon, tells him all he needs to know.

    I told this to a woman. We were dancing
At our 20th high school reunion, her thigh
    A presence against my own. I could barely

246

Remember who she was. I didn't remember
    Telling her, "Pretty soon, boys will be chasing
After you," though she did, and how solemn
    I'd looked, how she planned her future then.
Years later, standing before a mirror
    Brushing her hair, the memory shuddered
Through her like music through an empty room.

    On the night of my 40th birthday,
Far from home, I stayed up late and lonely.
    Snow fell on a city in the valley,
Lights in the windows went off, roofs blended
    Evenly with snow, evergreens with snow
Until the whole white valley dissolved.
    I could vaguely remember whom I'd loved,
Flake by flake snowing down, the courtesies,
    Undressing slowly, pleasure given, pleasure taken,
The nerves barely inquiring of each other.

    Not memory, but elipsis. Not the consciousness
Of afternoons, but gray light falling, Beethoven
    From the next room, the *Bagatelles* he wrote,
Not to be remembered by, but to be played
    Practice afternoons. On top of the piano
Some bric-a-brac given me by friends, a brass
    Whale paperclip, an ivory elephant no bigger
Than a child's lost tooth, and a globe
    With two polar bears seesawing in the snow.
When I turn it over, I see us years from now
    Talking on the phone. One says, *Remember this?*
And the other, rising white on white, *Remember that?*

A House

Their mouths blur like leaves caught
    In a crosswind. Lips barely, softly
Touching there, and behind the lips the hard

    White teeth, and further in, pink membranes
Pulsing to seize a breath. How deep is a mouth?

How far in before you find the other?

Some nights they fall asleep like that.
　　Then wake, walk out to check the weather,
Breakfast together, and off to the world

　　For a day. All morning and all afternoon
Inside the house shadows change places
　　With light. Noon, then twilight, dusk,

Until the shadows become one darkness.
　　How thoughtless it looks to a passerby—
Room by room the lamps go on

　　As though to repair the harm
The hours have done. But what can you say
　　In dark or light that hasn't been said?

Good morning, good night, a kiss again?
　　Then, in the body's deepest place—as in a room
Revisited after years away, some space

　　You thought of as your own, same radio, same bed
And sink, same view—you meet another
　　Passing through, a pilgrim, not quite

Familiar, not quite a stranger. What
　　Will you say? *This is where things change,
Sometimes.* This is how some people love.

Put Your Mother On The Ceiling

In the schools of Arizona
we used to play a game
put your mother on the ceiling.

What is she wearing?
What does she have in her hands?
Is she happy or sad, or can you tell?
If she is speaking, what is she saying?
Is she looking at you or looking away?

Some days the walls backed off,
the ceiling lifted, and there were
many women, real women
over our heads held up
by the light in our eyes.
They wore long turquoise dresses,
bright sweaters, beads
and concho belts, T-shirts
that said Kiss, Phoenix Suns, Ford.
They held babies, knives, baskets,
cans of beer. They were laughing
or weeping or watching TV.
They said shut up, be good, I love you
in English, Spanish, Navajo, Apache, and Pima.

Now and then
one of the women whose name
might have been Nina Pancho, Charlotte
Keesay, or Josie Allison,
one of the mothers
who wore a white dress
and perhaps a hat of live
hummingbirds and held in her hands
wild flowers and dollar bills
looked down on all of us
smiling, saying, "Come home, come home."

On other days some of the mothers
failed to appear. They were hidden
among other concerns.

A girl by the window might say,
"I can't put my mother on the ceiling,
my mother is dead."
Then she would look out
over the schoolyard toward the motherless mountains
and the ones who were there above us
would close their eyes, go mute
in mid-sentence, and fall
embarrassingly in the aisles,
all of them having died a little
in the finality of the words of the girl.

The Flower Farm

At the end of Avenue B
Masuda, the flower farmer,
brightened the hills with iris,
daffodil, chrysanthemum—acres
of swaying flowers. An occupation,
and a beauty, that came of necessity.
Flowers for lovers and funerals.
Flowers to forget the war
and the people who disappeared
leaving only their shadows printed on stone.

Born afterwards, having nothing to forget,
I tortured those flowers. I stuffed them
in my pockets, crushed them in my fists
and held them to my nose, bit them,
pulled them apart petal by petal
and swung the long stalks in the air like swords.
And when I came home, fingers smeared with pollen,
I handed my mother a perfect flower
and offered her my cheek.

When she kissed me, too hard sometimes,
I didn't know if it was from pleasure or pain.
But everyone had their job, my new father told me,
and mine was to help her forget.

Our house, like everything,
was temporary: a board shack propped on blocks,
tar bucket for toilet, pastel bed sheets
tacked up for curtains, and at night
the smoky light of kerosene and the sounds
they couldn't conceal.

One night I saw him
stroke her belly with his big hand
and touch the four purple scars, a map of loss.
I pressed that image into my pillow
as a flower is pressed in a book.

When I asked her
she told me. She told me to go out
and pick four flowers, one for each of my brothers,
who had refused the world.

That morning at the end of Avenue B
I failed my first job while Masuda's farm
claimed the air for miles.

Endless Nights Of Rain

Did you have relatives
among the dead? the man
in the black felt hat is asked.
His dark poncho hanging like a shroud
over his clasped hands, he stands
in the little cemetery
on the edge of the village of San Mateo Ixtatan.
Around him the green walls
of the mountains and the conspiring shadows
that circle his world like bad weather
won't let him answer.
On the other side of his gaze
under his hat the leaves
are bloated with rain and he
is a man waking again
to the sound of gun fire
and the cries of his neighbors.

251

Relatives among the dead?
He does not answer. He no longer
trusts the simple truth.
It is 65 kilometers to Huehuetenango.
Where he stands it is 36 lives
away from the first of June
and all the living and the dead
are relatives where he stands.
Rain drips from his black hat
and a small shadow covers his eyes
where a whole country is hiding.

No one seems to know
who they were: the army
of the rich, the army of the poor,
the army of the rich
dressed in the clothes of the army of the poor.
No one knows whose souls
are tangled in the trees and vines
in the darkness of the mountains
outside the towns
or why the soldiers came
to kick in the doors of the sleepers
and gather the players and deal the hands
in the game called endless nights
of rain. For blood or money,
no one's sure. But the soldiers,
trained in forgetfulness, must have agreed
that their mothers were whores
that their own bodies were weapons
with which to stab out the lights.
And it goes on every night,
the rain and the killing
in some foreign country of the heart.

Boquillas

Along that tract of the Rio Grande
where the river flows
out of one steep-walled canyon
and into another, braiding its waters

over the desert rocks, there's a town
called Boquillas. Boquillas—little mouths,
openings in a river or canal
for irrigating the lands, mouthpiece
of a wind instrument, holes
in the knees of children's pants.
The town stands on a rocky bluff
above the river near the mouth
of a canyon. To get there from
the north you must cross
the desert and walk down a dirt path
through the reeds to the river,
that border the birds ignore.
There's a boatman on the other side
and a few burros standing
saddled in the shade of a mesquite.
The crossing is cheap. The *Aduana,*
the customs house, is closed. Everything else
is open—the two bars, the church,
the hands of the children.
There's a woman
who will not meet your eyes
wiping her hands on a black apron.
She is whispering to the children
sending them out to offer
quartz pebbles for the coins
in your pockets embossed
with the heads of presidents.
There's a man smiling
or squinting under a white sombrero
catching the sun on his one
gold tooth. He could be the man
who, years ago, taught you the word
boquimuelle—tender-mouthed
as applied to a horse
or, unwary, easily imposed upon.
Yes, Amigo, she is beautiful,
but she is boquimuelle, be careful.
You are careful as you enter
La Tapia, the Hideout. A couple of tourists
sit at the bar drinking *Superior*
occasionally saying a few words
into the stillness of the desert air
drifting in at the open door.

The bartender waits for another round
and listens in his own language.
From the posters on the wall
naked blond *Norteñas* sulk
or smile or stare with half-closed
eyes and open mouths.
Drink your beer, Señor. Listen
to the voice of the dust.
The church on the same dirt street
has something else to say. Come in,
but come in quietly, there's a service
in progress. The door is open
so the birds fly in, black-throated
sparrows from the desert
and canyons of the Sierra del Carmen.
There's an altar with candles
and four rows of pews decorated
with sparrow droppings.
Above the crucifix and framed prints
of bleeding Jesus and sad-eyed Dolorosa
the birds are up in the rafters
building nests of weeds, bits of
pink yarn, discarded cigarette packs.
Their voices loud and confident
under the tin roof of this church
in the town of Boquillas
that could be named for them
or for all the small openings
into the life of the spirit
that may be lost or found here.
You could live here.
You could be the mayor of this place
whose job is to do nothing
but listen to the little mouths,
be careful, and leave the doors open.
Evenings you could watch
from the bluff above the river
as the dark grows out of the mouths
of the canyons, that dark
that is peace or terror or nothing,
that spreads, as it always has,
until it covers half the earth.

ROBERT PINSKY

The Figured Wheel

The figured wheel rolls through shopping malls and prisons,
Over farms, small and immense, and the rotten little downtowns.
Covered with symbols, it mills everything alive and grinds
The remains of the dead in the cemeteries, in unmarked graves and oceans.

Sluiced by salt water and fresh, by pure and contaminated rivers,
By snow and sand, it separates and recombines all droplets and grains,
Even the infinite sub-atomic particles crushed under the illustrated,
Varying treads of its wide circumferential track.

Spraying flecks of tar and molten rock it rumbles
Through the Antarctic station of American sailors and technicians,
And shakes the floors and windows of whorehouses for diggers and smelters
From Bethany, Pennsylvania to a practically nameless, semi-penal New Town

In the mineral-rich tundra of the Soviet northernmost settlements.
Artists illuminate it with pictures and incised mottoes
Taken from the Ten-Thousand Stories and the Register of True Dramas.
They hang it with colored ribbons and with bells of many pitches.

With paints and chisels and moving lights they record
On its rotating surface the elegant and terrifying doings
Of the inhabitants of the Hundred Pantheons of major Gods
Disposed in iconographic stations at hub, spoke and concentric bands,

And also the grotesque demi-Gods, Hopi gargoyles and Ibo dryads.
They cover it with wind-chimes and electronic instruments
That vibrate as it rolls to make an all-but-unthinkable music,
So that the wheel hums and rings as it turns through the birth of stars

And through the dead-world of bomb, fireblast and fallout
Where only a few doomed races of insects fumble in the smoking grasses.
It is Jesus oblivious to hurt turning to give words to the unrighteous,
And is also Gogol's feeding pig that without knowing it eats a baby chick

And goes on feeding. It is the empty armor of My Cid, clattering
Into the arrows of the credulous unbelievers, a metal suit
Like the lost astronaut revolving with his useless umbilicus
Through the cold streams, neither energy nor matter, that agitate

The cold, cyclical dark, turning and returning.
Even in the scorched and frozen world of the dead after the holocaust
The wheel as it turns goes on accreting ornaments.
Scientists and artists festoon it from the grave with brilliant

Toys and messages, jokes and zodiacs, tragedies conceived
From among the dreams of the unemployed and the pampered,
The listless and the tortured. It is hung with devices
By dead masters who have survived by reducing themselves magically

To tiny organisms, to wisps of matter, crumbs of soil,
Bits of dry skin, microscopic flakes, which is why they are called "great,"
In their humility that goes on celebrating the turning
Of the wheel as it rolls unrelentingly over

A cow plodding through car-traffic on a street in Iasi,
And over the haunts of Robert Pinsky's mother and father
And wife and children and his sweet self
Which he hereby unwillingly and inexpertly gives up, because it is

There, figured and pre-figured in the nothing-transfiguring wheel.

History Of My Heart

I.

One Christmastime Fats Waller in a fur coat
Rolled beaming from a taxicab with two pretty girls
Each at an arm as he led them in a thick downy snowfall

Across Thirty-Fourth Street into the busy crowd
Shopping at Macy's: perfume, holly, snowflake displays.
Chimes rang for change. In Toys, where my mother worked

Over her school vacation, the crowd swelled and stood
Filling the aisles, whispered at the fringes, listening
To the sounds of the large, gorgeously-dressed man,

His smile bemused and exalted, lips boom-booming a bold
Bass line as he improvised on an expensive, tinkly
Piano the size of a lady's jewel box or a wedding cake.

256

She put into my heart this scene from the romance of Joy,
Co-authored by her and the movies, like her others—
My father making the winning basket at the buzzer

And punching the enraged gambler who came onto the court—
The brilliant black and white of the movies, texture
Of wet snowy fur, the taxi's windshield, piano keys,

Reflections that slid over the thick brass baton
That worked the elevator. Happiness needs a setting:
Shepherds and shepherdesses in the grass, kids in a store,

The back room of Carly's parents' shop, record-player
And paper streamers twisted in two colors: what I felt
Dancing close one afternoon with a thin blonde girl

Was my amazing good luck, the pleased erection
Stretching and stretching at the idea *She likes me,*
She likes it, the thought of legs under a woolen skirt,

To see eyes "melting" so I could think *This is it,*
They're melting! Mutual arousal of suddenly feeling
Desired: *This is it: "desire"!* When we came out

Into the street we saw it had begun, the firm flakes
Sticking, coating the tops of cars, melting on the wet
Black street that reflected storelights, soft

Separate crystals clinging intact on the nap of collar
And cuff, swarms of them stalling in the wind to plunge
Sideways and cluster in spangles on our hair and lashes,

Melting to a fresh glaze on the blood warm porcelain
Of our faces, Hey nonny-nonny boom-boom, the cold graceful
Manna, heartfelt, falling and gathering copious

As the air itself in the small-town main street
As it fell over my mother's imaginary and remembered
Macy's in New York years before I was even born,

II.

And the little white piano, tinkling away like crazy—
My unconceived heart in a way waiting somewhere like

Wherever it goes in sleep. Later, my eyes opened

And I woke up glad to feel the sunlight warm
High up in the window, a brighter blue striping
Blue folds of curtain, and glad to hear the house

Was still sleeping. I didn't call, but climbed up
To balance my chest on the top rail, cheek
Pressed close where I had grooved the rail's varnish

With sets of double tooth-lines. Clinging
With both arms, I grunted, pulled one leg over
And stretched it as my weight started to slip down

With some panic till my toes found the bottom rail,
Then let my weight slide more till I was over—
Thrilled, half-scared, still hanging high up

With both hands from the spindles. Then lower
Slipping down until I could fall to the floor
With a thud but not hurt, and out, free in the house.

Then softly down the hall to the other bedroom
To push against the door; and when it came open
More light came in, opening out like a fan

So they woke up and laughed, as she lifted me
Up in between them under the dark red blanket,
We all three laughing there because I climbed out myself.

Earlier still, she held me curled in close
With everyone around saying my name, and hovering,
After my grandpa's cigarette burned me on the neck

As he held me up for the camera, and the pain buzzed
Scaring me because it twisted right inside me;
So when she took me and held me and I curled up, sucking,

It was as if she had put me back together again
So sweetly I was glad the hurt had torn me.
She wanted to have made the whole world up,

So that it could be hers to give. So she opened
A letter I wrote my sister, who was having trouble

Getting on with her, and read some things about herself

That made her go to the telephone and call me up:
"You shouldn't open other people's letters," I said
And she said, "Yes—*who taught you that?*"

—As if she owned the copyright on good and bad,
Or having followed pain inside she owned her children
From the inside out, or made us when she named us,

III.

Made me Robert. She took me with her to a print-shop
Where the man struck a slug: a five-inch strip of lead
With the twelve letters of my name, reversed,

Raised along one edge, that for her sake he made
For me, so I could take it home with me to keep
And hold the letters up close to a mirror

Or press their shapes into clay, or inked from a pad
Onto all kinds of paper surfaces, onto walls and shirts,
Lengthwise on a Band-Aid, or even on my own skin—

The little characters fading from my arm, the gift
Always ready to be used again. Gifts from the heart:
Her giving me her breast milk or my name, Waller

Showing off in a store, for free, giving them
A thrill as someone might give someone an erection,
For the thrill of it—or you come back salty from a swim:

Eighteen shucked fresh oysters and the cold bottle
Sweating in its ribbon, surprise, happy birthday!
So what if the giver also takes, is after something?

So what if with guile she strove to color
Everything she gave with herself, the lady's favor
A scarf or bit of sleeve of her favorite color

Fluttering on the horseman's bloodflecked armor
Just over the heart—how presume to forgive the breast
Or sudden jazz for becoming what we want? I want

Presents I can't picture until they come,
The generator flashlight Italo gave me one Christmas:
One squeeze and the gears visibly churning in the amber

Pistol-shaped handle hummed for half a minute
In my palm, the spare bulb in its chamber under my thumb,
Secret; or, the knife and basswood Ellen gave me to whittle.

And until the gift of desire, the heart is a titular,
Insane king who stares emptily at his counselors
For weeks, drools or babbles a little, as word spreads

In the taverns that he is dead, or an impostor. One day
A light concentrates in his eyes, he scowls, alert, and points
Without a word to a pass in the cold, grape-colored peaks—

Generals and courtiers groan, falling to work
With a frantic movement of farriers, cooks, builders,
The city thrown willing or unwilling like seed

(While the brain at the same time may be settling
Into the morning *Chronicle,* humming to itself,
Like a fat person eating M&Ms in the bathtub)

IV.

Toward war, new forms of worship or migration.
I went out from my mother's kitchen, across the yard
Of the little two-family house, and into the Woods:

Guns, chevrons, swordplay, a scarf of sooty smoke
Rolled upwards from a little cratewood fire
Under the low tent of a Winesap fallen

With fingers rooting in the dirt, the old orchard
Smothered among the brush of wild cherry, sumac,
Sassafrass and the stifling shade of oak

In the strip of overgrown terrain running
East from the train tracks to the ocean, woods
Of demarcation, where boys went like newly-converted

Christian kings with angels on helmet and breastplate,
Bent on blood or poaching. *There are a mountain and a woods*

Between us—a male covenant, longbows, headlocks. A pack

Of four stayed half-aware it was past dark
In a crude hut roasting meat stolen from the A&P
Until someone's annoyed father hailed us from the tracks

And scared us home to catch hell: We were worried,
Where have you been? In the Woods. With snakes and tramps.
An actual hobo knocked at our back door

One morning, declining food, to get hot water.
He shaved on our steps from an enamel basin with brush
And cut-throat razor, the gray hair on his chest

Armorial in the sunlight—then back to the woods,
And the otherlife of snakes, poison oak, boxcars.
Were the trees cleared first for the trains or the orchard?

Walking home by the street because it was dark,
That night, the smoke-smell in my clothes was like a bearskin.
Where the lone hunter and late bird have seen us

Pass and repass, the mountain and the woods seem
To stand darker than before—words of sexual nostalgia
In a song or poem seemed cloaked laments

For the woods when Indians made lodges from the skin
Of birch or deer. When the mysterious lighted room
Of a bus glided past in the mist, the faces

Passing me in the yellow light inside
Were a half-heard story or a song. And my heart
Moved, restless and empty as a scrap of something

Blowing in wide spirals on the wind carrying
The sound of breakers clearly to me through the pass
Between the blocks of houses. The horn of Roland

V.

But what was it I was too young for? On moonless
Nights, water and sand are one shade of black,
And the creamy foam rising with moaning noises

Charges like a spectral army in a poem toward the bluffs
Before it subsides dreamily to gather again.
I thought of going down there to watch it a while,

Feeling as though it could turn me into fog,
Or that the wind would start to speak a language
And change me—as if I knocked where I saw a light

Burning in some certain misted window I passed,
A house or store or tap-room where the strangers inside
Would recognize me, locus of a new life like a woods

Or orchard that waxed and vanished into cloud
Like the moon, under a spell. Shrill flutes,
Oboes and cymbals of doom. My poor mother fell,

And after the accident loud noises and bright lights
Hurt her. And heights. She went down stairs backwards,
Sometimes with one arm on my small brother's shoulder.

Over the years, she got better. But I was lost in music;
The cold brazen blow of the saxophone, its weight
At thumb, neck and lip, came to a bloodwarm life

Like Italo's flashlight in the hand. In a white
Jacket and pants with a satin stripe I aspired
To the roughneck elegance of my Grandfather Dave.

Sometimes, playing in a bar or at a high school dance, I felt
My heart following after a capacious form,
Sexual and abstract, in the thunk, thrum,

Thrum, come-wallow and then a little screen
Of quicker notes goosing to a fifth higher, winging
To clang-whomp of a major seventh: listen to *me*

Listen to *me*, the heart says in reprise until sometimes
In the course of giving itself it flows out of itself
All the way across the air, in a music piercing

As the kids at the beach calling from the water *Look,*
Look at me, to their mothers, but out of itself, into
The listener the way feeling pretty or full or erotic revery

Makes the one who feels seem beautiful to the beholder
Witnessing the idea of the giving of desire—nothing more wanted
Than the little singing notes of wanting—the heart

Yearning further into giving itself into the air, breath
strained into song emptying the golden bell it comes from,
The pure source poured altogether out and away.

STANLEY PLUMLY

With Stephen In Maine

The huge mammalian rocks in front of the lawn,
domestic between the grass and the low tide—
Stephen has set his boat in one of the pools,
his hand the little god that makes it move.
It is cold, the sky the rough wool and gaberdine
of pictures someone almost talented has painted.
Off and on the sun, then Stephen is wading . . .

Yesterday we saw two gulls shot out of the sky.
One of them drifted into shore, broken, half-eaten,
green with the sea. When I found it this morning
all I could think to do was throw it back. One wing.
Its thin blood spread enough that Stephen is finger-
printed and painted with washing and wiping dry.
Even his boat, at the watermark, is stained.

I lift him, put him up on top of my shoulders.
From here he can watch the deep water pile, turn over.
He says, with wonder, that it looks like the ocean
killing itself. He wants to throw stones, he wants
to see how far his boat can sail, will float.
The mile or more from here to there is an order of color,
pitched white and black and dove- or green-gray, blue,

but far and hurt from where he is seeing.

After Whistler

In his portrait of Carlyle, Whistler builds
from the color out: he calls it an arrangement
in gray and black and gives it a number in order
to commit us to the composition—to the foreground
first, in profile, before we go on to a wall
that seems to be neutral but is really the weather.
Carlyle is tired, beyond anger, and beautiful,
his white head tilted slightly toward the painter.

He is wearing a long coat and rests his hat on his knees.

When I was born I came out holding my breath, blue.
The cord had somehow rotted at the navel—
I must have lain alone for hours before they would let
my father's mother, the other woman there, give blood.
She still had red hair and four years to live.
The place on my arm where they put the needles in
I call my mortality scar. When I think of my grand-
mother lifting me all the way to the kitchen counter
I think of the weight by which we are doubled or more

through the lives of others. I followed her
everywhere, or tried to. I was her witness.
When I look at Whistler's portrait of Carlyle
I think of how the old survive: we make them up.
In the vegetable garden, therefore, the sun is gold
as qualified in pictures. She is kneeling in front
of the light in such a way I can separate skin from bone.
She is an outline, planting or preparing the ground.
For all I know she will never rise from this green place.

Even the painter's mother is staring into the future,
as if her son could paint her back into her body.
I was lucky. In nineteen thirty-nine they still
believed blood was family. In a room real
with walls the color of buckwheat she would sit out
the afternoon dressed up, rocking me to sleep.
It would be Sunday, slow, no one else at home.
And I would wake that way, small in her small arms,
hers, in the calendar dark, my head against her heart.

Wildflower

Some—the ones with fish names—grow so north
they last a month, six weeks at most.
Some others, named for the fields they look like,
last longer, smaller.

And these, in particular, whether trout or corn lily,
onion or bellwort, just cut

this morning and standing open in tapwater in the kitchen,
will close with the sun.

It is June, wildflowers on the table.
They are fresh an hour ago, like sliced lemons,
with the whole day ahead of them.
They could be common mayflower lilies of the valley,

day lilies, or the clustering Canada, large, gold,
long-stemmed as pasture roses, belled out over the vase —
or maybe Solomon's seal, the petals
ranged in small toy pairs

or starry, tipped at the head like weeds.
They could be anonymous as weeds.
They are, in fact, the several names of the same thing,
lilies of the field, butter-and-eggs,

toadflax almost, the way the whites and yellows juxtapose,
and have "the look of flowers that are looked at,"
rooted as they are in water, glass, and air.
I remember the summer I picked everything,

flower and wildflower, singled them out in jars
with a name attached. And when they had dried as stubborn
as paper I put them on pages and named them again.
They were all lilies, even the hyacinth,

even the great pale flower in the hand of the dead.
I picked it, kept it in the book for years
before I knew who she was,
her face lily-white, kisses and dry and cold.

Ground Birds in Open Country

They fly up in front of you,
suddenly, as in allegory, black
            and white, by the handful.
    If it's spring, they break
back and forth in a blur,
                in new air warm

266

        down to the ground. Lark
or longspur, starling or sparrow.

    My life list is one bird at a time long.
What Roethke calls *looking.*
        The eye, particular for color,
    remembers when a whole treeful
would go gray with applause.
            In the middle of nowhere,
      in a one-oak field.
I clapped my hands just for the company.

    As one lonely morning, green under glass,
a redwing flew straight at me,
            its shoulders slick with the air.
      It was that close,
and brilliant. In the birdbook, there,
    where the names are,
         it is always May,
and the thing so fixed we can see it,

    even the yellow margin halving the wing.
Magnolia, Blackpool, Palm and Pine—warblers:
        the time one got into the schoolroom
      we didn't know what it was,
        but it sang, it sailed
along the ceiling on all sides.
    And blew back out, wild, still lost,
before any of us, stunned, could shout it down.

    And in a hallway once a bird went mad, window
by closed window, the hollow length of the building.
        I had to break it, finally, with my hand.
        They fly up so quickly
in front of you, without names,
        in the slurred shapes of a wing.
        Or they fly from room to room,
having already gathered in great numbers on the ground.

After Rilke

(1)

There is the poverty of children shy with child—
the girl who will not say what is already
part of her breath, like a second wind, another mouth.
And there is the poverty of rain, in spring,
clean on the streets, the small roofs of the city.
And poverty of desire in prison hallways, cell by cell . . . .

And poverty of the wheelchair and the deathbed
and the blind who tow them where they're told.
Or flowers along the railway and the river,
poorer with every passage.

               You should look
into your hands right now—they'll hold
the poverty of grief until you let it go.

You should look into the light—it is the dust made whole.

The poverty of the bird that flies in the window
or the yard-dog tied to the ground—rooms with doors
locked on the dumb who talk to themselves . . . .
These are the stones that will shine.

For the poor own the houses you will not visit;
they own the trees that are dead all day.
They own the table and the chair and the glass of water.

And they let their children go hungry who will eat all the
      bread.
And they let their children go cold who will take what is
      warm.

You should look around you how the dark is poor.

(2)

And, Masters, how all this city planning comes
to one dead-end or another—block after block
abandoned, as in the loneliness after a fire.
This could be snow falling through the roof, nineteen

268

hundred and one, or the air that will open above Dresden.

I have seen people stunned, sitting in the center of their rooms,
watching the street like children who have sinned.
I have seen a child's shadow, the shadow of a child,
at the same sill the same each day.
And nowhere in the mind of that child

nor in what its father sees
is the shade tree rooted where the ground is green
or the wind off water and the sea rose bending.
The sad eyes looking back at me
give nothing for nothing.

And the girls, so young they still bloom toward the future
and seem almost beautiful with memory,
though we know what they long for is beyond desire,
their bodies burning even as they close,
they will be mothers, year after year,

and will sit at tables half in, half out of light,
waiting for something as at the hour assigned
in a room adjacent where they can be alone
and be at peace and let themselves lie down in a long death,
still married to need and the needs of others.

BIN RAMKE

The Magician

From up my own sleeve I came
and chose my father,
a volunteer from the audience.
I told him to stand
there, in front
of the buzzing saw.
I grabbed him by his long
ears and pulled him
into the hat with me.
There in the silky dark
we slept.

I used to know lots of tricks.
Pick a card, any.
I memorized a card a week
for a year. I turned
rabbits into plowshares.
I escaped from every kind
enclosure.

In the hat we slept together
dreaming each our games
of solitaire.
We awoke old;
forgetting everything
we bowed goodbye:
I last saw him walking away
trying to wipe his eyes
with a white handkerchief
that kept becoming a pigeon.

Eclipse

Recall the light
that moved under the bedroom door,
that sifted through the dust-mice caught

beneath the bed, then was gone.
It was your mother in the hall,
deep in the night—the sound of water
from the bathroom, the whine of plumbing
like the torturer's bride escaped
into the wall.

                    *

                    I could not turn
away from their flash when distant
visiting relatives took pictures:
I stared at the blue bulbs
they licked then stuck in steel
sockets. Afterward, the seared spot
still floating in my eye,
I would secretly peel the plastic
coating off—a safety device,
they told me, in case the glass globe
should explode.

                    *

                    My father held
the black, nearly opaque sheets for me
to protect my eyes, he said, but that
I would remember this eclipse forever.
The papers carried stories of two boys
gone blind from unprotected staring.
They should have had such a father
as mine, I said, but wondered
what it was like, that last moment
of sun, that ring of corrosive light
just at that moment beyond recall.

Another Small Town in Georgia

This is the future, what we feared.
It could have been worse. For instance,
the woman you spied on in your first madness,
you a boy of seventeen, is gone, but walk

down any street and look for that golden
incandescence in some window, see a woman there
combing her hair and dreaming of a man
who might as well be you.

And in your favorite restaurant, in the afternoon,
you can still sit in that place that lets you see
an occasional breast, the slimming movement of thigh
eclipsing the sunlight through diaphanous dresses,
blouses thin as the film of tears in your eye,
as they pay their bills at the counter.

Note how the dandelion grows in front of your house
through the cracked, unkempt sidewalk,
signaling to the neighbors the depth of your failure
and despair, reminding them daily of the disgust
they felt when they passed your open door and saw
you in your stained underwear watching television.
Note how the dandelion's glory is a halo, a sphere
of seed surrounding nothing, aimed only at
its own tight, perfect circle of future.
It is possible to be brave.

Jacob

The first light of the day, milk-
colored, flattens the landscape
into eternal present; headlights
yellow weakly while legitimate business
begins to open; workers return
after a night's sleep little suspecting
the adulterer riding among them.

The worst of it is
I asked for it, adventures in the night
skulking with other men's wives,
wrestling us both into skeletons,
sad confessions, burning the flesh
from the bones.

With the morning star shining
the milkman leers in his small-town way
tinkling down the sidewalk as I leave.
She, at the door anyway, clasps
her peignoir close and reaches
through the door ajar for the bottle.

*

The texture thickens, the houses
grow smaller and more closely packed,
the potholes breed mosquitoes
seven months of the year.
I live here. My children
know me, the dog licks my hand.
My wife sleeps alone: we've not
touched in a decade.

It's less unusual than you'd think:
I see the condition in many men's eyes,
the love that burns brighter for wives
they've wronged than for all
the young things in Biloxi, end to end.

We're irresistible: nothing attracts
like the smell of despair from married men.

*

I have no friends to speak of,
or to. Contrary to what women think,
my kind doesn't talk about women.
No bragging in the locker room.
We're not proud, just doing
what flesh demands in secret,
gliding through the night driven
by ancient needs, deeds, despairs.

Alone in strange rooms listening
to the sounds from the bathroom,
we dream of release,
of the time when the body becomes
a shadow weaving
along the surface of things

like a flag on wind. A body
beyond itself, a body borne
by force of clean intellect,
a ghost haunting nothing
but mind vast and noble.

*

I could never say no to a woman,
the homely especially, so full
of ghosts we couldn't bear it,
baring their thin arms,
their thighs so wide apart, like
clothespin dolls. Like children.

I have more than once conducted
complex affairs with women
whose names I never knew;
was too polite to interrupt,
they had so much to say.

*

It often begins in a bar, a face
looms mirrored over my shoulder,
a smile. I know nothing then
will stop it, nothing save us.
I touch her elbow so slightly
it might have meant nothing.

I'm always attentive to weakness,
their shame. Scars, missing fingers,
prostheses, limps, lumps, ravaged
spoils of small lives. Sometimes
as in old movies they drape scarves
over the lampshade. Sometimes
they cry as I hold them.

I have read all their women's magazines,
all the articles on living alone,
or with brutish husbands, or husbands
who travel, or children filled
with terrible lust and languor.

I can name their perfumes
shyly smeared with trembling small
hands in the ladies' rooms,
the bottles later hidden
beneath the panties in the dresser.

I know more about panties and bras
than any salesman, I know the brands
by texture, by their sheen in moonlight.

I have seen the sad flash of cotton
crotches, medically approved,
in the flickering moth glow of streetlight.

    *

On the cool drive home I see mist
fog the windows: the word made water.
I talk to myself as I wipe
the windshield with a Kleenex:

                Oh woman,
isn't this just what you wanted,
the silent twining anonymous,
the sweat? How physically,
how solid with flesh you know this world;
flash of synapse, fold of firm
muscle, and that's the birth of it.

      Day unto day uttereth speech,
      and night unto night showeth knowledge.
      —Psalm 19

ALBERTO RIOS

The Purpose of Altar Boys

Tonio told me at catechism
the big part of the eye
admits good, and the little
black part is for seeing
evil— his mother told him
who was a widow and so
an authority on such things.
That's why at night
the black part gets bigger.
That's why kids can't go out
at night, and at night
girls take off their clothes
and walk around their
bedrooms or jump on their
beds or wear only sandals
and stand in their windows.
I was the altar boy
who knew about these things,
whose mission on some Sundays
was to remind people of
the night before as they
knelt for Holy Communion.
To keep Christ from falling
I held the metal plate
under chins, while on the thick
red carpet of the altar
I dragged my feet
and waited for the precise
moment: plate to chin
I delivered without expression
the Holy Electric Shock,
the kind that produces
a really large swallowing
and makes people think.
I thought of it as justice.
But on other Sundays the fire
in my eyes was different,
my mission somehow changed.
I would hold the metal plate

276

a little too hard
against those certain same
nervous chins, and I
I would look
with authority down
the tops of white dresses.

Combing My Hair in the Hall

Each time the doors to her room were opened
a little of the gathered light left
and the small room became blacker
moving somewhere in a twilight toward night.
And then a little of the light left
not her room, but her falling face
as each time she opened the smaller doors
that were her wooden eyes.
She talked only with her mouth then
no longer with the force of her wild eyes
and that, too, made her less,
each word leaving her now
as the way her firm bones had abandoned her.
Then she spoke with her woman's hands
only, no words left, then only with her smell
which once had been warm, *tortillitas,*
or like sugar breads just made.
In the half-words of our other language,
in the language of the new world
of which she had had time to show me
only half, I tried to speak to her,
to fill her up, to tell her the jokes
of the day, and fill her too much
with laughing, fill her fat like she had been,
and my brother Tomás tried too, we
touched her, were made to touch her,
we kissed her even, lips trying
to quickly press back the something
as children even we could feel
but whose name she had not told us,
and as we kissed her, bent and kissed her,
we could smell her, I shivered, and we both

breathed out hard when we had to
put our lips there, like later we would learn
to drink *pulque* and be men, trying even that
to push her back into herself.
But she was impatient with us, or smarter,
or quicker, so that we did smell her,
she made us, and taste the insides of her,
and take her in small parts with us
but not like drink, not like men— instead,
like the smell of bread taken by the heart
into the next day, or into dreams.
Every night she wanted to be young again
as she slept there on her bed
and in the night, in the minute she could
no longer talk, and did not smell, or wake,
she was, again, young: we
opened our mouths
and asked words about her, cried
bits of ourselves out through our eyes,
each sigh expelled, each tear,
each word said now making us,
us less, not here, each word gone
making room in ourselves for her,
so that one day, again, she laughs hard,
a Thursday, four voices stronger, five,
laughs at something none of us understands,
standing there, comb in hand, laughs
at something silly, or vain, or the story
of the six sisters of mercy, perhaps, she
just laughs looking at all of her new faces
full in the mirror at the end of the hall.

I Would Visit Him in the Corner

He was the uncle who when he was young
and lying down had a spider crawl
into the large hole of his left ear and stay

through the night. Even after it was crushed
on the side of his head and he saw the legs
he never could believe it was gone

and so that ear was always stopped up
even though he would stand sometimes
like a swimmer jumping up and down

with his head cocked. It kept him from dying
in the war because they would not take him.
But he said he died anyway, and had nightmares

that crawled. And his ear grew bigger
because he kept hitting it, and when he was old
it became his habit, even when it bled.

Finally in the red night scratching
with no one to see and nothing to hold
the spider carelessly left him.

In the Woman Arms of the Ground

His breath smelled when he spoke
because his insides were rotting.
As a child he had eaten dirt
and his mother had said all right.
He eats it, she would say,
because there is something there
that he needs.
He grew, but not much
and his mornings became apples
and black coffee out of one cup.
His secret was that the apples
from the orchards grew
from trees, and trees grew in dirt.
With each apple he swallowed
his insides chased each other,
the little chases of children,
quick, out of breath, the chases
of boys playing tag, back
and forth and back without plan,
boys running and falling,
kicking the slowest, too many times
laughing, and then too hard
like a father who has worked

since birth and then one day
must punish his son, but goes too far,
as the boy starts to cry,
to feel pain, and they, too,
can feel it, these tag boys,
these insides of the man, aching,
yet they will not stop,
even out of breath, Ricardo,
Pachi, Julio, Rubén and every one,
the boys he remembers, the boy
he was, who fell to the ground
and held onto it as they kicked him,
held it like later he would hold
a woman, too long, too desperately—
himself young and all of them
running so fast still, but now
out of him, out of his old mouth,
each one yelling with the pain
memory brings, into the sink.
I would watch this man
who had the face of my uncle
come out of the bathroom on these days.
These were his insides he left
and he was glad to trade them,
to trade these pieces of what he was
in exchange for the power to eat
another apple, to build himself again
from the beginning with new pieces
of earth, to hold the earth near him
as apples, but these were the green,
wild apples that made the pain
that was his woman inside.
But that was what his woman was
he told me every morning,
so I dream of him happy now
in the woman arms of the ground.

PATTIANN ROGERS

The Pieces of Heaven

No one alone could detail that falling—the immediate
Sharpening and blunting of particle and plane,
The loosening, the congealing of axis
And field, the simultaneous opening and closing
Composing the first hardening of moment when heaven first broke
From wholeness into infinity.

No one alone could follow the falling
Of all those pieces gusting in tattered
Layers of mirage like night rain over a rocky hill,
Pieces cartwheeling like the red-banded leg
Of the locust, rolling like elk antlers dropping
After winter, spiraling slowly like a fossil of squid
Twisting to the bottom of the sea, pieces lying toppled
Like bison knees on a prairie, like trees of fern
In a primeval forest.

And no one could remember the rising
Of all those pieces in that moment, pieces shining
Like cottonwood dust floating wing-side up
Across the bottomland, rising like a woman easily
Lifting to meet her love, like the breasting,
The disappearing surge and scattering crest of fire
Or sea blown against rock, bannered like the quills
Of lionfish in their sway, like the whippling stripe
Of the canebrake rattler under leaves.

Who can envision all of heaven trembling
With the everlasting motion of its own shattering
Into the piece called honor and the piece
Called terror and the piece called death and the piece
Tracing the piece called compassion all the way back
To its source in that initial crimp of potential particle
Becoming the inside and outside called matter and space?

And no one alone can describe entirely
This single piece of heaven partially naming its own falling
Or the guesswork forming the piece

That is heaven's original breaking, the imagined
Piece that is its new and eventual union.

Justification of the Horned Lizard

I don't know why the horned lizard wants to live.
It's so ugly—short prickly horns and scowling
Eyes, lipless smile forced forever by bone,
Hideous scaly hollow where its nose should be.

I don't know what the horned lizard has to live for,
Skittering over the sun-irritated sand, scraping
The hot dusty brambles. It never sees anything but gravel
And grit, thorns and stickery insects, the towering
Creosote bush, the ocotillo and its whiplike
Branches, the severe edges of the Spanish dagger.
Even shade is either barren rock or barb.

The horned lizard will never know
A lush thing in its life. It will never see the flower
Of the water-filled lobelia bent over a clear
Shallow creek. It will never know moss floating
In waves in the current by the bank or the blue-blown
Fronds of the waterclover. It will never have a smooth
Glistening belly of white like the bullfrog or a dew-heavy
Trill like the mating toad. It will never slip easily
Through mud like the skink or squat in the dank humus
At the bottom of a decaying forest in daytime.
It will never be free of dust. The only drink it will ever know
Is in the body of a bug.

And the horned lizard possesses nothing noble—
Embarrassing tail, warty hide covered with sharp dirty
Scales. No touch to its body, even from its own kind,
Could ever be delicate or caressing.

I don't know why the horned lizard wants to live.
Yet threatened, it burrows frantically into the sand
With a surprisingly determined fury of forehead, limbs
And ribs. Pursued, it even fights for itself, almost rising up,
Posturing on its bowed legs, propelling blood out of its eyes

In tight straight streams shot directly at the source
Of its possible extinction. It fights for itself,
Almost rising up, as if the performance of that act,
The posture, the propulsion of the blood itself,
Were justification enough and the only reason needed.

Love Song

It's all right, together with me tonight,
How your whole body trembles exactly like the locust
Establishing its dry-cymbal quivering
Even in the furthest branch-tip leaves
Of the tree in which it screams.

Lying next to me, it's all right how similar
You become to the red deer in its agitated pacing
On the open plains by the sea, in its sidling
Haunch against haunch, in the final mastery
Of its mounting.

And it's all right, in those moments,
How you possess the same single-minded madness
Of the opened wood poppy circling and circling,
The same wild strength of its golden eye.

It's true. You're no better
Than the determined boar snorgling and rooting,
No better than the ridiculous, ruffled drumming
Of the prairie chicken, no better
Than the explosion of the milkweed pod
Spilling the white furl of the moon deep
In the midnight field. You're completely
Indistinguishable from the enraged sand myrtle
Absurd in its scarlet spread on the rocky bluffs.

But it's all right. Don't you know
This is precisely what I seek, mad myself
To envelope every last drupe and pearl-dropped ovule,
Every nip and cry and needle-fine boring, every drooping,
Spore-rich tassle of oak flower, all the whistling,
Wing-beating, heavy-tipped matings of an entire prairie

Of grasses, every wafted, moaning seed-hook
You can possibly manage to bring to me,
That this is exactly what I contrive to take into my arms
With you, again and again.

Inside God's Eye

As if his eye had no boundaries, at night
All the heavens are visible there. The stars drift
And hesitate inside that sphere like white seeds
Sinking in a still, dark lake. Spirals of brilliance,
They float silently and slowly deeper and deeper
Into the possible expansion of his acuity.
And within that watching, illumination like the moon
Is uncovered petal by petal as a passing cloud clears
The open white flowers of the shining summer plum.

Inside god's eye, light spreads like afternoon spreads,
Accepting the complications of water burr and chestnut,
The efforts of digger bee and cuckoo bee. Even the barest
Light gathers and concentrates there like a ray
Of morning reaching the thinnest nerve of a fairy shrimp
At the center of a pond. And like evening, light
Bends inside the walls of god's eye to make
Sky-wide globes of fuchsia and orange, violet-tipped
Branches and violet-tinged wings set against a red dusk.

Lines from the tangle of dodder, bindweed
And honeysuckle, from the interweaving knot
Of seaweed and cones, patterns from the network
Of blowing shadow and flashing poplar, fill
And define the inner surface moment of his retina.

And we, we are the only point of reversal
Inside his eye, the only point of light
That turns back on itself and by that turning
Saves time from infinity and saves motion
From obscurity. We are the vessel and the blood
And the pulse he sees as he sees the eye watching
The vision inside his eye in the perfect mirror
Held constantly before his face.

First Notes from One Born and Living in an Abandoned Barn

Every dusty bar and narrow streak of brilliance
Originating from white slits and roof-crevices
Or streaming to the floor all day in one solid column
From the opening directly overhead
Is only light.

The rising tatter of weed-ticks under the door
And the quick unseen banging of shingles above
Are named the sudden and the unexpected.

Silence is understood to be the straw-flecked
Morasses of webs consistently filling the corners
With a still grey filigree of dirt, and meditation
Is called orb-weaver and funnel spider tugging
At their ropes, working and stitching
With the synchronization of their flexible nails.

The furthest limits to which the eyes can see—
The rotten board walls and the high wind-stopped
Eaves—are the boundaries the mind clearly recognizes
As the furthest edges of itself, and the steel-blue forks
Of the swallows bumping and tapping along the ledges
Of the rafters all afternoon define again
The barriers of the acknowledged. Realization
Is simply the traceable expansion gradually filling
All the spaces known as barn.

And at night the point at which the slow downward swoop
Of the bat first begins its new angle upward is called
Proof of the power of the body's boundaries.
And what it is believed the snake experiences as it slides
The line of its belly along the thigh
Is thigh. The length of the arm is nothing more
Than the length the mouse crawls before its feet
Are felt no more. And what it is imagined the owl sees
As it stares from the eaves directly into the eyes
Of the one it perceives is called identity.

What appears in the opening of the roof at night
Is only what the barn envelopes and holds.
What the mind envelopes and holds in the opening
Of the roof is called the beyond.

And the beyond is either the definition of disappearance
Discovered by the bats, or else it is the rectangular
Body of stars defining the place of the roof, or else
It is the black opening looking down on the starlit
Rectangle creating the eyes, or else it is the entire
Inner surface of the face composed of stars, or else
It is the first lucky guess of the mind at the boundless
Which is exactly what has caused the need to begin tonight
The documented expansion inherent to these notes.

Trinity

I wish something slow and gentle and good
Would happen to me, a patient and prolonged
Kind of happiness coming in the same way evening
Comes to a wide-branched sycamore standing
In an empty field; each branch, not succumbing,
Not taken, but feeling its entire existence
A willing revolution of cells; even asleep,
Feeling a decision of gold spreading
Over its ragged bark and motionless knots of seed,
Over every naked, vulnerable juncture; each leaf
Becoming a lavender shell, a stem-deep line
Of violet turning slowly and carefully to possess exactly
The pale and patient color of the sky coming.

I wish something that slow and that patient
Would come to me, maybe like the happiness
Growing when the lover's hand, easy on the thigh
Or easy on the breast, moves like late light moves
Over the branches of a sycamore, causing
A slow revolution of decision in the body;
Even asleep, feeling the spread of hazy coral
And ivory-grey rising through the legs and spine
To alter the belief behind the eyes; feeling the slow
Turn of wave after wave of acquiescence moving
From the inner throat to the radiance of a gold belly
To a bone-center of purple; an easy, slow-turning
Happiness of possession like that, prolonged.

I wish something that gentle and that careful
And that patient would come to me. Death
Might be that way if one knew how to wait for it,
If death came easily and slowly,
If death were good.

KENNETH ROSEN

The Flaying Of Marsyas (after Titian)

If I had eyeballs up my asshole I could watch
Apollo's faggot angel—Erato, the love muse—

play his suck-ass violin. Oh yes, watch the fiddle
unriddle in fire for him to celebrate the president,

his master's, crooked win. Oh Jesus, sh, that's
my skin. The whisper of his razor I can hear,

the slit, click and tear, my woodflute scorned
and my poor fork of fur unpeeling like a peach

to be that sonofabitch's treasure: I SALUTE
YOU, MR. SOAP, MR. RULE OF RHYME AND MEASURE!—

feet yoked into trees, hands bound each to each,
and calm as if crucified, as if in a love thrill's

paralysis, while underneath my elbow my lady's
lapdog laps up blood where I leak. Maybe Phoebus

will make a lampshade from my leather, and me,
thinking these thoughts, beyond pain and shame,

how god and dog are not daunted by my buffalo
face, while every nymph I kissed was hushed.

What I feel is my frown tight down like a kid's
horseshoe that grins into eternity. Me, I'm

upside down, soon to be naked as Apollo is,
but in a glaze of pus. Soon this century

of gold, forest of lust, will be lost to progress,
and horror, and god's honor—a simple apocalypse.

The White Egret

In a marsh lake
a white egret
stares sideways

until a little fish
excites the swift dip
of its bitter lips

its beak. Its beak
breaks the lake
into a glitter now

less a mere morsel
of breath. Like flight
to make a word clear

a hand pauses
on a breast of air
and the egret rises

flies to blue pines
across the grave gold
marsh grass

to another lake.
Oh little white bird,
little fish

in every beginning
a sliver of silver,
a death and a hunger.

Jack & The Beanstalk

> "It is late. The Evacuation still
> proceeds, but it's all theatre."
> —*Gravity's Rainbow*

A door opened and a gust of mandolins
flew across the road like a flock of swallows.

Crosswinds rippled the flooded meadow,
and on the road two men, arm in arm, stalked

into the gravelly dawn with no clouds yet in sky
as if no angels there or milk cows, and there were
no milk cows. And yet the sky loomed over the village
houses and abandoned market stalls like a ship's wall,

sluice of the lemon moon streaming like a gold chain
from a porthole, dawn falling like sand
in an hourglass, or like an iron ship slips
irresistibly to sea, fog sucking at trouser legs

and low fields, a bird flying swiftly past,
woodsmoke and white morning. The boy was orphan stupid,
orphan glad, and he strode slowly, the lame salesman's
hand burning at rib and elbow like a baked potato.

"You'll like these," he whispered, fondling
the brown cow's twisted ear, its crumpled horn, "these
magic beans?" he persisted, limping away, spavined
beast obese, pair into darkness plowing the square.

"What are they?" his mother asked, as if the hostage
dove brought Noah olives back instead of a sprig,
a rainbow sign, a fish splash, a fairyland forlorn.
Talking to a giant state trooper over routes down the neck

to the shore, trooper membling all were about the same,
who was it he was looking for? He was fooled again, fooled,
trapped in the music that webbed heaven in *non sequiturs,*
giant's eyes quarried of moon bone and ocean skies,

and he knew he'd never recover his mother's brown cow
or live anymore among the cottages, or all day long
watch the marsh grass sway, the ocean charge, change
and retire, the sun at the horizon play with his hopes:

to saw at the stalk's root, to carry home the singing harp,
the eggs of gold, the goose. Nobody cheered
and nobody reckoned. The giant, greenstalk, and sky castle
fell, and all of his intelligence was accidental.

Crow

In this world of poison corn,
farmer dolls in backyard gardens,
death cassettes, birdlime, the owl

nailed live to the barn door
beside the weasel and the rat,
shotguns, nylon snares and broken glass,

the crow is well pleased in a cemetery
with well-spaced trees. There the brethren
can relax, nod a gang of heads to feed

like monks in hoods on nuts of the tamarack
and aspen seeds. Up at a tiptop crotch
of twig, one sits. Portland Harbor lies

in silver light like vinegar at a dinner
table, the tugboat guided tanker a portent
of leviathans remote right now, like sight

of a fireball in the trees quietly leaping
forward precedes its roar. An airplane
crosses the sky like a board on a river.

The sick elm is prolific of branches,
a tree of eyes. It sees the jogger and someone's
stone separate at dusk a thousand times.

My Tea

At the end of the path a schoolhouse
with white shutters, brown shingles, a path
of glisten-kissed stones and jointed tree roots
climbing boots have torn orange, ivory—oh,
you know the way, to raw silk whitenesses,

to scars of silver—lift up, lift up
my head off dewy trail dimples and gouges
to see needled boughs of forest-marine my

head makes bob bob as I jog, head criminal,
head hobnailing old rubber ocean, old

watery wonder—oh the moon is my thimble,
the stars shall not prick me!—with well-sunk
shining iron: (sexual glee). I allowed,
I could hardly believe, rendezvous alone
with her, my old squeeze, to retrieve

still smoldering chestnuts of desire, the moist
saucer and china fire—her hair is gray today,
Chocorua, and behind
her legs glaze of blue lines, her thighs
clumps of uncertain cumulus. But up there,

at the end of the path, fresh paint and faintly
aromatic cedar shakes, cornerstone
foursquare, solar plexus opening like
a door, and there, the dark red sky—no, a golden
chamber, a quiet stove, school desk, strawflowers

in a jar, chairs and sofa, corners of dawn
already paling, slowly unbuttoning
the gingham sky, her ladyfriend grinning like a
loose tooth—how, honey, sugar, lemon, milk—
naked legs pocked like a bombed pasture—

my tea. "Plain and with cream," I say.

MICHAEL RYAN

Winter Drought

P. K. (1957–1977)

First you cut your wrists and throat
then after they had sewn you up,
after three months of hospitals and talk,
after those who loved you cried themselves out
and their faces changed to sculptures of mistrust
in the early light, in the breakfast nook,
as you told them each day point-blank
how you felt about this life,
after they could no longer answer or look up,
you stole your father's car and drove it
to the bridge across the bay near Jamestown
where the police found it three days before
they found your body, bloated and frozen.
How could anyone so young want to die
so much? we asked, as if loneliness
tightened its death-grip gradually with age;
but we felt much older and lonelier ourselves
for a few days, until your terrible final image
began to fade and even your close friends
became again content enough
in that vast part of life
with families and earthly concerns
where your absence had never been noticed.
Such were the limits of friendship
you railed against, cursing its "ersatz intimacy"
one evening after a reading: in a crummy Cambridge bar,
with our uncomfortable group of ten
trapped in a half-moon booth,
you climbed onto the table and screamed
and we heard you and could do nothing
but pick up broken glass and take you home.

Now it has been years.
You were nearly nothing to me— a friend
of a friend, a pushy kid who loved poetry,
one more young man alone in his distress—
but last week when I went out to where I sometimes walk,

across a field of chopped stalks yellowed and dried
by months of snowless winter,
you rose abruptly from the undercurrents of memory
dredged in a steel net, and I was there
where I never was, amid boat noise
and ocean stink, your corpse
twisting as if hurt
when the net broke the surface,
then riding toward me, motionless
pale blue against the water's black.
And I've seen you here every day since,
as if I were walking the beach
the moment you balance on the iced, iron railing
and jump. Does such rage for pain
give immaculate clarity to things?
Like winter sunlight day after day
showing this field for what it is:
dust and splintered
stalks about to become dust?
Tell me what you want.

Tourists On Paros

for Debra

If I die or something happens to us
and a stray breeze the length of the house
takes you alone back to that June on Paros
when we wrote every morning in a whitewashed room
then lay naked in the sun all afternoon
and came back at dusk famished for each other
and talked away the night in a taverna by the water—
I hope the memory brings you only pleasure.

But if you also suddenly feel the loss
snap open beneath like a well covered with grass,
remember our stumbling in T-shirts and shorts
onto that funeral party in the cafe at breakfast:
not the widow, barely sixteen, in harsh wool cloth,
or the grief that filled the air and seemed boundless,

but the brawny, red-haired orthodox priest
whose shaggy orange beard over his black-smocked chest
was like an explosion from a dark doorway
of a wild, high-pitched laugh.

Larkinesque

Reading in the paper a summary
of a five-year psychological study
that shows those perceived as most beautiful
are treated differently,

I think *they could have just asked me,*
remembering a kind of pudgy kid
and late puberty, the bloody noses
and wisecracks because I wore glasses,

though we all know by now how awful it is
for the busty starlet no one takes seriously,
the most attractive women I've lunched with
complaining no one sees past the body,

they can never trust a man's interest
even when he seems not just out for sex
(eyes focusing on me above the rim of a glass):
and who *would* want to live like this?

Then I guess what beauty does to a man—
Don Juan, Casanova, Lord Byron—
those fiery eyes and steel jaw lines
can front a furnace of self-loathing,

all those breathless women rushing to him
(while hubby's at the office or ballgame)
primed to be consumed by his beauty
while he stands next to it, watching.

So maybe the looks we're dealt are best.
It's only common sense that happiness
depends on some bearable deprivation
or defect, and who knows what conflicts

great beauty could have caused,
what cruelties one might have suffered
from those now friends, what unmanageable
possibilities smiling at every small turn?

So if I get up to draw a tumbler
of ordinary tapwater and think *what if this*
were nectar dripping from some maenad's naked fingers,
will all I've missed knock me senseless?

No. Of course not. It won't.

Portrait of a Lady

> ". . . because she was in that state so many
> young girls go through— a state of sexual
> obsession that can be like a sort of trance."
> —Doris Lessing

Was it only the new, old chemical stirrings
that caused her to shoplift purple corduroys
and squeeze into them out of her mother's hearing
to discover what noises could come from boys?

Like sleepwalking on stilts, she laughed years later
(the cheap spiked heels wobbling under her feet).
The lip-smacks and wolf-whistles she remembered
fainter than the slamming of her own heartbeat

when she appeared to herself in the bright mirror
that Saturday afternoon in the shopping mall john.
All the stoned girls quit primping and stared.
And time stopped. Then one stuck out her tongue.

Our lady flipped that little whiffet the finger
and gave all strength to yank open the door
and promenade bravely past Sears and What-A-Burger
down the white-hot, phosphorescent corridor

to draw a boy to her who would answer her anger.
Of course, what she got was bruises from their pawing,

fast rides, dirty jokes, and thorough ignorance of her.
But what was she to do when need came gnawing?

Then one day there was a stranger playing Space Invaders
whose fury charged his body like a thick, hot wire.
And she'd meet him there and do anything he told her
until for no reason he didn't show up anymore.

This is the time she marked as her awakening,
the slow hours picking through the heart's rubble
and finding only bits of incomprehensible pain.
Then *she* broke hearts, got a teacher in trouble,

and never gave herself easily to anyone again.
But cruelty was a drug she needed less with age.
She read books, became accomplished, had children.
At the end, stepping out of the wall, was the damage.

When I Was Conceived

It was 1945, and it was May.
White crocus bloomed in St. Louis.
The Germans gave in but the war shoved on,
and my father came home from work that evening
tired and washed his hands
not picturing the black-goggled men
with code names fashioning an atomic bomb.
Maybe he loved his wife that evening.
Maybe after eating she smoothed his jawline
in her palm as he stretched out
on the couch with his head in her lap
while Bob Hope spoofed Hirohito on the radio
and they both laughed. My father sold used cars
at the time, and didn't like it,
so if he complained maybe she held him
an extra moment in her arms,
the heat in the air pressing between them,
so they turned upstairs early that evening,
arm in arm, without saying anything.

SHEROD SANTOS

The Evening Light Along The Sound

I

As if the sky could no longer hold its color,
that pale blue light sifts down onto the water
like talcum onto a tabletop, or like the fine powder
of memory settling again in the mind in that hour
toward sleep, in that season toward autumn
when the trees begin to fill with a sorrowing air.
Still, there's a moment then when it all seems
so impersonal: no sign that something difficult
is reappearing in our lives, no image
of a feeling, but a feeling itself, like a mis-
directed letter from someone sad and faraway.

II

And it doesn't matter that in that quiet hour
you forget yourself awhile, that the sky
becomes a kind of mirror in which the face
grows dim, then disappears, like a coin
receding underwater. Even the early arrival
of the moon on the horizon only magnifies
the light's desire to turn all things
to light: how quickly it absorbs the sea-
birds drowsing on the air, although, tonight,
the evening star, like a bread-crumb dropped
on the water, is enough to bring them back again.

III

And the night is usually carried in on a breeze,
so that each time the water ripples the light
will darken, as if sprinkled with ash, and become
more fully a part of the air. But the truth is,
the light is sinking into itself, as we, in an absence
of light, will sink back into ourselves—
and it isn't a question, then, of how we feel,
but of how we hold ourselves out to the dark
when the dark closes down around us, and when,

momentarily, what light there is only glitters
in the mind, like a cluster of stars on the Sound.

Death

(after Elizabeth Bowen)

Although great in passing, although suddenly enlarged
    The frightened heart puts up its proud defense,
        Still, it always leaves you feeling
    A little smaller somehow, and living becomes a little
        Meaner then, necessitous, and preoccupied
With harder pleasures, like the lives of the poor.

It's as though your childhood house had been gutted
    By fire, the blackened walls left standing there,
        The windows gaping under an open sky,
    And suddenly one day you find yourself standing out
        On the lawn without the heart or ambition
To rebuild. And in that hour, with its one idea

Of releasing you from some part of yourself, you think
    You can see it unfolding there: how the maple
        Trees that line the yard are all cut
    Down, the land itself sold out in parts, how before
        Too long small apartments will appear
In a long red row, each one a home for someone

You don't know. And after dark, where once was silence,
    The maples' shadows drawn slowly across the grass
        By the moon, or, if no moon, then
    An exhalation of darkness—you find, instead, a string
        Of porchlights have come on like stars,
And the bluish glow of television screens has filled

The windows from street to street. And then it happens
    That in your mind a gate will click, a door swing
        Shut, and bicycling children drift home
    Like birds from the avenues and the birdless dark,
        Until your childhood house seems gone
For good into the dead center of some memory's glow.

But years from now, when the smell of spring is still
    Sweet in the air, or when snowdrops are beginning
        To gather under the palings, when the blue
    Autumn first blurs the narrow streets, or the low
        Sun in winter dazzles the windows gold,
You'll discover inside, in that vague way you're still

Drawn to the air, that something has remained, something
    Which, now silent and unseen, still touches
        The heart—and there is someone, too,
    Someone perhaps just returning from work, who will
        Pause a moment, in sorrow or love, a hand
On the apartment gate, but not to wonder: What was here?

.

The Enormous Aquarium

(after Proust)

All morning long from inside the lobby
Of the Grand Hotel, the empty sea shore
Hung suspended there like a tapestry
Of no particular interest or value,
And it was only at intervals, while cards
Were shuffled and dealt around the tables,
That one of the players, finding nothing
To do, might turn his head to glance outside
At an occasional sail on the horizon.
And so, too, the afternoon hours, immutable
And bland, would pass before the windows
That more and more, as the sun declined,
Came to seem like mirrors in which you look
And find no other face but your own.

But then the evening arrived, the heat
Of the day settled onto the sand,
And suddenly it happened—as though
At the gesture of an imaginary hand—
That a great hidden stream of electricity
Would flood the dining rooms and halls
Until the hotel became, as it were,
An enormous aquarium against whose glass

The fishermen's and the tradesmen's families,
Clustering invisibly in the outer dark,
Would press their faces to look in—how like
Strange fishes or mollusks the occupants
Now seemed as they floated past on those
Golden eddies of unrippling light: there,

A Serbian officer whose organdy plume
Was like the blow of spume off some great
Blue whale; and there a young man who,
From his earliest years, had obviously moved
In the freshest waters of Faubourg Saint-Germain;
Or there, grand and aloof, the dowager Duchess,
Her powdered jaws closing on a morsel
Of food, like a primitive shell fish closing
On a spore . . . And the question now
Lingering in the air was how the glass contained
A world so vastly different from the poor,
A world where tea-gowns and sable, grosgrain
And *crepe-de-Chine,* topaz and silver
And the enameled ring that encircled a wrist

All spoke of a life grown infinitely
Distant and unreal . . . Yet if, from out
Beneath the eaves, the unwearying, gentle
Flight of the sea-martins and swallows
Had not arisen just then—one beyond another,
To shiver the air like a playing fountain,
Like dying fireworks strewn out along
The shore—without the sudden lull
Of that brief interruption, they might easily
Have stayed much later at the glass,
Instead of turning, as they did, beneath
A disc of moon as round and white as an eye,
To walk back home down the darkened streets
Like some ancient and magnificent tribe.

Betrayal

There were two of you in the dream, you
And another woman, both intimate and apart

As in the circle of a lens, and both seated
In identical high cane-backed chairs
Out in a garden where the redbuds and asters
Formed a backdrop so still, my unexpected
Presence throbbed on the footpath like some
Gross and inexplicable flower. Then I
Came forward. I could almost feel the wheel
Of the seasons turn in my heart. I could almost
Feel your quiet indifference in that thick
Noon summery air. Then a door was shutting
Gently behind me; then the rain gauge
Made a click like a key in a lock. It seemed
The light, too, had grown weary of me,
And you, as if tired of waiting for the theme
To this hour, reached out toward the woman
And ran a hand through her hair. Then a palm
Tree in the garden began to sway its head,
And the voice which caressed her was my own.

Eurydice

Waiting beside the window while you were brushing
Back your hair, I looked out across the empty
Hotel boardwalk: only two gas lamps still burned,
Their twin pools of oval light lying undisturbed

In that warm, tea-leaf colored dawn, and out beyond
The shadows of the eelgrass, the shore went on
Increasing, drawing slowly at those endless
Gray acres of the sea . . . And I remember, too,

How the tall sea pines, heavy with lichen, now sank
Beneath the stand-still of the morning air . . . how,
When you rose from your chair, naked in lamplight,
You rose, all the same, out of a break in those trees,

As though some sudden disaffection had taken
You there: and already you were part of it,
Already passing into that underworld
Of tide-pull and unraveling dark—and it was

As if the small shore birds flew away from you then,
As if my dull stare now drove you out of reach.

HERBERT SCOTT

Early Love

for Emma

Your skin was blue-
puddled snow, I mean
so fine I could trace
your flow from every
tributary. Your breasts,
yes, they were truthful,
freckled and new
beneath your shirt
that summer afternoon
we climbed the ladder
to the barn's dark loft.
We lay down
in the sweet straw
your body
granting the darkness
such mercy
until your brother,
shouting,
brought us down
to fish for crawdads
below the garden.
Your brother,
and your dead sister,
forever between us.
To be with you
I had to pretend
your brother
was my close friend.
On summer nights
we three slept on the lawn
beneath the open sky,
your brother
the dark body
in the center,
we, like wings,
never touching,
unless

I would fling
one arm
in a long arc
across the sky,
perhaps I saw a meteor,
my descending hand
brushing your shoulder,
and you would laugh
and touch my hair
in tender retaliation.
I suppose
you were lonely,
put up with us,
with me
who tugged at you,
innocent and severe,
wanting your skin
to grow around me.
Then your older sister
married and died
within the year.
After the funeral
her husband came for you,
claimed you
from your father
as if you were payment
for that death.
You were sixteen
the day you were taken
by a man in a straw hat
straight-backed
your arms full
of folded clothes
on the front seat
of his car.
I could see everything
from the south pasture
where I lay
tear-shaken, spying
on your leaving,
your solemn descent
from view. I never again
slept with your brother.

Achilles' Heel

The foot slides open, disjointed,
toes askew, arteries spurting
legions of Greeks, Romans, the tribes
of Israel, Alexander, Hannibal,
and the long river we call *Helen.*
And the river rich with bodies, little flags
of hands protruding, the baby Moses, silt
that builds deltas at the mouth of darkness.

And the foot marking the throat of the slave
for the axe, for the hand to lift
the unencumbered head,
for the fingers never to be free again
of that wrath of hair.
The four-clawed foot
digging its terrible furrows . . . .

Or the slender, high bridge,
lacy, intricate arch, the lover's mouth
laid against the instep,
that curve of air, delicate slippage
along the long slip of thigh . . .
until all collapse
as the heel comes down,
shatters, as cities splinter,
as the foot turns, disembodied,
almost its own master.

The Man Who Would Be A Mother

The stirrings in his chest
are maternal, mild. He imagines
giving suck, the gentle ooze,
the child's lips still forming
around his nipple. He wipes away
the last drop with his thumb,
lifts it to his tongue. Milk.
The first taste in his mouth again.

He would say to his children,
You were once in my belly. This
is how you fed before you were born.
This is where I held you,
child on a rope of blood.
This is my mark on your belly.
I pushed hard and you came into your life.
They held you up for me to see,
as if I were dangling from you, your child.

If I am not your mother,
and you do not rise from my body,
it is not because I would not have it.
Take my hands, as if they were
your face, and when I am dead,
and this flesh unlocks the bones,
imagine birth from my body,
a garden of children blooming.

Fathers Of Desire

We are fathers of the child
at its mother's breast,
the child who sleeps
in our doubled arms,
heavy and sweet.
This is a love we bless.

We are fathers of the child
on fire, who bears
no lips, no nose, no hair,
whose eyes will never close;
and fathers of desire.
No. We cannot forgive ourselves.

We are fathers of the child
who turns to stone, no heart
to moan into our ears
laid like flowers
against its chest. No one
loves us more than this.

The Woman Who Loves Old Men

She loves the brown moles
widening to pools of oil
on their faces, their eyes
turning to milk, the tiny
forests of their ears;

and the shoulders,
wearing thin as skulls,
the slow glaciers of flesh
sliding from bone;

and oh the white bellies,
the pure salt of their bellies,
she could bury her face forever
in such perfect snow.

Yes, she marries them,
and they roost in her arms
like tired birds as she listens
for the last drawn croak
before that certain stillness.

And they, thankful, never know
it is their deaths she loves,
their bodies she lays out
like polished wood, as she dreams
of the one who will marry her twice.

MICHAEL SHERIDAN

Michael

It's late afternoon and already dark.
At this hour a smoky smell
Hangs in the air along the river bank,

And there's a haunted silence here
Like the quiet after a party.

I think it should have been this way
In mid-November, 1942,
When my father stepped from a steam engine
And hurried to the roundhouse,
Hands raw from shoveling coal.

His signature on the log that day
Would be delicate, almost frail.

Later that night, in bed with Mother,
Maybe he recalled how the river looked
From his window on the train,
And turned to her . . .

So in August, holding me the first time,
He searched my body all over
For some flaw, then named me

After the fiercest angel in heaven.

In America

There is always a lonely farm on the prairie.
At night, behind the house,
A father ties his daughter to a tree by her hair.
The father, mean drunk, warns her to pray.

She is so pretty I would deface her
With consolation until her heart

Became a shambles, until
The sun put down its big foot and the dead
Stopped treating us with contempt.

I drive by this place a dozen times a day.
On a summer dawn the few trees
Are full of birds and near hills rise
Like the tanned backs of swimmers.
Sometimes she waves and smiles
From the front porch and my breath
Turns gauzy and my hands are double locks.

Other times, today for instance,
Mist hides the house, hides the hills and trees,
And though sun gnaws my skin
I don't know if I imagine this world
Or it imagines me, or neither.

From The Illinois Shore

On a beach too small to have a name
I stand and watch the sunlight
Cast my shadow on the Mississippi.
The shadow drifts over sunken stones
As if trying to get away.
Across the river, in mist,
Fort Madison looks faded, amorphous,
Like a woman who dresses to be ignored.

When white settlers arrived there in 1834—
After Chief Black Hawk lost
The Battle of Bad Axe—
They felled trees, trimmed and notched them,
Dragged them into squares.
They became resigned to long silences.

A century later my father came
To work the Santa Fe.
We've both known the greed
That keeps this country going, the wives
Who weep and cannot tell you why.

We've stood before bosses, heads bowed,
While great engines whined and thumped
In a landscape boring as someone else's dream.

From the Illinois shore the world's a mouth,
A sad, raw, gaping thing.
Me? I'm only less than ordinary:
I dance when no one's looking.
I'll dance until the last light
Gleams on the river and on the roofs
Of houses across the river,
Until the sky's so red it wants to scream.

Shooting The Loop

My wife sleeps soundly beside me.
Outside, the boys drive souped-up cars
Maniacally through the streets,

Toss empty beer cans till the sun comes out,
Then spit on the sidewalks and idle.
The boys, the drunken boys who cruise down Main—

I walk through the echoes they leave
And examine their skid marks,
Teach in their school and live beside them,

Feeling like a passenger.
All day I think of graves, the digging,
Listen for the clink of shovels,

Then rise from thought when the casket falls,
Heading again towards the combustion of evening
And my wife sound asleep beside me.

Homecoming

after the anonymous Chinese

At sixteen I joined the army.
I returned home at thirty
and found only one man who remembered me.

He led me to father's house
where rabbits were darting from floorboards,
pigeons gliding from roofbeams, wild rice
sprouting in the yard
and wild ducks floating in the well.

All right, I thought, I'll gather the rice
for gruel, shoot the ducks for soup.

I cooked the rice & duck.
Alone, I tried to eat.

After dinner I walked outside, gazed east,
and cried until my gown was soaked.

JOHN SKOYLES

Knockout

Sometimes two people together
cancel each other out,
and are left dizzy and alone,
as if hesitating outside an office door
where they might not be wanted.
Those seconds are so conspicuous,
slower than the whole long day,
just like that instant in a slow round
when a good left connects,
and the crowd so silent
before it sinks in
that even the aggressor takes a while
to follow it up. And who knows,
his opponent might want to be alone now,
now that the boredom of vertical life has tasted him,
pulling him down like a lover
the way God floored St. Teresa
so she woke up not recognizing anyone,
but content she went through
something glorious and came out even.

Evidence

I used to pray in furnished rooms,
rooms where only my conscience
waited up when I came in late,
but since I'm with this woman
I hardly ever pray. I think of my childhood,
my parents back home, and maybe raising
a daughter like the woman beside me.
And I remember what it's like
to live alone, with nothing but fantasy,

and what living with a woman's like,
with its special loneliness,
and the two lives not that far apart,

like this world and the next.
Men and women with no place to go
make God less alone, and couples
walk the same streets as the homeless,
both having someone to point to
when asked what they did with their lives.

Burlesque

after Weldon Kees

The day the dancer in the loud red dress
tossed her hair and said "What else is there to do?"
I remembered what my father told me.
She looked into the mirror applying makeup
while the traffic lights went on and off outside.

What my father told me was this:
women look into mirrors looking for men;
blondes toss their hair indifferently all night
but finally settle down; changes of heart
flicker like the traffic lights.

We fall in and out of love in rooms
where women wearing makeup
reflect our fantasies and lust:
so we're to blame for whatever they become.
And looking back, how could we

have taken that dancer so seriously?
But the way to forget
how she stepped out of her dress
was something our fathers couldn't tell us.
The lights go on and go off.

No Thank You

Who'll be the lover of that woman on the bench?
If she wants to hurt someone, she can use me.

Did she mean it, or was she trying to be unforgettable?
If she wants to use someone, she can hurt me.

I'll use my manners to stay in one piece,
but I end up believing every excuse that I make.

I always sigh when I see a woman like this;
I don't know where it comes from and I don't know where it goes.

I thought I'd enjoy a beautiful day like today.
I took a walk in the park and then something like this happens.

Once Or Twice

1
You never let me have you
more than once or twice.
I guess these things
don't mean that much to you,
and I don't want to say
they have to be meaningful
in some silly psychological sense;
but for me, at those times
watching your face,
for a moment each feature
took on a life of its own.
And I loved those little lives
in you, being someone
whose life is steady and controlled.
So it was a release for me
to see you lose yourself
passionately, once or twice.

2
Leaving your house one morning,
after a night with you,

I saw children dodging
each other's snowballs.
One said "Where did I get you?"
I mention this only because
I have nothing else to say to you,
and there's a chance this detail
might soften up your heart a little.

If You Have An Enemy

If you have an enemy, picture him asleep.
Notice his shoes at the foot of the bed,

how helplessly they gape there.
Some mornings he needs three cups of coffee

to wake up for work;
and there are evenings when he drinks alone,

reading the paper down to the want-ads,
the arrival times of ships at the docks.

Think of him choosing a tie,
dialing wrong numbers,

finding holes in his socks. Chances are
his emptiness equals yours

when you thoughtlessly hurry a cashier
for change, or frown to yourself

in rush hour traffic,
and the drivers behind you

begin to remind you
the light has turned green.

GARY SOTO

Saturday Under The Sky

This morning, with the rain tapping
The shoulders of everyone we will ever love—
Your mother for one, those dogs
Trotting for leaves—
We could go to the aquarium—
Angel fish and eels, the gray plop
Of toads among rocks. We
Could walk slowly, with a balloon
Banging against my head,
Walk with other fathers and
Daughters tapping the glass cases
That the lizard should waken
And the snake roll from
One dried limb to the next. We
Could handle a starfish, lift
A spiney thing, green in the water,
Blue in our hands. Instead
It's the Hall of Science
Where we stand before mirrors
That stretch us tall, then squeeze us
Squat as suitcases bound for Chicago.
There are rocks, the strata
Of earth, a black cut of oil far down.
There are computers, a maze of lights
And wires, steel balls bouncing
About—they could be us, if we should make
The moon one day. But you tire
In a room mixed up with stars
And it's juice and a pretzel
On the bench, with me thinking
I'm a good father. When we leave
Rain is still tapping shoulders
With everyone looking around,
Hunched in their coats.
The wind picks at the trees,
At the shrubs. The sky rolls and
The balloon tied to your wrist is banging
Unfairly against my head: *What else! What else!*

Between Words

Just what is there to do? Eat
Is one, sleep is another.
But before the night ends
We could walk under
These camphors, hand in hand
If you like, namedropping
The great cities of the past,
And if a dog should join
Us with his happy tail,
The three of us could talk,
Politics perhaps, medicine
If our feet should hurt
For the sea.

        Love,
The moon is between clouds,
And we're between words
That could deepen
But never arrive.
Like this walk. We could go
Under trees and moons,
With the stars tearing
Like mouths in the night sky,
And we'll never arrive.
That's the point. To go
Hand in hand, with the words
A sparrow could bicker
Over, a dog make sense of
Even behind a closed door,
Is what it's about.
A friend says, be happy. Desire.
Remember the blossoms
In rain, because in the end
Not even the ants
Will care who we were
When they climb our faces
To undo the smiles.

Where We Could Go

Happy that this is another
Country, we're going to
Sit before coffees and croissants
On Rue Lucerne
And watch the working fathers
Labor up the street,
A stiff loaf of bread
In each roughed up hand.
Some nod to us;
Others pass with the moist eyes
Of a strict wind.
This is France, daughter.
This is the autumn of calendars.
The sparrows are like
Those back home fighting
With the lawn,
Squealing and transparent
As their hunger.
They play at our feet,
Then climb to our knees
To hop like wind-up toys,
Until they're on the table
That's scratched with more
History than either of us—
Their beaks tap for crumbs.
But the waiter shoos them
With a dish towel.
This is a cafe for people,
Not birds, he says,
And so we leave because
We're like birds,
Transparent at love and deceit.
We hunger; we open our mouths . . .
We walk up the street, our shoes
Ringing against the stones,
To stare into a store window—
Clocks, coffee pots, an accordian
Longing for the sea.
But we're miles from the sea.
There are no boats or salt
Climbing our arms.
This is a country town,

And straw is what makes things
Go here—or so says our guide book.
And it says that there
Is a church, lit with gold
And rare paintings,
And we start off
Hand in hand, smiling
For no reason other than
Everything is new—
The stone buildings, straw
Whacked into bundles.
What's that? my daughter
Asks, and there's no greater
Pleasure than saying,
Beats me. Let's go see.

The Plum's Heart

I've climbed in trees
To eat, and climbed
Down to look about
This world, mouth red
From plums that were
Once clouds in March
—rain I mean, that
Pitiless noise against
Leaves and branches.
Father once lifted me
Into one, and from
A distance I might
Have been a limb,
Moving a little heavier
Than most but a limb
All the same. My hands
Opened like mouths,
The juice running
Without course down
My arm, as I stabbed
For plums, bunched
Or half-hidden behind
Leaves. A bird flittered

From there, a single
Leaf cutting loose,
And gnats like smoke
Around a bruised plum.
I climbed searching
For those red globes,
And with a sack filled,
I called to father
To catch—father
Who would disappear
Like fruit at the end
Of summer, from a neck
Wound some say—blood
Running like the juice
Of these arms. I
Twisted the throat
Of the sack, tossed
It, and started down
To father, his mouth
Already red and grinning
Like the dead on their
Rack of blackness.
When I jumped, he was
Calling, arms open,
The sack at his feet
For us, the half-bitten,
Who bring on the flies.

Behind Grandma's House

At ten I wanted fame. I had a comb
And two coke bottles, a tube of bryl-cream.
I borrowed a dog, one with
Mismatched eyes and a happy tongue,
And wanted to prove I was tough
In the alley, kicking over trash cans,
A dull chime of tuna cans falling.
I hurled lightbulbs like grenades
And men teachers held their heads,
Fingers of blood lengthening
On the ground. I flicked rocks at cats,

Their goofy faces spurred with foxtails.
I kicked fences. I shooed pigeons.
I broke a branch from a flowering peach
And frightened ants with a stream of piss.
I said "shit," "fuck you" and "No way
Daddy-O" to an imaginary priest
Until grandma came into the alley,
Her apron flapping in a breeze,
Her hair mussed, and said, "Let me help you,"
And punched me between the eyes.

When We Wake

Sometimes it's only the square light
Of window, white behind the bushes,
Yellow if it faces the street, in Autumn.
Sometimes it's a young woman with a book
In her mittened hand,
Off to work, a lover's house perhaps.
I cross the street
With my own book, with my own gloves:
A strand of hair from under her beret,
The eyes, her face flushed from
The rain we walk against in any weather.
Sometimes it's a grandfather on a bench,
Legs crossed, hands fiddling
In his sweater's pocket—
Face is happy, now worried, now happy again.
For years I have been asleep
But now I am awake to this life. The trees
Lowered across an indifferent sea,
Failing at the shore. I sat
With my eyes closed on a landscape

Of childhood—a chinaberry, the broken
Glass that gritted its many teeth
All summer. Now I am awake.
This city is filled with people with hats
In their hands or on their knees,
And I am amazed that I missed them—
Amazed at the women stepping onto

Buses, their calf muscles taut,
Their purses creaking with goods.
There are children, a waitress in a yellow
Apron, my neighbor bending down
To a tulip in the yard. I could approach
Any one of them with simple questions:
Is this Tuesday? Are pears in season?
If they said *yes* or *no* or *maybe*
If the dog made a noise, if the weather stayed
Where it was, it could be a start.
The cat is in the sun, the sun in the trees,
The trees against a blue to remember . . .

MAURA STANTON

At The Cochise Tourist Pavilion

Yesterday I saw my first mirage
Spreading for acres across a desert basin,
The water blue and flat, reflecting mountains.
The image lasted for miles. Astonished,
I searched my map for explanations,
Some new dam, or reservoir, or flood plain,
But only the black words "Bombing Range"
Crossed that white space beside the highway.
Of course I've seen the highway mirages
Even in the midwest, without sand or cactus,
When suddenly the road ahead turns into water,
Reflecting the slow passage of the clouds
Shaped like the cows and sheep of dozing giants
Until you blink or traffic breaks the illusion.
Wasn't this an illusion? Shading my eyes
I turned the lovely water into caliche,
That zone of calcium under the parched soil
Blown off by the practiced rake of the bombers.
But then I felt a chill. I could imagine
Some old prospector leaning down to view
The image of his own inverted face
Before he choked on a bright handful of dust,
For my lake reappeared, dotted with sails,
With houses on the far shore under the trees.

At the tourist pavilion, under a glass case,
I found the chart of ancient Lake Cochise
Where strange fish once swam, their starry tails
Imprinted on an occasional rock or cliff face.
The old travelers had seen this same mirage,
Leaning out the windows of the Butterfield stage.
And even Coronado may have crossed the ghost water,
The waves turning to sand around his ankles,
The first of his seven golden cities vanishing.

The air conditioned air stroked my face
While I stood there, feeling pale and watery
As if from certain angles I might disappear.
I'd been seeing backward (Eight thousand years!)

324

In a way I hadn't been able to see last summer
Passing under the Lion's Gate at Mycenae
When I strained my eyes, trying to find Helen
Or Agamemnon or the royal children
Buried with gold leaf on hands and feet.
All I discovered then was the roar of jets
Crossing the valley below the grave circle
At sonic speed, so that the tour guide
Shouted her list of treasures, the fluted cups,
The obsidian arrowheads, the child's rattle.

I remembered that famous doodle, or riddle,
Five ghosts looking into a pond,
Which I liked to draw in notebooks as a child,
Making the large circle perfect with my compass,
And the half-circles equal in size and distance.
I used to sympathize with those ghosts
Hovering sadly above their lost reflections.
The first year or so after I don't exist,
If I could feel, I'd feel about like this,
I'd think, holding the paper up to light
Which shone evenly through heads and water.

I saw my own head deep inside the glass
Protecting the map, the rocks, the fossils.
The old nun who taught biology
Seemed to be breathing at my elbow then
As if I were back in my girl's school
My hair combed into its stiff wave.
Once she lectured on the mystery of the body,
Moving her pointer over the skeleton
Hanging in the corner of the dark laboratory,
The wings of her white headdress shaking
As she explained the kneecap and the ribs
Curved to protect the lungs. She made us
Find the floating rib under our blouses
Then told us to look in our emptying bathtubs
For dead cells, those grey and spinning flakes.
We were totally new every seven years,
She said, and we understood by her tone
How the subject was moving finally to religion.

Even then I'd speculate about the brain
Spiraled inside its shell like the conch—

I never saw its cells drifting away,
And yet, whole sections of my life
Seemed to have disappeared in its interior.
I was already bleak and diluted
Like those mysterious and extinct fish
Whose bones reveal nothing of their color.
The father holding his daughter's hand
May have smiled to see me staring at myself
Caught in the wavy glass of the exhibits,
But some night he'd find he was listening
On the edge of her bed, as she described
A dream vanishing as she tried to tell it,
A whole landscape of marsh and greyness
Into which she sank with her arms raised.
I saw I'd drawn a circle in the dust
Powdering the display case, then five curves
Meant to suggest the hollow ghosts
Which the janitor might recognize as he wiped
The glass clean for tomorrow's tourists.
Driving home, again the shining lake
Stretched so clearly under the sun I gasped
Thinking I felt a breeze, heard cries of swimmers.

Good People

The sight of all these people in the street
Heading a dozen directions, in puffy coats,
Icelandic hats, in boots or rubber shoes,
All walking stiffly on the melting ice,
Necks bent against the wind, makes me giddy.
If we could hear each other think, the noise
Would shatter glass, break the best hearts.
A business man in a camel overcoat
Passes a red-haired girl with a yellow scarf,
And neither will ever see each other again

Or see me standing outside the florist's.
I'm buying flowers for my mother, who lies
In the hospital with a blood clot in her vein,
Almost recovered. I saw her yesterday
And through the doors of other rooms I glimpsed

Face after face I didn't recognize,
Twisting on wet pillows, or watching T.V.
How accidental my existence seemed—
I might have sat beside some other bed.
I might have loved that man in blue pajamas

Or kissed the silent child in the metal crib
Receiving a transfusion, as I did once,
Thirty years ago to save my life.
Then a car honks. A woman jostles me.
I stare in wonder down the crowded street.
I could be part of one of these strangers
Breathing hard in the cold, Kentucky air,
That tall man with gnarled, shaky hands
Or that heavy woman, or part of someone dead
Who thought that life was choice, not accident.

At The Landing

A few days before I die
I'll stand near a river that runs
a thousand miles with no bridge,
thinking back on today, on the greenish
dogwood petals, descending, in the woods
while my husband speaks of a friend
already only a shadow in conversation.
On that future day I'll see clouds
beyond the transparency of my hands
held to the sky's light,
knowing that if I undressed in the street,
children would see each other through my skin.

I feel nostalgia for the old woman
I'm growing into; I'll rise
stiffly from a bench on the long pier
many years from now, recalling the dogwood,
recalling myself, like this, at the window.
Then I'll watch for the ferry
although no friend ever gets off.
I'll have buried them all,
choosing exile in this town

because the streets smell of dying greenery
& once as a girl I dreamed
palms more glamorous than snow.
One day I'll enter the customs shed
with the women who work across the river.
At the rail of the ferry,
as the far shore rises up so blue,
they'll see me touch my heart, sadly,
then fall backwards on the deck,
mistaking their shocked faces for clouds
gathered over my last glimpse of the sun.

Visibility

I have no illusions.
When I roll towards you at dawn,
I can't see you in the fog.
We've simply memorized each other.
I read a story about a giant
who couldn't see his tiny wife
for all the clouds
drifting around his huge, sad head.
He'd stroke the tops of fir trees
thinking he'd found her hair.
In another version, his wife
turned into an egret,
her strong wings
brushing her husband's face;
then she fell into the sea
weighted down by his immense tear.
Let me tell you this:
I miss your shadow, too,
but I know it waits above the fog
black as the shadow of the oak
you saw in your dream
when you woke up, almost happy.
I know our town's invisible.
The pilots on the way to Alaska
think they're over the sea.
Even if they glimpsed a light
through a rift in the clouds

they'd call it a ship
loaded with timber for the south.
Still, I hear those planes.
Last night on the satellite map
I saw a land without clouds.
Remember, I groped for your hand.
Suppose the men go barefoot?
Suppose the women own fans?

Atlantis

Our new house isn't steady.
I feel water below the floors.
When we sleep, I think it rises
slowly through the cracks.
I'm afraid it's the ocean
for I've found salt on the walls.
When it reaches our windows
we'll cut gills into each other's throats,
just like our neighbors,
then bend our heads into our new element
a mile below the sun.

I think we may carry an umbrella
for the first year
against the immense pressure of waves.
We'll even tap the shells
until tiny air bubbles float out
toward the surface,
which we'll imagine bright with ships.
I'll describe all the clouds I remember,
trying not to notice
how the seaweed tangles in my hair.
We'll dream ourselves on earth.
When you point to the sun,
I'll watch your blurred face,
your eyes closing with disuse.
I won't tell you that the shadow
floating above us is a whale.
I'm turning dark and strange.

Sunday Graveyard

"Walks in graveyards
Bore me to death,"
Says the old woman
Walking beside me
Who reads the sunken gravestones
Clucking, clucking—

"Such odd engravings,
A stairway to heaven,
Naked cherubs."
She shakes her head.
Her own stone is smooth,
Paid for, wordless,

"A solid slab
Of grey marble
Thick as a wrist,"
She tells me, pointing—
"No poetry like this."
Just her name

"Elizabeth"
Cut so deep
It won't blur
For two centuries.
"Time enough," she laughs,
"For judgment day."

She calls her husband
Who lags behind us.
She wants her dinner,
Complains of cold.
Half-blinded by cataracts,
She can't read

Fainter inscriptions
Meant to console
Women like herself,
Or warn the ironical
Like me, who think they'll face
Death more honestly.

DAVID ST. JOHN

33

This is where I wanted to be
Today, on this hotel balcony, three
Stories above the boulevard
Watching the end of a summer's rain;
Here, on this plush wrought iron
Chaise, a bottle of "33"
In my hand, my favorite French beer,
Its label the same two tones of
Black-and-gold as the beat-up Ford
I used to coax up the coast
Highway, hellbent for San Francisco,
Fifteen years ago in California.
And just as nothing could
Save that '33
Ford, I know, this evening, looking
Down on a parade of students,
Models, pickpockets, cinéastes, cab
Drivers, terrorists, and a single
Priest making their ways down St. Germain,
Nothing can save me from this
Birthday. Those sullen
Numerals stare out at me from these
Dead soldiers, each empty bottle
I've stood at attention
In a snaking line
Over the bare floor of the bedroom,
Then across the tiny Bokhara at my
Feet: with this last,
An even thirty-three! Christ, I
Know—don't tell me—it could be
Worse. I could be thirty-four . . .
And dead. Or home alone. Or even more
Wounded, and alive.

The Orange Piano

Plainly one's fears are never
Punishment enough

One must also live the life that proves
Each fear was justified & if
Like me one's ambition for a life is failure
Then the work is hard in order to fail
So completely
No doubts remain in the eyes of one's friends
& therefore only a truly fine career

Is worth destroying

It was a day the color of an oboe
That is   the voice
Of Noah's dove as it skims the newly
Bared reeds of the world
A voice that considers & remains
The echo of rain
Across the staunch oaks & maples
That rim this lake more emerald than
Her rings

& she has taken the early cable car

Up to the peak
To sketch & drink tea on the veranda

Of the cramped lounge filled with tan
Young women with skiing gear & used Leicas
& beside them the severely **angular** boys
Without expressions

& over a dinner of lake trout in lime spokes

Before I take up my nightly post
At the orange electric piano in the hotel's
Balcony bar & jazz
Up some standards for the drunks   here
As the chandelier of the dining room
Begins to sway in the heat
Of the huge fireplace where the waiters

Have stacked an especially precarious
& intricate rack of logs

The gold of their flames shaking the cut glass

Above us   I'll turn
& take out the small diary embossed with a dove

& ask about her day up
Where the view from any prospect she says
Is simply of these somber trails & random traces
Of those of us below   *a world*   still going

Its many predictable & ordinary ways

                        * *

Orange is the color of the soul no
That's wrong orange is the color of the *eccentric*

Soul like that of the old man who rings
The Angelus bell at odd hours before sitting
Down on his unmade bed to play the violin
Until at his open window the gray & the brown
Squirrels arrive with their daily
Curiosity picking
Through the scattered rinds & peels he leaves

Along the sill to encourage his audience
To return   *to return*

Orange is the memory of smoke as it recalls

Flames rising off the bones
Which is only to say that lovers make
With their own figures a special
Figure for the imagination that pleases anyone
Whose loneliness each morning might seem

As resolute as mine   as I walk with

My cup of coffee to the ballroom now empty
& dusty with disuse   where the only real piano
Stands in this "Old & Formerly Regal" hotel

333

Once known for its sulpher baths & lakes
Shaded in layers of green   *chartreuse emerald*
The unreal dead greens of envy & remorse

& as I sit at the old Bechstein grand

I try working over again
The closing passage of a concerto
I could never quite get right   that is never
With that proper shade of *orange* to it

Though at concerts no audience seemed ever
To notice   or to care

& one evening during my last season
& on my last tour   somewhere in the Midwest
I went onstage drunk   & as I was playing
That concerto I knew suddenly she was *there*
In the anonymous darkness of the night

& I felt her body calmly

Settling beside mine in the narrow spotlight
& slowly fine grains of sweat blew all around me
In the air   above the keys   & over my stiff cuffs

& as I finished the final passage at last

I looked up without thinking to where
I knew she'd be sitting   still as far from me
As ever in the deepest row *high* on the right side

Of the paradisal third balcony

                    * * *

Music is the voice of time

& therefore my father told me also the voice
Of God our greatest teacher & so

I was taught to play with reverence the solemn
& ecstatic notes measuring God's voice

As my father

Stood above my right shoulder himself
The greatest living teacher   critics agreed
Of Chopin & also ("perhaps") Liszt   commenting
In his precise & endless way on the mistakes
One brother hand inflicts so often
Upon the other

This morning outside my window

The sparrows are stringing their invisible
Chains between the branches of the last
Budding silver birch

My father is dead now & I imagine

In heaven playing concerts for God the father
In His own voice of course forever

& I'm here   watching
The sparrows swell in the bitter dawn like pure
Notes held in some bare rehearsal hall

& beside me she is still asleep

Her arms hooped perfectly above her head
As if she were   a girl at her morning class
About to go on pointe before

The mirror & as

The sparrows repeat their annunciations
Of the day   I hear my father saying
Music is the voice of time

Describing our hesitance   the ease
With which a day passes or is held for us
Even as
The tones of every passage reflect & mingle
In the simple rhythms of decay

& by *measure* we mean always *time*

As when the actor
Steps downstage to persuade the gods there is
No measure to his love   we sympathize

& as I look again at her body in the light

I can see it's a light as unworldly & orange
As the memory of my own hands leaving
Her shoulders

& I know the sun must understand
There's only one immediate music to a life

Only one body truly held by

That voice my father now in heaven
Always said would be the final measure of all
That might someday allow

Such time as to forgive oneself one's pain

Providence

A little drunk he walked back slowly
Along the bank of one of the outer canals
Until he saw painted in a prim Dutch hand the sign
Of an ornate tankard   the sign of his hotel
& in the unlit hallway he took out his skeleton key
& opened the door to the wrong room
Urgency without remorse   light flooding the frame
& inside the room she stood engaged in a particularly
Secular form of self-discourse   naked before
A full mirror   a few muffled apologies   he turned
& paused in the hallway wondering if this wasn't
An accident of fate   perhaps   the hand of providence
& then the door slammed firmly behind him

PAMELA STEWART

Jack Yazzie's Girl

Dawn, with its scant
plateful of stars.
From the west,
brief flint-bright winds
where rainbows
whet their knives on stone.

Jack Yazzie
pockets a handful of blue meal
and leaves his hogan.
Small deer might be waiting
on the mountain.
But Annie won't wait.
She packs, and why not.

In the arroyo,
old blackskirted women
claw flat water into pots.
They know how a day begins.

Thin-legged Annie shrugs past
the bird-pecked pools, the
clicking roadside lambs.
Thumb-up, she turns toward Gallup
where riverbed shacks
jitter with love, or rain.

A trucker stops. Annie smiles.
His hand falls like dust
into her skirt.

Deep, in the red-eyed barroom,
Annie tilts between tables
that welcome any girl
who's left the flintblue air,
green corn, bony
ol' jackrabbit in the pot.

Again and again, Annie laughs.

White music, white fists, jade
folds of paper tucked into her dress.
Here, days are short
and through any long night,
no dry ancestral stars.
Annie shrugs, lifts
a glass of red water on fire.

The Wind Of Late Summer

At first, what flew hard from my grandfather's mouth
into my mother's ribs was a feeling,
no more, no less.
Call it anger, call it love,
call it thunder cracking against the pines.

She never spoke of that moon looking up from the lake,
or the loons with their terrible noise.
The doorknob turned. His hands
became two red knots slipping at her breasts
while the wind rose on its hind legs.

Don't tell me I can't speak of this. My mother
hummed in her sleep as the mist off Sebago
sucked all the light from the windows.
Grandfather stomped through the house
like he was still outdoors.

My mother, who wakes now over and over,
is rattling about in the kitchen. She never thinks
of those sheets once pale beneath her storm bound hair,
how they've rotted and gone. The house
still stands in its timber. It's August again
and wind brushes the pines with the blurred
sound of a girl's dress, torn
and falling. But Mother doesn't listen.

Postcard

Dusk, the sea is between colors
and our medallion star is ready to leave for China.
This is the brushstroke hour
you have already befriended.

I am here for the first time
taking a rush of water into my mouth.
My ribs fold with a white salt weight.

Centuries ago, Mu Ch'i slipped his eye
from fog to indigo. A grain of sand
dislodged from a monastery wall.

His six bitter orbs of fruit
are still blindingly pure.
And everyday
his seventh, unpainted persimmon
ripens across the sky.

The bell-blossom moon follows behind.

Here, in California, the day shakes once
and falls. The ocean pulls closer.
With luck, you say,
a sudden streak will flash toward the stars

as the flaming persimmon dips into salt.

In this way the eye will complete the day.
It will root in the heart.
My hands return from water, the water
returns from China.

I would unstain my heart to carry it with me.

Spring

The scent is back, a bridal weave
across the city. All night

the kiss won't leave our mouths
and memory steps, with dark measure,
between us and the flowers.

If we rise to this, the white
budded stars will shake,
the sky fall back to air.

I know what I've worn in my bones since birth,
hands at my throat, hands
at my knees, that swift red stain
between my teeth.

The future of memory flares.

We age, the flowers return. The trees I pass each day
fill up with birds. I pick
a single orange blossom which I crush to my wrist.

I could rub its skin to music, break
a man's bones to get to the heart.
I have only
one slow breath riveted to breath —

The stars stammer back their light
oil of flowers, bright enemy, heart.

The Damaged Aria

When a song goes wrong behind
a piano's foamy, indifferent ledge —
staccato. F sharp, or E. Even
one cruel note happens to a room,
a mark or disturbance opens the wall.

You can watch lightning's
unpredictable stitching of heaven
to earth, but what you hear, what's felt
lifting your hair, slamming your skin
wields more damage. Force ten

across the moors, harbor, houses and church.
At times like that you need two hands
just to hold down your head. All smart winds

remain invisible, and with their wild
singing get away from us. The sky
only looks seamless. The sea is another story.

*

You stand at cliff's edge thinking
Look at all that sea! (That's nothing,
that's just the top of it.) How many worlds
the sea keeps from us. She finds, takes,
then forms herself again. At dawn, she'll be
as glassy and silver as a lover's thumbprint
dragged along sex-moist skin. The skipper's eyes
clench with such deep white fires
from having looked straight into the wind,
into that solid spray and light. Then
the sea becomes the all-and-only world
as the weariness of too much wanting
lessens in a deceptive chant of waves.
How often, in our hearts, we fare
just that shoreless, indefinite as God . . .
and when, with precision and fury, the sea
claims cargo, iron, wood and men to seed
their ornament and bone across her hidden floors,
we may know nothing of it. We simply say
they've disappeared as, sky-sheeted
and at peace again, the sea lies back down.

*

We're catching up. Our inventions
are closer now to God's. You know how rooms,
streets, cities wear their damage — not just
as accessory, but as style — how levees,
a bloodied shirt, or broken books remind us
of the body wrenched from its ideal?
Today, the hummingbird bruise below a cashier's eye
is familiar, and some friends
have sandbag legs that cannot feel their jeans
or the tightening of a shoelace.

When the original song gets away from us
it hurtles, singlemindedly, forward —
or clear back to Merlin crouched beneath Peredur's tree:
There, still rising, is half a spray of moist
green leaves, the other side on fire.
From the hidden cleft of seeds, our first
passion splits to embers and early snow.
But our bodies must have skin
to hold our blood and spirit in. This

the magician warns as he imagines the planet
spinning through gritty air. Our faces
splayed to angel husks beneath the blank
shadows of doves rushing by. Twigs
flake ashen in their beaks. Look —
beyond the ancient hills, now breaking,
just infinite oceans of steam.

*

Between the finding and the losing
our future's hedged with fire. What the world says
is a birdnote, what it throws across
two lovers is a long quill of original light.
Hope has no house but this woven air. It goes
everywhere, within and without the dance of streets
or standing stones. It calls the walking fires
from the swamp, lifts wind-bitten thorns
to shelter lambs from the wolf's-paw cold.
Up through the beaded center of lakes, cities,
hearths or the sea's own bed, it links
root-laced ancestral faces back to us.
No more than a reed can help the wind
of God blowing through it, this world
is a world of facts. The day,
grey or blue, is yet itself
and the damaged aria with its firm white tongue
still yearns to sing clear through,
and from within, the only selves we have to use.

Man Dancing With a Baby

Before balance, before counting, before
The record glistens and the needle slides,
Grating, into the overture, there is the end
Of weight, the leaning into nothing and then

A caught breath, the record listens, the needle slides
Over slowly, and, all at once around us, a woman's voice
Stretches weightless, leaning into nothing,
Like a clothesline, the taut chorus: oh, hilarious

Oh baby, all around us, over slowly, a woman's voice
Gathers above the pick me up, pick me up
And the desperate put put me down. First the tightrope,
Then the light foot, and the taunting chorus

Pick me up, pick me up. Oh, oh baby.
The slippery floor shimmers and spins like a record while
The light is swinging footloose on its rope
Out of time. The shadows

Slip, shimmering black, and spin across the floor,
Then turn back and pick up again. Oh seedpod stuck for just
One moment on the cat-tail, out of time, out of shadows,
Downy cheek against a beard: oh scratches

On the record, oh baby, oh measure
Oh sweet balance that grips us
On this side of the world.

Consecration

The man in the yellow hard hat,
the one with the mask
across his nose and mouth,

pulls the lever that turns

the great arm of the crane up
and over and sideways

toward the earth,
then the wrecking ball
dangles crazily,

so delicately, like a silver fob
loosened from a waistcoat pocket;
shocking to see

the dust fly up and the timber
sail up, then so slowly
down, how the summer air

bristles with a hundred splinters
and the smallest is a splintered flame,
for it takes so many lengthening

erratic movements to tear away
what stands between the sidewalk
and the bell tower,

where the pigeons now rise
in grand indignant waves
at such poor timing, such

a deaf ear toward the music;
in this way the silence
between hand and lever is turned

into a ragged and sorely-lifted
wing, the wrecking ball lurches
in a narrowing arc until only

the dust resists—the rest
comes down, story by story,
and is hauled off in flatbed trucks.

Meanwhile the pedestrians come
and go, now and then glancing
at their accurate watches.

Gradually, the dust

becomes the rose light
of autumn.

But one evening a woman
loses her way as she's
swept into a passing wave

of commuters, and she
looks up toward the perfectly
empty rectangle

now hanging between
the rutted mud and the sky.
There along the sides

of the adjacent building, like
a set for a simple
elementary school play,

like the gestures of the dead
in her children's faces,
she sees the flowered paper

of her parent's bedroom,
the pink stripes leading
up the stairs to the attic

and the outline of the claw-
footed bathtub, font
of the lost cathedral of childhood.

Secret Ceremony: The Sailboat

There were thirty-six streets between us
and the moon and the weeds lay tangled,
the timothy broken off like a half-remembered song.

I walked so slowly toward you,
toward the lights beyond the river,
but then the night came

Toward me and took away
my breath. What we meant to say:
how the seven stars assembled

Far above the vacant lot
where the tramps were burning paper,
gray boxes,

Bursting in the rusted
oil drum. That fire was forbidden,
yet they called out to a woman,

Pointing to the tangled moon;
she turned her head. The scene they never
show is the two of us

Pulling away, as the arms come down
untangled, like separate leaves
in November air, or a train

Circling forever beneath the high vault
of the station, a hand half-raised,
a look no one recalls.

Since that time I've seen
a small blue sailboat falling,
always, when I close my eyes.

What I meant to say: how some nights
I close the window and turn down
the thirty-six streets, and then the flimsy

Paper states, the cardboard expanse
of a country without you;
what flares up suddenly from

The stillness of the heart,
like an oil spill—secret faces
in the surface of the river.

The Evening of Montale's Death

A green light trailed through the park at dusk
like a lantern slowly lifted
by a search party, but it was only

A fisherman starting out
to avenge some private grief.

Two by two, the couples hurried
into the inn with its warm music of spoons
against linen. That was the first

Evening of autumn when
the dogwood smouldered at its edges;

Soon every shadow would be blazing
against the black winter rains.
That was the last summer evening; a mist fell

Softly on the benches and on the lightning-scarred faces
of the pine trees. What the sun had tried to make simple

The night was about to obscure.
Because out of that mist with its promise
of darkness rode all

The mistakes of God:
the june bugs carrying their swollen bellies

On frail and skeletal wings, while above
the mulberry trees tried to hide
their sorry patchwork leaves.

A pair of runners limped by, their arms thrown around
each other, and a small woman

In a large winter coat dragged her
wheel-less bicycle beside them.
There was a Boy Scout troop whose marching song

Was in the fabulous alphabet of the deaf,
and a man who swore over and

Over to himself that he would never again
go home. They all ran after the trailing
green light and toward the promise of winter,

Away from some warm place of beginning
which one by one

They had neither remembered nor forgotten;
just as at dawn a search party
gathers in an open field

And a lantern is held up to each face
to be sure that nothing has changed.

JAMES TATE

Mystic Moment

I faced the Star Maker, the candy butcher
from the window of a Pullman car
just outside Pueblo, Colorado,
from a plush and velvet world
with plugs of tobacco
outside a jelly factory.
The vibration of names, a cardinal—
Behind me, Gabriel.
Rounded up like rats
on Metacombie Kay.

First leap at Little Steel,
and the invaders vacuumed
with a ferocity of elegance
seldom encountered, and never
in circles or indifferently.
The Sante Fe Railroad was really something in those days.

The mountains had long ago crumbled away,
erased by some soft artillery on the radio.
I thought I saw my twin, limbless on the desert,
drowning near a herd of angels; I reached out the window
and killed him with a single blow.

The momentousness of the moment demanded it:
there were organs in the post office
and weapons in the organs.
The angels signaled for pandemonium
and soon I was engulfed with temptations,
I was invested with contact with
the populous interiors of many dying stellar worlds.

I faced the Star Maker, the candy butcher,
swarms of burnt-out stars,
from the window of a Pullman car.

Summer Night

"If you raise canary birds," my grandfather said to me,
"feed them birdseed." Indeed, it is certain disaster
to not give them water as well, I figured out for myself.
And sonic booms will give them a headache, they have no taste

for coffee. "No, Zosine," I moaned softly, "No, Zosine."
Long after his death, one man arose to defend his memory.
Unfortunately, that man's character and writings made him
certain to do more harm than good. Brittle stars,

sea lilies, I sit here at the window and gaze back at the waiters
on the kitchen porch of the Chinese restaurant, getting cool
after a hot spell. They don't know how to interpret what they see,
dinosaurs two feet long, worms thirty feet long, a one-ton

jellyfish. "Must they not have terrible, cold hearts,"
Zosine again whispered, "to figure out everything like that?
And to go on, day by day, carrying out their scheme."
I longed for the gift to shake loose rain, but only briefly.

Variations, pigments: next door the painted lady and the red
admiral, the spangled fritillary, cannonsmoke and sewing machine.
My grandfather also said, "The brightness of the colors is said
to depend upon the emotions of the insect. What a beautiful way

to express one's feelings, to be able to glow like melted gold
when one is happy." He obviously did not want to take
his own business seriously, but all the same his voice had changed.
The Lion hath not prevailed. To open the book, and to loose

the seven seals thereof (to judge every one according to his state):
the wings of the male are velvety black and those of the female
are smoky in color, with a distinct white stigmata spot on the tip
of each wing. Common as Tasmanian grasshoppers. Common

task, water. Dreadful fantasies chattered, laughed. Metallic
black, the storm was on the right path. The race of Edwin—
a long, mild, intense glance. Moss animals, labor, hinged
shells. Lake monsters, nobody really knows what to do with them.

There is no other name, backboneless. Adults that emerge
during wet weather are frequently darker in color than adults

that emerge during dry weather. Aquatic labor, ribbon-shaped,
coiled. "Nay, Zosine, be quiet," I whispered, "you have been
  dreaming."

"If you are right," said Zosine, "if you are right, if all this
is possible, what are we to do then?"

Spring Was Begging to Be Born

After a winter of seclusion
I curtsy farewell to my pagoda:
Friend, tinfoil gangster, deviant silo,
I leave you to your own stale resources
to wander this spring in my disguises,
in my new naked zigzagging across
the pulsating battlefields of my own kind.
                    *
Murmur of cherry blossoms, I winced, glassy-eyed:
Had not I dreamed their color in my fairy tale?
Then hush; homeless now, I am arriving
at my one true home, the barricades melting.
The further I delved into these murderous zones
the more crisscrossed and woven became
the life within my fussy warehouse and that
beside this celebrated outer cherry.
                    *
Your wish is my command, I said to no one special.
Feeling festive now, and somewhat fraudulent,
I waited for the zodiac to sneak a glance
at my horoscope. Was this to be, spluttering,
with the plumes of raspberry light
erasing my hearsay and stifling my double?
I picked a thread from the zillion squiggles
and followed it around the corner to where
an orchestra was looking askance and
asking for complete silence.
                    *
Men sat outside their factories playing dominoes.
Their bodies were swollen, as after a hurricane.
I had dreamed of this hour; and yet, standing there,
my dream seemed suddenly, monotonously, attenuated,

351

as though a tugboat were the wiser to ignore
this sinking ship. I moved on, sobbing, giggling,
and looked back more than once to no hands waving.
Spring was truly begging to be born
like a cipher that aspires to the number one.
Hush. It is all hearsay, irresistible hearsay.

The Horseshoe

I can't read the small print in the scrapbook:
does this say, *Relinquishing all bats, feeling faint
on the balcony?* There is so much to be corrected here,
so many scribbles and grumbles, blind premonitions.
How does one interpret, on this late branch, the unexpected?

I can see just here that strength was gathering, perhaps
even an excess, and, specifically, the heart-rending detail
of the horseshoe found propped against the windowsill.
Years of toil to find the right angle, I'm almost rigid
with anticipation, maneuvering as at an opera intermission.

Stropping the razor, occasional whining, exploits of idleness—
all are clenched against a teatime eventuality, the progenitors
with their inspired plaintive skeletons engulf us here
for several pages, then sink, like migrating hooves.
What happened to them? I trusted their wings, their
heroic gusto methods. I am shaving this gossipy impetus

like rigid articles away from my face. I see the corrections
penciled in, I'm privy to their forgetfulness, a sprawling
design: I look away and project streaks of hesitant chance
wherever I look. Pulsating veins of thin planks to help me
bridge this muscular aria. Aslant the tone of Life's dialogue,

between siestas, the horseshoe diversion is polished, its legs
degenerating, athletically anyway. It's all in the ankle
or the wind, in breeding bones. Scrapbook, I am in the middle
of your hive, I must take back your corrections to the mute
and inform stretches of my own big shave, swell the parallel
world with your murky burden, still betting against this charm

nailed to the sidedoor of a photograph to ward off, what was it,
was it me?

Poem for the Sandman

The child begins to walk
toward her own private sleeping place.
In the pocket of her bathrobe
she clinches a hand grenade.
She is lumbering through the lumberyard
like a titmouse with goosebumps.
She waves goodbye to the orthodox dart games.
The noodle shops have returned
to their antholes, gulp, and a single spoor
has traveled all the way from Wichita
to tuck her in and tell her a story.
There, at a juvenile crossroads,
livestock are dragging their saliva
in a semicircle, it is like pulling taffy.
The child stands there for a moment,
sees herself as an ancient washerwoman
playing bingo on Saturday nights.
She, the child, is counting lemons
and squirming before a quiz.
She is standing in a vestibule,
an airless, gravelly vestibule,
when a hearse pulls up and offers her a lift.
Audibly aching, she swerves to miss
some typhoid victims (being shampooed by
an uncle on furlough?) (who pampers her
with infinitesimal sighs?) and bounces
into bed at last as into a cedar bough.
And the sandman stops playing pinball
to mend her cocoon, to rinse her shroud.
He has had his eye out for her all along.
Her tired little soul could not survive another war.

Poem to Some of My Recent Poems

My beloved little billiard balls,
my polite mongrels, edible patriotic plums,
you owe your beauty to your mother, who
resembled a cylindrical corned beef
with all the trimmings, may God rest
her forsaken soul, for it is all of us
she forsook; and I shall never forget
her sputtering embers, and then the little mound.
Yes, my little rum runners, she had defective
tear ducts and could weep only iced tea.
She had petticoats beneath her eyelids.
And in her last years she found ball bearings
in her beehive puddings, she swore allegiance
to Abyssinia. What should I have done?
I played the piano and scrambled eggs.
I had to navigate carefully around her brain's
avalanche lest even a decent finale be forfeited.
And her beauty still evermore. You see,
as she was dying, I led each of you to her side,
one by one she scorched you with her radiance.
And she is ever with us in our acetylene leisure.
But you are beautiful, and I, a slave to a heap of cinders.

RICHARD TILLINGHAST

Fossils, Metal, and the Blue Limit

"Thou anointest my head with oil."

The sky, out of reach, unexpected,
like the curved ceiling of a mosque—
us motoring up the long freeway
north from San Francisco:
a promise, yes, a blue ribbon.

We navigate privileged space in the fast lane,
two men and two boys in a Volkswagen van,
alongside families getting a jump on the weekend heat
in cushy, portable, air-conditioned interiors
that rolled down suburban drives
hours and miles ago.
My big, hot-rodded, 1700-cubic-cemtimeter engine revs
fast, loud, and *comme il faut;*
the van lunges eagerly northstate

breezing through a river of air—
inches above the concrete slabs that,
dove-tailed by sky-colored slicks of asphalt, *are*
the freeway.

Three fiberglass poles, and a nine-foot, willowy fly rod
of the lightest material made
bounce easily to the even pace of the engine
as my customized classic
1966 VW microbus, forest green
with white trim,
or as I might call it
in moments of gloom,
"decrepit old wreck,"—
burns through the blue fumes
with bumperstickers advising contradictorily "Bomb Iran"
and "Think Trout."
Tolstoy would have loved it.

Everything the round eye sees

355

suggests the absence of limitation
as we uncork the day with coffee and Bushmill's ,
even what the shapeless, mind's eye
imagines and recalls:
the view to limestone in the pine-shadowed creek
under Mt. Lassen,
our destination;
even the fat, springy, uncoiling, muscular
earthworms I dug at first light out of odorous humus
with a clean-tined pitchfork.

Ayub, *né* Borsky,
companion on many an outing,
fair or foul, poaching or sport, trout or shark—:
street artist, carpenter, taxi driver, mystic, bad cook,
with a face like a rained-on rock,—
rolls a cigarette out of thick, dark
Dutch tobacco,
smokes it through his Mosaic beard
(his grey hair thin, stretched and stranded,
three wavy pencil-lines over his crown),
and gives his well-considered philosophy of life
and trout
to his two sons,
Eric—dark, humorous, fourteen,
maker of fine model airplanes—
and Dylan—blond, ten—:

about "feeding stations," about how
the big trout take the choicest spots
("Just like you, Dad")
how they face upstream, treading icy water,
and don't blink—
about the trout's "window of vision"
wherein the fisherman looms huge, dark, and threatening
("Just like you, Dad")
unless he treads softly, and relies on concealment—
and how "the freeway is a river,"
the cars swimming in four diverted and weaving currents,
how everything is like that really,
and how—
quick as a rainbow trout
flashes sunlight

out of a deep pool—
right at the top of a grade
past Cloverdale,

the green warning signal on the dash flickers
and stays lit!
Blue smoke congregates behind us,
I veer across two lanes,
slide to a stop on the sandy shoulder,
hood
(in the back in a Volkswagen, remember?)
up,
head under hood,
smoke in eyes:
OIL! the engine-opening black
as the underground streams
of Arabia, black
as the fingernails and secret dreams
of the Ayatollah.

We glut it with an extra quart, then another,
and point it toward the exit
though it smokes
like a pointillist painting of London weather
and early Marxist pollution-stacks.

Like those long first paragraphs of *Bleak House*,
creeping, deliberate, ominous,
we nose the cloud
into the town of Weed
along a cyclone fence and frontage road,
up a little paved crescent of street,
then down another one, plain and straight,
in view of the bleached, horizontal, meandering river—
then straight down, miraculously, a yarrow-wild drive:
two wheel-thin slabs of concrete wheelwise
downhill, beside an abandoned, pink, shotgun house.

Down a slanting, weed-jungled drive,
beside a pink house that is having no trouble
falling apart,
under two shapely, identical camphor trees
and one disreputable sycamore,
next to a grey picket fence and a rained-on, broke-down couch,

we squat on our heels like two aborigines
sun-squinting at the engine: black, oil-flooded.
Groping behind it blind I scorch
the first, second, third knuckles on overheated steel,
grabbing for the burst, expensive cooler hose
splashing black fossil-oil
over every inch of metal,
where it burns off as blue smoke
into the clogged atmosphere.

My Piscean friend grins
in the dirty face of disaster
(Of course it is not *his* car.)
Hi-temp rubber hose, this size (handing it),
the three quarts 30-weight oil;—
the boys are out of the van then,
skateboarding down the long street.
For them, unscheduled adventure,
and 50¢ each for something cold.
"The sky's the limit"
is the thought I imagine
for them.
For us, a problem, a headache, gloom.

We take in the panorama
of blue-collar suburbia:
cheap, 1950's houses
dwarfed even more than they anyway would be
by "recreational vehicles," evil-looking, smoked-glass vans,
reptilian-fendered hot rods, a vintage Airstream
trailer, jacked-up
Camaros and Mustangs, souped-up
otherworldly Harleys with chrome out to here,
a single, monstrous, ark-sized, blunt-nosed speedboat,
ready to lumber off into the next flood.

Then a (unique in my experience) residential used-car lot,
where we endeavor to borrow,
and end up renting for five bucks,
a floor-jack
from the thirtyish, drunkish ex-biker
slouched in the doorway,
with "Born to Lose" and "WHITE

ON" and prison-art swastikas
tattooed asymmetrically across his belly,
latitude unknown, longitude uncertain,
where "Save the Whales"
would have seemed more appropriate.
"Hitler's Revenge," he calls my car.

I see the look of concern
drift across my face,
mirrored in the blue sky
of his mirror shades.

But everything's cool!

The procedure:
battery disconnected, jittery, wires pulled
off and labeled with bits of brown tape.
Yank off the gas-line, gas spurts,
choke it fumblingly with an old pencil (not knowing
to clamp it first
with your small vise-grip),
and it dangles there sealed—

pass the Bushmill's around
(cuts the fumes):
then to get the bumper and assorted pieces of tin,
cunningly shaped,
from around the engine, *then,*
passing the big wrench back and forth between us,
and dropping it once, twice, clangingly on cement:
four nuts haltingly and bothersomely
twisted off the engine-studs,
while the neighbors—two Bahai housewives,
the over-the-hill Angel, and an off-duty postman—
drink beer and make free with advice,
we ease, rock, nudge
the engine onto the ton-and-a-half
Hein-Becker floor-jack,
hulking and out of place,
mired and sliding already
in the sweet grass
becoming mud.

The disconnected engine broods there like a primal force,

the metal like a fifth element,
like an alien life-form from a slower planet
putting in down-time—
earth-morning becoming midday
as the metal ticks and bangs, cooling, contracting,
under twin camphor trees and sky.

Were days like this foreseen
in the Platonic heaven of machinists?—
or by the generations of men,
with boots and soiled caps and wire-rimmed eyeglasses
and daughters and sons,—
who brought iron-ore out of the earth,
learned to smelt it, and formed it into steel,
then refined oil to cool
every frictive articulation of that wonder,
an apparatus (1637) *for applying mechanical power,*
consisting of a number of parts, each
having a definite function, —
which they had named *Machine.*

The day heats up,
mare's tails braid across the blue.
The boys skate back into sight down the long, straight street
exhilarated, with motor oil and lengths of hose.
At first it seems simple:
pull the old hoses off,
fit the new ones on true,
tighten the clamps to a turn,—
but *then:* to pump the jack,
grunt, puff, and stagger,
bring the boys and neighbors into it,
struggle, despair, and struggle,
to work the heavy, lumbering mass of old technology
onto the four, eccentrically-placed engine-studs,
tighten the four nuts back on,
cross-eyed with concentration,
feeling humbly resigned
and at the same time in some sense weirdly lucky,
that nothing worse than this
has gone wrong,—
                    fit
the tin back on,
hook up the gas-line,

plug the wires back in,
replace the bumper, and our job is done.

Now the blond, virgin oil
inside the newly tight engine.
I reach out my hand
and turn on the key.

The engine kicks to life,
no oil leaks,
the stream awaits.
In a moment, you who read this,
you can drive it to the carwash and clean it up for me.

My hand, arm, shoulder muscles rebound
with freedom, reflexively,
from the work they have done:
and the quaint construance of the word *nut*
which follows its botanical meanings
in the Oxford English Dictionary
(I wish I had it right here at my elbow)—
a small block of wood, iron, etc.,
pierced, and wormed with a female screw—
drifts into my mind,
suggesting the history, and the slow romance
of machinery.

Maybe what I mean to say is the way oil
looks on skin:
black, verging on chemically murky translucence,
the little human hairs bravely standing up half-bent
beneath the grime, the irreducible petro-dirt,—
or maybe it's what is going to happen
to Joe Borsky,
how two weeks from now
he will take a knife in the gut
and be in all the papers
as he and the passenger in his cab
go after a man who is trying to further
the evolution of the human race
by raping a nurse
as she goes home from work,
for God's sake,
on Nob Hill at four in the morning.

He's one of the lucky ones, however:
only his flesh is wounded.
He'll soon recover.

Waiting for you,
so we can get on up the road,
I loaf here in the bruised, oil-shiny grass,
with a green pen that writes blue,
while my friend meditatively smokes,
as unaware as I am of what lies ahead of him.
The boys are quiet now, the neighbors
have gone home
with their jack, their help, and their noise.
Smells of crushed grass, beer, hot oil, scorched metal
hang in the air.

I hear the river
loop and crook back on itself
over its sandy-bottomed channel
through the nearby field,
where shattered cinderblocks
and an old transmission sprawl.

Between the river and the sky,
the mountains:
the Sierra—a myth, a truth,
the hard backbone of the West,
distances extending untraveled
a thousand miles or more from here
up switchbacked roads
with pine needles dusted over them,
over daylong, empty deserts,
past granite diners that say more
than will easily go into words—
to the eastern slope of the Rockies,
half of America away.

Stained with the bodies of half-billion year-old plants,
releasing my breath upward,
I stare upward uncomprehendingly,
at the blue, cloud-woven limit of the sky.

LESLIE ULLMAN

Private Acts

My father promised,
as he shut my room
dark, night
was the sun's eye

blinking. I promised
I wouldn't chew paper
again, or leave the damp wads
like amulets under the bed.

I shut my eyes. The guests
raised their drinks and told stories
downstairs, laughing in their
bracelets. Their rings of smoke.
Their strange breath bloomed

with attention. I opened my eyes
but the paisley sofa print
rose still, a copper wave that filled
and kept filling my eye's
black room.

I crept to the stairs where light
floated up, and sometimes
a string of words I would
wear for the night . . .

He tucked me in again.
He promised me dark
as a pair of arms, rocking
water, a blanket my size . . .

The paper tasted salty,
the taste of my first lie.
Then I crept among scented
furs on the bed no one

made my parents sleep in—
no, I slept all night

in the bed where I
belonged, while turquoise threads

branched like bits of sky
through my mother's water-colored
gown, and morning came
slow, grey, through every window at once.

Running

i
Lately my neighbor wheezes
pounding dough, her forearms
glazed with sweat and flour.
"At your age," my mother
writes, "I wanted babies.
I got pregnant
each time one of you
learned to walk."
I circle the block again
and again, until I run
outside my body.
This time last year
my husband stopped
speaking of the other woman
who slept poorly inside him.

She promised in another town
to give him up. All night she
tossed and tried to speak
until he spoke of his
father, who drank himself
into the cracked
well of his voice
and never touched bottom.
She made him wake sweating
and brooding in the close
room of his departure
while I ran myself past
my neighbor's lawn and plump

loaves settling in their heat
to an early shape of myself.

ii
I've forgotten whose apartment
stretched like a tunnel,
shapeless and dark
the way my good dress hung
too large, a formal
body outside my body.
The other men drifted
alike behind their drinks
while he stood in one place
and spoke to me of THE MOVIEGOER
which spoke, he said, to his very soul.

Sometimes I run in Louisiana,
where I've never been,
where the hero saw an egret gather
itself over swamp mist
and settle in a single oak
that rose to meet it.
Later he married his cousin
whose agile mind wandered,
glittering at the family table.
The dense mahagony.
The black butler
wheezed as he passed buttered beans.
She couldn't sleep, she
said, without pills.
Sometimes she slept for two days.
She promised she could
be like anyone, if he
would tell her each morning
how to pass that day.

That night, my skin
held me like liquid glass.
I wanted to slip
my hand beneath his elbow,
to dance,
to see the other women naked
inside their clothes.

iii
Every morning I run
through pollen, late-summer
haze, or rain. My husband
is an illness I had
in another country.

The day he left
again and again he said
it wasn't my fault.
I circle the block, pump
and sweat until I run
outside my body.
My ribs ached.
He ran his hands
gently over them.

Inside my running
I write to him, breaking
the silence we keep
for his new wife:
I saw the sun disappear
into mist as it reached
the horizon. I saw an egret
airborne, circling all
this time.

The morning bus gathers
husbands and children
and leaves for a moment
a soft rope of exhaust.
I draw breath over breath
as the children

must breathe in their sleep.
My neighbor waves
from her doorway, watches my
easy stride: "Your waist,"
she says wistfully,
"fits the dress I wore as a bride."

Loyalty

Our eyes meet over other
couples' shoulders, and another

lovesong launches its views.
His body lists

in my direction but not
I assure myself, without

grace. I offer my ringless
hand: "Shall we dance?"

On his waist my hand meets
the roll of flesh, the wife

who let her body go.
I remind myself there's no such thing

as a badly-made man.
"Your eyes . . ." he says

and my glasses slip into their silk
purse. His chin settles into

my neck. "The pearls," I
say, "were a gift

from the man I didn't marry."
Tall, dark, and riddled

with beauty, he spent my ardor
to please, pressing any

knees under glass
tables. This one

breathes in my ear
with the two-step. I

rise to my toes to
follow on air. Oh, I

learned to stay calm on that phone
while a stranger breathed hard

words of love. Now my life
is about to change.

He tells me his mistress,
all legs and caramel

skin, just left for the Coast.
We dance, we drink, we doze

on each other's shoulders.
We stare at stars

which stay in their dark
and gather ourselves towards

morning, the hard sun, the
rough ride out of our clothes.

MICHAEL WATERS

Anniversary Of The Air

Past storefronts lit among the dusk-swept avenues
where those broken grandmothers spit
or straighten their babushkas in the smoky light
            of sausages, streaked windows
hung with strings of red and green peppers,
bluefish gazing through galaxies of pink glaze,

she groans up the bursting, rubble-strewn path
where Our Lady of the Ascension
glistens in rain—
to light one candle, by habit, for her husband
who no longer rests, even in memory,
with any detail,

though tonight she might remember his hair,
red as the candle, or
his alert, political mind flickering
like the flame on its black wick.

The seraphic coloratura of the choir
lulls her . . .

She'll hear them later, distinct, bordering
            her bed, cold water
whispering through the walls, whispering
her name— *Anna*— across the vast
privacies of so many years

so that, in sleep, those tongues start to storm
            through her breast and cross the narrows
            of her lips,
cries of homesickness overwhelming the vermilion
            sky of her arrival,
cries of wrenching in bone-weary orgasm mixed
            with the animal cries of her husband,
cries of her daughters awash in the headlights
            of automobiles racing the rose-blown
            wallpaper (or were those her cries too?),
old-language cries across back alleys
            of rug-beatings and boiling laundry,

the last cries transforming into birdsong
in the crenellated dawn
as she awakens, light-struck, this swallow
of a woman, to celebrate the past,
this anniversary of the air
issuing forth
with the now-recalled memory of his hair:

yes, *red,* and for this anniversary —
with thanksgiving to Our Lady —
the color is enough.

Singles

I don't know anyone more lonely
than the woman listening
to the late news, memorizing
baseball scores for coffee break.

She must undress so carefully,
folding her beige blouse
as if for the last time,
not wanting to be found unkempt

by detectives in the morning.
Sometimes I hear her talking
as she roams from room to room
watering her plumeria,

the only splash of color.
She sets two places at the table
though no one ever comes,
then turns to the boredom of bed

thinking *Indians 7 – Yankees 3,*
Cardinals 11 – Mets 2
until she rises before dawn
and drives crosstown to work.

Could anyone be more lonely?
She doesn't acknowledge, again,

the man in the toll-booth
who's spent the whole night there,

not even a magazine before him,
grateful now to be making change
and touching fingers, briefly,
with such a beautiful stranger.

Dogs In The Storm

after Akhmatova

When this slow heart was raging
and I could tell no one, especially you,
I would abandon the exhaustion of sheets,
this woman tossing like damp leaves,

and storm a few miles into the country.
I wanted to memorize the silhouette
of each branch, the chorus of stars,
the uproar of the willows' shadows,

the stiff mailboxes bearing witness
to such immense drift and flux.
I wanted to not think about you.
But each time some stray bitch

came limping along the highway,
eyes iced shut in the wind, nose
scenting the hunger of wild couplings,
I wondered: Whose lost lover is this?

And how far away is my distant brother
who howls for us both in such savage moonlight?

Negative Space

When you press next to me
on the downtown local, calm
in the clamor of secretaries,
the vast alarum of wheels,

toting your new sketchpad,
I imagine the flexed muscles
of the male model, the art
class you audit each night.

No one else notices you,
not even when the lights fail
and the train halts between stations,
when the air in the car grows stale

and, aloud, you begin to count
express trains flickering toward Queens.
Their lit windows bear faces
schoolchildren draw

in pencil on each fingernail,
though these faces are dimmer,
thinking of supper, thinking of bed,
the four hours of boredom between . . . .

The lesson this evening will be
to see what is *not* there,
to draw "negative space,"
the space, say, between two bodies,

say yours and mine, so palpable,
milky as the pulp
of the wet, green pears
ignored on the stool before you.

Their odor inhabits the air
so that, hours later,
entering your apartment,
the key still fixed in the lock,

you stare at the familiar furniture—
the sofa-bed with its worn print,

the table with one leg
propped on newspaper,

the vase with its red, silk flower—
and see, not these still-lifes, but
the terrible, torn spaces between them
you must, this moment, begin to fill.

The Furniture-Maker

On nights I can't sleep
the moon unlicks the house
like an ex-wife
removing the furniture.

She has her own key,
no one understands it.
Stick by rotting stick
she carts away the darkness.

Soon light settles in corners
like soft chairs,
or gathers in a quiet beauty
to suggest a white piano.

I play sonatas till dawn.
I weave rugs onto the floor.
I try to hammer something too heavy
for a woman to carry on her back.

Drunk With Pavese

for John Skoyles

Already this life is no fun.
The breasts of my girlfriend droop
and she is not even a woman yet.
In the large bed that shakes the world

she tells me she loves me.
I don't know.
She tells me she is afraid to die.
I am not afraid to die.

I believe the women in the next life
have breasts that stare God in the face.

In His large bed
the women laugh at weak bastards like me.
I worry about this all day.
So this life is not so much fun,
not the next one either.

BRUCE WEIGL

A Romance

The skinny red-haired girl gets up
from the bar and dances
over to the juke box
and punches the buttons as if
she were playing the piano —
below the white points of her pelvis
an enormous belt buckle
shaped like the head of a snake
with two red rhinestone eyes
which she polishes with the heels of her hands
making circles on her own fine thighs
and looking up
she catches me staring, my lust like a flag
waving at her across the room
as her big mean boy friend
runs hillbilly after hillbilly off the table
in paycheck nine-ball games.

It is always like this with me in bars,
wanting women I know
I'll have to get my face
punched bloody to love.
Or she could be alone,
and I could be dull enough from liquor
to imagine my face interesting enough to take her
into conversation while I count my money
hoping to jesus I have enough
to get us both romantic.
I don't sleep anyway so I go to bars
and tell my giant lies to women
who have heard them from me,
from the thousands of me
out on the town with our impossible strategies
for no good reason but our selves,
who are holy.

1955

After mass father rinsed the chalice with wine
Again and again.
Drunk before noon
He'd sleep it off in the sacristy
While the other altar boys and I
Rummaged through the sacred things, feeling up
The blessed linen and silk vestments,
Swinging the censer above us so it whistled.
We put our hands on everything we could reach
Then woke the father for mass.

In summer the wool cassock itched
And I sweated through the white lace surplice.
My head reeled from incense
So I mumbled through the Latin prayers
And learned to balance the paten
Gracefully under their chins, my face
Turned away from the priest
Who dipped into the cup
As if to pluck a fish
And just like that something took me by the brain
And I saw myself
Torn loose from the congregation,

Floating like an impossible
Balloon of myself and I thought
This must be what my life is
Though I didn't know what it meant
And I couldn't move or swallow and thought I'd panic
Until father scowled and nudged me down the altar railing
To the next mouth
Open in the O of acceptance
So much like a scream
That can't get out of the lungs . . . .
I don't know why my hands should shake,
I'm only remembering something.

The Man Who Made Me Love Him

All I know about this man
is that he played the trumpet
from his bedroom window.
Evenings we could hear him
trying to play something
while we laughed at the din
and called him names.

I want to sing about this
but all I know
is that it was near dark
so I missed the way home
and stopped to rest in the churchyard
where gold carp lolled in the holy pond.

I was seven and the man who played the trumpet
took me to the roundhouse
where he said the hobos slept,
and though I knew the tracks
and the woods surrounding them,
I didn't know that secret.

He made me take him into my mouth,
my face rose and fell with his hips
and the sun cut through boxcars
waiting to be emptied.

Regret For The Mourning Doves Who Failed To Mate

I passed the window and saw their lovely flash of wings
In the ivy all tangled and fluttering.
Something about gravity is deeply important
To whether or not it works for them
And gravity keeps these two from mating.
Even in the rain he tried
His small dance up her back
As she clung to the ivy
Easing the angle for him.
But I'm sorry,

I'm here to say they didn't make it.
Their nest stays empty
And the wind eats it up bit by bit
The way they constructed it together —
Some twigs, some brown grass woven,
A bit of color from a scrap of paper
Returned to litter the street.
And the winter keeps us locked indoors
Where we peck at each other,
Our voices thin and cold
Saying always what we don't mean,
Our hearts all future,
Our love nearly gone.

ROGER WIENGARTEN

Sometimes, at Thirty-Six

I'm walking a side street
looking down at the pattern
of tiny deaths on the orange-and-mica
granite slabs that slope

into the river or nodding the bearded
geography of my head at the light gray
figures of the evening becoming paper
cutouts pushing carts. Leaf season

overwhelms the sharp cheese, the year
of the near suicide and the amber
jewel bobbing in the apple jack
and sometimes, approaching the half

submerged railroad ties
rotting in the path to the quarry,
suffocated with leaves everywhere
gone yellow, I look up at the stained

fingers of my old friend yellow birch,
who had a fatal yen for gossip, heights,
and exported blends, and imagine
the two of us pacing that nun's cap

of a hill looking east at the soft-bellied
mountains, or heaving the bone-weary
branches high over the dark
brown water, and sharing smoke, an apple

gone soft in my pocket,
and quiet praise for the spirit
of poetry climbing on hands
and knees into middle age.

Two Sons Drowning

The bottom clawed out of a canvas boat,
a wave and a reef. I take the towheaded

struggling thief of my heart into the slippery
crook of my arm and the blue-faced

medicine man of my moods, his collar
between my teeth. And with a free hand

reach for the Adam's apple
laughing from a cloud that breathed

this scene into the unwilling
lungs of my dream, and try to crush

the larynx flailing until I wake in nightsweat,
that hand around my throat, teeth and arm

holding on to the legacy
of my father's love, looking

at the pregnant falling and rising
of my wife's belly under the sheet. I want

to wake her now, shake her arms, and say
what a thick-skinned, elusive stranger

I am to myself and the selves I meet
in the early light, as if I

were older, my own father, and sleeping next
to the son in me, and have her touch

the pulse climbing my neck, and say
forgive yourself, go back to sleep.

Shadow Shadow

I, too, once spouted yards of poetry, and rushed
the sunrise into my sister's giggle, slamming the door
of one chamber into another until my father, rabbi
of the only synagogue in the Berkshires, collared us
by the scruff and swore
there would be no honey cake if we
woke mother (two of her could have sailed
to America in Emily's housedress) the smell of schnapps
hovering in his beard's underbrush. I
never hung back at the top of the stairwell, drawing
pictures in my head of anyone's
parlor shenanigans, *especially*

my father's, who firmly said never to pisch,
pardon his Yiddish, in the pot you eat from, but like her
my intensity gathered in my belly,
the hearth, the staircase
spiralling to the cupola, where I cried and choked
on father's refusal to bless
my first marriage: You remember that northwest
window in our room? Where Emily
lowered ginger
and almond cookies to the little ones squinting
up at the sun and reaching for the shadow
that became a bride lowering herself on old shoestrings
braided for strength and magic

out of that white whale of a house, no velvet
neckpiece to set off the mixture of fear
and desire glazing my wide, brown irises—not yet
puffed and diminished into wrinkles, or mocked
by rouged dark bags of tears I've held in check
in case you, or any young man with a pen
or tape recorder would break the dry
monotony of this retirement
city named for the sun, without an oak or the little ones
to carve the acorns for Halloween; the sun
my second husband willed to me
after scattering ashes into winds
that slapped a few
white fragments back in my face. Emily

and I share a secret. We knew the same loose board, nearly
equidistant from the stove and closet
where the curators display her dress. There was a poem
folded twice; so bitter; so simple.
I put it to memory. It became—like a lapis lazuli

scarab carved by some ancient Hebrew craftsman
and welded by time to the breastbone
of a pharoah—our poem. Breaking faith, if I let it go.
However, I'll tell you this: You are young; you have
my father's mouth; his high forehead, wrinkled and glowing
stain in the night, and absolutely
no one gradually withdraws from life. Someone inside,
like a seed breaking free of the groundfallen fruit,
puts out her own
taproot like a wing, and either flies or doesn't.
We didn't. It was all a dream. Linen or gabardine.

The Night-Blooming Cereus

When you spoke to me—wrapped in your faded, perennial,
black raincoat that embraced
the connective tissue to those shadowed,
meditative, mossy paths that laced the interior
of the Vermont woods, where we found each other leaning

over the railing of a rickety bridge, an amber
bottle tipped in the air, the neck
pressed and forming a vacuum around your tongue
in the stern of this; austere, beam-and-stucco
vaulting past the blue, all

too familiar stained glass
figures of your youth, watching your father
gesture to his parishioners—you said that I, as unlikely
a friend, and vice versa, am the only
one of them (You illustrate, tossing a prayer,

bound in black, the gold-rimmed pages
ruffling into swan-feathers) in twenty-odd years that you didn't

push away; If I arrived at a bus terminal, the dry
taste of sleep on my tongue, took a room
with a skylight and no windows, furnished

in the middle-class fashion, a corridor
and a kitchen that I could share with a semi-bald
Jehovah's Witness, my landlord, his atheist daughter
for a neighbor, and never left, I'd remember;
first, the cold maple pressing my heel into ice
uncrossing my feet over the back of that pew, then
the adolescent portrait
you drew of yourself; "In the high
polish of my Sunday shoes and a cranberry jacket, I could touch
the reflection of a man who could see all the way through

the architecture of his faith
to his son, the son of a nurse, who pursued me
through the rock-swollen catacombs of childhood, which I fled,
barefoot and half-asleep with poetry, up the wild
strawberry and dew-slick

hill of night, her arms shaking
like a corn crib being devoured by raccoons,
like brooms holding
up the moon, relentless and high into the New England
claustrophobia." In this weather

we left the six pack, almost empty
and floating prenatal
in its own liquid, inside
the baptismal font, one for the pastor. Years later,
in a town without weather, we were living

in cave-dark Siamese apartments, the wall we shared,
white and thin as a moth wing, me
sleeping by night, and you by day; we kept a vigil,
someone always clearing their throat or tapping the keys
of a typewriter. Once you woke me
with a chocolate bar glowing in the vehement

yellow of a birthday candle; another time
to warn of a neighbor twisting
his wife's hair around his fist through the broken glass
of a window, and again to insist

that I stereotype you in my poems, proving
that I didn't love you.

The History of the World

Ectoplasm in the air! A partial eclipse
of the moustache and a nineteenth-century
German idealist climbs a fever, giving birth
to the phenomenology of the nose

that understands what's written on the wind
of the right nostril is engraved in the ring
around the left . . . In San Francisco
strange handkerchiefs travel under the counter

at the speed of light. A nose at birth begins to die
and the end begins at the beginning. The imperfect
shadow of a stuffed nose is the new poetic.
Believing the soul resides in the nose, a fourteenth

century wife of a Castillian aristocrat, having learned
her husband was going to guillotine her nose
as a wedding present for her successor, stuffed it
with holy water, myrrh, and a wad of honeycomb. Wilhelm

Reich stuffs his with a mixture of fermented sharks meat
and illuminated scrolls that describe St. Joseph
riding a tortoise around a recumbent Virgin
submerged in a goblet of steam glazing her Wedgewood

nostrils. A nun, lowering the drawbridge
for a priest, wore a black handkerchief over her face
for thirty years that lifted in the wind
of her devotions. You can't xerox a stuffed nose

leaping from a Lady Godiva
chocolate-covered peach to a bowl of gelatinous
red and yellow antihistamines. Raiders of a nose-shaped
pyramid of the Upper Nile opened a delicatessen

on the Lower East Side. In Los Angeles, unemployed
dairy farmers injected silicone into the clear passages
of go-go dancers until both nostrils filled to Renaissance
proportions. As the golden trumpet of the herald

bloomed in the stratosphere, the imperfect
shadow of a horn of plenty was set in heaven
and sat on a throne. Doc Holiday and Wyatt Earp
filled theirs with lead balls, black powder,

and spun the chambers. If the eye
of the nose intercedes for the rectum,
can the state of repose achieved by Erasmus,
fallen from his mount with kidney stones in 1506,

be far behind? In Palm Beach, a full nostril's
looked upon as a sign of breeding. Speaking
from the nose is regarded as more etheric,
godlike . . . Another poet, believing his nose

was haunted by W. H. Auden and Jesus Christ,
relied on an Ouija board to speak for the spirits.
Black market transistorized nose hair cutters
laundered off the coast of Florida are highly prized

by libertines and vegetarians tumbling
out of one nose into another. Queen Victoria
negotiated a liquor license for the Prince of Wales'
nose, the swinging doors of his nostrils opening

into the twentieth century, where Frank
Lloyd Wright was waiting to model the first skyscraper
after a cue tip. An old man with three nostrils
and a bad cold is looked upon with no little reverence

in the back rooms of the Kremlin. How sweet the aroma
rising from the appetite of one who wished
Weingarten's nose was filled with nickels. Whither
the years and who can remember. O sinusitis, mingling

with love and poetry, lead the way through ivy-covered
stations of the cross into the inner sanctum of the eardrum
where I may live out my life, holding up the cocoon
of my nose to the inner light, like a glass paperweight

to a window, watching the wings of my godlike self, my hermit
almost ready to fly. My stuffed nose I do bequeath
to our great brother Villon and to the earth our mother
I bequeath a tincture of goldenseal and the common cold.

Nicolai Vasilievich Gogol dropkicked a nose
baked in a piroshk and wearing a uniform
down Nevsky Prospect, swearing under his breath
that a stuffed nose can live twenty-seven thousand

days without a hankie, but a clean handkerchief
will die of heartbreak in a dark pocket.

C. K. WILLIAMS

Still Life

All we do—how old are we? I must be twelve, she a little older;
      thirteen, fourteen—is hold hands
and wander out behind the barn, past a rusty hay-rake, a half-collapsed
      old Model T,
then down across a barbed-wire gated pasture—early emerald rye-
      grass, sumac in the dip—
to where a brook, high with run-off from a morning storm, broad-
      ened and spilled over—
turgid, muddy viscous, snagged here and there with shattered branches
      —in a bottom meadow.

I don't know then that the place, a mile from anywhere, and day,
      brilliant, sultry, balmy,
are intensifying everything I feel, but I know now that what made
      simply touching her
almost a consummation was as much the light, the sullen surge of
      water through the grass,
the coils of scent, half hers—the unfamiliar perspiration, talc, some-
      thing else I'll never place—
and half the air's: mown hay somewhere, crushed clover underfoot,
      the brook, the breeze.

I breathe it still, that breeze, and, not knowing how I know for cer-
      tain that it's that,
although it is, I know, exactly that, I drag it in and drive it—rich,
      delicious,
as biting as wet tin—down, my mind casting up flickers to fit it—
      another field, a hollow—
and now her face, even it, frail and fine, comes momentarily to focus,
      and her hand,
intricate and slim, the surprising firmness of her clasp, how judiciously
      it meshes mine.

All we do—how long does it last? an hour or two, not even one whole
      afternoon:
I'll never see her after that, and, strangely (strange even now), not
      mind, as though,
in that afternoon the revelations weren't only of the promises of
      flesh, but of resignation—

all we do is trail along beside the stream until it narrows, find the one-
    log bridge
and cross into the forest on the other side: silent footfalls, hills, a
    crest, a lip.

I don't know then how much someday—today—I'll need it all, how
    much want to hold it,
and, not knowing why, not knowing still how time can tempt us so
    emphatically and yet elude us,
not have it, not the way I would, not the way I want to have *that*
    day, *that* light,
the motes that would have risen from the stack of straw we leaned
    on for a moment,
the tempered warmth of air which so precisely seemed the coefficient
    of my fearful ardor,

not, after all, even the objective place, those shifting paths I can't
    really follow now
but only can compile from how many other ambles into other woods,
    other stoppings in a glade—
(for a while we were lost, and frightened; night was just beyond
    the hills; we circled back)—
even, too, her gaze, so darkly penetrating, then lifting idly past, is so
    much imagination,
a portion of that figured veil we cast against oblivion, then try, with
    little hope, to tear away.

Spit

. . . then the son of the "superior race" began to spit into the Rabbi's mouth
so that the Rabbi could continue to spit on the Torah . . .
The Black Book

After this much time, it's still impossible. The SS man with his stiff
    hair and his uniform;
the Rabbi, probably in a torn overcoat, probably with a stained beard
    the other would be clutching;
the Torah, God's word, on the altar, the letters blurring under the
    blended phlegm;
the Rabbi's parched mouth, the SS man perfectly absorbed, obsessed
    with perfect humiliation.

So many years and what is there to say still about the soldiers
        waiting impatiently in the snow,
about the one stamping his feet, thinking, "Kill him! Get it over with!"
while back there the lips of the Rabbi and the other would have brushed
and if time had stopped you would have thought they were lovers,
so lightly kissing, the sharp, luger hand under the dear chin,
the eyes furled slightly and then when it started again the eyelashes of
        both of them
shyly fluttering as wonderfully as the pulse of a baby.
Maybe we don't have to speak of it at all, it's still the same.
War, that happens and stops happening but is always somehow right
        there, twisting and hardening us;
then what we make of God — words, spit, degradation, murder, shame;
        every conceivable torment.
All these ways to live that have something to do with how we live
and that we're almost ashamed to use as metaphors for what goes on in
        us
but that we do anyway, so that love is battle and we watch ourselves in
        love
become maddened with pride and incompletion, and God is what it is
        when we're alone
wrestling with solitude and everything speaking in our souls turns against
        us like His fury
and just facing another person, there is so much terror and hatred that
        yes,
spitting in someone's mouth, trying to make him defile his own meaning,
would signify the struggle to survive each other and what we'll enact to
        accomplish it.

There's another legend.
It's about Moses, that when they first brought him as a child before
        Pharaoh,
the king tested him by putting a diamond and a live coal in front of him
and Moses picked up the red ember and popped it into his mouth
so for the rest of his life he was tongue-tied and Aaron had to speak
        for him.
What must his scarred tongue have felt like in his mouth?
It must have been like always carrying something there that weighed
        too much,
something leathery and dead whose greatest gravity was to loll out
        like an ox's,
and when it moved, it must have been like a thick embryo slowly
        coming alive,
butting itself against the inner sides of his teeth and cheeks.

And when God burned in the bush, how could he not cleave to him?
How could he not know that all of us were on fire and that every
        word we said would burn forever,
in pain, unquenchably, and that God knew it, too, and would say
        nothing Himself ever again beyond this,
ever, but would only live in the flesh that we use like firewood,
in all the caves of the body, the gut cave, the speech cave:
He would slobber and howl like something just barely a man that
        beats itself again and again onto the dark,
moist walls away from the light, away from whatever would be light
        for this last eternity.
"Now therefore go," He said, "and I will be with thy mouth."

Floor

A dirty picture, a photograph, possibly a tintype, from the turn of
        the century, even before:
the woman is obese, gigantic; a broad, black corset cuts from under
        her breasts to the top of her hips,
her hair is crimped, wiry, fastened demurely back with a bow one
        incongruous wing of which shows.
Her eyebrows are straight and heavy, emphasizing her frank, un-
        introspective plainness
and she looks directly, easily into the camera, her expression some-
        where between play and scorn,
as though the activities of the photographer were ridiculous or be-
        neath her contempt, or,
rather, as though the unfamiliar camera were actually the much more
        interesting presence here
and how absurd it is that the lens be turned toward her and her
        partner and not back on itself.
One sees the same look—pride, for some reason, is in it, and a sur-
        prisingly sophisticated self-distancing—
in the snaps anthropologists took in backwaters during those first,
        politically pre-conscious,
golden days of culture-hopping, and, as Goffman notes, in certain
        advertisements, now.

The man is younger than the woman. Standing, he wears what looks
        like a bathing costume,
black and white tank top, heavy trousers bunched in an ungainly

heap over his shoes, which are still on.
He has an immigrant's mustache he's a year or two too callow for,
   but, thick and dark, it will fit him.
He doesn't, like the woman, watch the camera, but stares ahead, not
   at the woman but slightly over and past,
and there's a kind of withdrawn, almost vulnerable thoughtfulness or
   preoccupation about him
despite the gross thighs cast on his waist and the awkward, surely
   bothersome twist
his body has been forced to assume to more clearly exhibit the genital
   penetration.
He seems, in fact, abstracted—oblivious wouldn't be too strong a
   word—as though, possibly,
as unlikely as it would seem he had been a virgin until now and was
   trying amid all this unholy confusion—
the hooded figure, the black box with its eye—trying, and from the
   looks of it even succeeding
in obliterating everything from his consciousness but the thing itself,
   the act itself,
so as, one would hope, to redeem the doubtlessly endless nights of
   the long Victorian adolescence.

The background is a painted screen: ivy, columns, clouds; some muse
   or grace or other,
heavy-buttocked, whory, flaunts her gauze and clodhops with a half-
   demented leer.
The whole thing's oddly poignant somehow, almost, like an antique
   wedding picture, comforting—
the past is sending out a tendril to us: poses, attitudes of stillness we've
   lost or given back.
Also, there's no shame in watching them, in being in the tacit com-
   merce of having, like it or not,
received the business in one's hand, no titillation either, not a tangle,
   not a throb,
probably because the woman offers none of the normal symptoms,
   even if minimal, even if contrived—
the tongue, say, wandering from the corner of the mouth, a glint of
   extra brilliance at the lash—
we associate to even the most innocuous, undramatic, parental sorts
   of passion, and the boy,
well, dragged in out of history, off Broome or South Street, all he is
   is grandpa:
he'll go back into whatever hole he's found to camp in, those higher-
   contrast tenements

with their rows of rank, forbidding beds, or not even beds, rags on a
   floor, or floor.
On the way there, there'll be policemen breaking strikers' heads, or
   micks', or sheenies',
there'll be war somewhere, in the sweatshops girls will turn to stone
   over their Singers.
Here, at least peace. Here, one might imagine, after he withdraws, a
   kind of manly focus taking him—
the glance he shoots to here is hard and sure—and, to her, a tenderness
   might come,
she might reach a hand—Sweet Prince—to touch his cheek, or might
   —who can understand these things?—
avert her face and pull him to her for a time before she squats to flush
   him out.

Tar

The first morning of Three Mile Island: those first disquieting, un-
   certain, mystifying hours.
All morning a crew of workmen have been tearing the old decrepit
   roof off our building,
and all morning, trying to distract myself, I've been wandering out to
   watch them
as they hack away the leaden layers of asbestos paper and disassemble
   the disintegrating drains.
After half a night of listening to the news, wondering how to know
   a hundred miles downwind
if and when to make a run for it and where, then a coming bolt awake
   at seven
when the roofers we've been waiting for since winter sent their lad-
   ders shrieking up our wall,
we still know less than nothing: the utility company continues mak-
   ing little of the accident,
the slick federal spokesmen still have their evasions in some semblance
   of order.
Surely we suspect now we're being lied to, but in the meantime, there
   are the roofers,
setting winch-frames, sledging rounds of tar apart, and there I am, on
   the curb across, gawking.

I never realized what brutal work it is, how matter-of-factly and harrowingly dangerous.

The ladders flex and quiver, things skid from the edge, the materials
are bulky and recalcitrant.

When the rusty, antique nails are levered out, their heads pull off;
the under-roofing crumbles.

Even the battered little furnace, roaring along as patient as a donkey,
chokes and clogs,

a dense, malignant smoke shoots up, and someone has to fiddle with
a cock, then hammer it,

before the gush and stench will deintensify, the dark, Dantean broth
wearily subside.

In its crucible, the stuff looks bland, like licorice, spill it, though, on
your boots or coveralls,

it sears, and everything is permeated with it, the furnace gunked with
burst and half-burst bubbles,

the men themselves so completely slashed and mucked they seem al-
most from another realm, like trolls.

When they take their break, they leave their brooms standing at
attention in the asphalt pails,

work gloves clinging like Brer Rabbit to the bitten shafts, and they
slouch along the precipitous lip,

the enormous sky behind them, the heavy noontime air alive with
shimmers and mirages.

Sometime in the afternoon I had to go inside: the advent of our vigil
was upon us.

However much we didn't want to, however little we would do about
it, we'd understood:

we were going to perish of all this, if not now, then soon, if not soon,
then someday.

Someday, some final generation, hysterically aswarm beneath an at-
mosphere as unrelenting as rock,

would rue us all, anathematize our earthly comforts, curse our sur-
feits and submissions.

I think I know, though I might rather not, why my roofers stay so
clear to me and why the rest,

the terror of that time, the reflexive disbelief and distancing, all we
should hold on to, dims so.

I remember the president in his absurd protective booties, looking
absolutely unafraid, the fool.

I remember a woman on the front page glaring across the misty Sus-
quehanna at those looming stacks.

But, more vividly, the men, silvered with glitter from the shingles,
clinging like starlings beneath the eaves.

Even the leftover carats of tar in the gutter, so black they seemed to
   suck the light out of the air.
By nightfall kids had come across them: every sidewalk on the block
   was scribbled with obscenities and hearts.

DAVID WOJAHN

Satin Doll

It's probably the year her marriage
fails, though the photo, blackened now
on the edges of its sepia, doesn't say:
my aunt on the hood of the blue Chevy coupe,

straw hat and summer dress. It's the year
she carries the novels and notebooks
into the backyard to burn them, and when she finishes
her dress and apron are covered with ashes, rising

in what she wants to call a pillar of fire
but is only smoke on a damp day.
She walks back to the house and her first
sickly daughter, feeling the one

inside her kick. She thinks of going
back to her maiden name, and the daughter
cries in her crib like this passionless
wind up the St. Croix River bluffs.

And when she was a child there, the day
of the grade school picnic, they found
a woman drowned on the banks. Everyone stared
and no one closed the eyes staring back.

But now it's raining on the first spring night
of 1947, six years to my birth,
and I don't want to leave her here. I want
the kitchen radio to murmur

some slithering big band and *Satin Doll*
from the Casablanca ballroom, high in Chicago's clouds.
I want her to see the women floating
in their taffeta, chilly red corsages from

their pencil mustached men, ivory tuxedos, lotion
and bay rum. She can almost touch them now. Duke Ellington
rises from the sprawling Steinway as the four
trombones begin their solo, horns glittering

under the spinning globe of mirrors. And now
she's dancing, isn't she? Until the cupboards shake,
until the window, already trembling with rain,
hums its vibrato, and she's holding herself in her arms

so tightly she can feel the veins
in her shoulders throb to their separate music,
until this is a song she can dance with too,
and I can let her go.

Cool Nights of October

I wanted to spare you this, the lying alone,
        the moon as it rises,
                watery and diffuse

like a washcloth pressed to the forehead
        of a girl so still she can barely breathe.
                I read of her now on page

four hundred and seventy-eight.
        I've wakened in the TV's bluish light
                and the noise my neighbor

the one-eyed Cuban makes,
        sharpening a stick against the sidewalk.
                He wears the battered face I saw last week

above the gate of St. Louis Cemetery —
        a marble angel with a broken trumpet.
                In the dampness after rain

it had no eyes or forehead.
        On page four hundred and seventy-nine
                Turgenev lets the girl die. The mother

had been reading to her, a novel in French.
        Turgenev does not tell us how the woman
                drops her book, cups her daughter's face

and cries out softly. The death scene,

like Bazarov's, is unsentimental.
          These are the first cool nights of October.

The Cuban beats his wife. I hear them
          over car horns and samba records,
                    the spas of Baden-Baden, the roulette tables,

the calculating Russian gentry. Turgenev
          was fat and lived alone. His brain
                    is in the Guiness book,

having weighed nearly seven pounds.
          Ivan Turgenev, I am David Wojahn
                    and some nights I can't sleep.

I read of you in English
          and tire of the word and heavy mind.
                    I wanted to spare you. A mother weeps

beside a still, consumptive daughter
          and some angelic Cuban, his eye-patch askew,
                    strikes his wife again across the face.

The Bicycle

He held her as she wavered
          and grabbed tight to the handlebars,
                    a woman in her fifties,

learning it for the first time,
          both of them, I was sure, in love.
                    Watching like that, I thought

I knew nothing about love,
          nor how to be alone.
                    All that spring he taught her

to coast awkwardly with him
          down their alley to the town pier
                    where usually she fell.

Maybe then he kissed her,
    I can't remember.
        I went home. I didn't

believe in the bicycle
    or in Petrarch, who wanted love
        simple: moral and wounded. Always

this need for yearning and blame,
    and always there's a part of you
        giving unasked-for advice

because you think that everything
    believed in is betrayed.
        You fall until you get

the hang of it, and finally
    you have no wrath for anything,
        though you've still

discovered only
    the small, persistent skills
        you thought impossible to learn.

The Betrayal of Christ in Tucson and Brussels

Beyond us, the Garden of Gethsemane
borders the Santa Cruz, which isn't a river,
only the grainy record of one.
The Betrayal of Christ is made of cement,
a public park with sleeping attendant,
the life's work of a single
fanatical veteran, a plate in his skull
from World War I. Vandalized,
God's face lacks a nose,
but seen more than once
He's almost endearing
and gestures toward houses
brick and absolute. Yards made of sand,
Who would live here?

This week we will part again
as if by habit for different coasts
and walking like this, late afternoon,
we are gestures the landscape makes,
a blur by riverbank willows. This morning
we argued with change.
I hurled the gray ceramic mug
against the bedroom wall. Silent,
you bent to shards the way
you now bend down to sift through stones
and I call you until I falter.
Nothing singular will help.
Not the sunlight grazing your face,
not the gazes—cat's eye marbles—
of the four astonished apostles, who must not
see change, only dispersal,
the evenings before them, the distant rooms.

               *   *

In Ensor's greatest painting, *The Arrival
of Christ into Brussels, 1889,*
the streets spill over with a tide
of masked cacophonous figures—
red skull in a derby, Death
in a washerwoman's bonnet, the Saviour
barely distinguishable
under a broad red banner inscribed:
VIVE LA SOCIALE. He's trying His best
to remember miracle and order,
stories that might
be personal. A man on a donkey
at a strange city's gate, who even now
cannot be distinct,
only alone on some impossible
sunlit evening, small and feckless, haloed.

               *   *

Why, between the figures
of Saul Struck Down by God
and the Sacrifice of Isaac,
this couple making love in Spanish?
And the park attendant, ready to close

the cyclone fence for the night,
winking at us as he watches.
Orange sky, the streetlights
coming on in unison against the dark.
In the parking lot, we watch them kiss again,
blanket on her shoulders,
the radio and Mexican hit parade.
When you turn to me, I only want you
to say my name, to tell me
you are sick unto death of change,
the evening whose plainness
we have just now entered, individual
and unprepared.

Evening Snow

(for My Mother)

I want to tell you how the light bends down
to touch the cars and abstract
December trees, and of the moment when
it stops itself and lets each shadow go
to die on the snow-choked porches.
I want to find the light you read by,
a romance on your lap, in 1961.

But today I woke late
in the too-familiar room, afternoon gone,
my visit nearly over. You curse at poets and sauces
and the fogged kitchen window
is half your world. On the feeder
sparrows and chickadees
flicker from a greedy squirrel.
You cough and stub a cigarette:
I am less your son. Coffee steam,
the kitchen table. Each visit,
you judge my life as more complex and wrong,
the marriages, the cities I've lost count of.

Returning home at last, the mansard
and its yellow light, we want to believe

the rooms and faces all have changed
the way faces flare out from portraits
as the edges darken with age.
But age, says Rilke, is not change. And the son
has grown too difficult to love.

Tonight I'll stand with you to watch
sunset ignite the windowpane and fail
before the spray of evening snow.
Then walk the dogs beneath the backyard pines
where I'll watch your silhouette behind the curtain
gaze out at me, where only one of us can see
the other, where the cord that bound us once
will bind us again,
one to darkness, one to pain.

CAROLYNE WRIGHT

The Custody of the Eyes

(for Madeline De Frees)

"Those who love uprightness of life diligently guard
their eyes from all inordinate glancing about . . ."
—St. Bonaventure, *Speculum disciplinae
ad novitios.*

It's the lie I've grown used to.
My plainclothes sisters still negotiate
the cut-rate aisles of the world
in their impeccable habits. They march
according to the anthems, spines
straight as hardback editions.
Their glances veer neither to the romance
nor the crime, their right brains
know not what their lefts are doing.
They have learned perfectly
the Custody of the Eyes.

                    I
don't have such advantages,
born so astigmatic the stars
never blinked at the proceedings.
In dreams, I follow the right-turn signs
that go left. The Japanese have a verb
for the way I lean toward one companion
or the other as I walk.
                    In my aquarium,
young flounders' bottom eyes
migrate; adult, they look up to heaven
double from the bottom-colored up-side
of their bodies. I, too, have practiced
the Migration of the Eye.

                    First grade,
the ophthalmologist brought back my wandering
left eye like a lost sheep: I put hundreds
of cartoon birds in cages, threaded red beads
through rose-colored windows. Every morning

I crossed my eyes like a devotion.
Every ball on the playground
aimed for my plate-glass lenses.
In the class photograph, I'm the one
with the Captain Kidd patch, my good girl's
curl falling in the middle of my forehead.

Thirty years, my pupils still round
and innocent as integers,
mascara on the lashes
fussy as parents who never could afford
the contacts. The fiance who wouldn't pass
the wire-rims, who told me
Take Them Off.
I did. He stumbled in the sudden blur.
I imagine he wanders still, calls
what he thinks my name is,
holding his aviator shades before him
like a flashlight in Hades.

          Now the left side of my skull
aches when that weak eye loses faith.
I make pilgrimages to strange cities,
Basilicas crammed with bad Italian
statues: Saint Lucy carrying her eyeballs
in a trencher. I look both ways.
When no one's watching, I steal them
like a coffee kitty's loose change.

Back home, I drop the eyeballs in the flounders'
cloudy water, listen for the telephone
to accuse me, ringing the syllables
of my lost love's name. I glue a postcard
on the notebook from which I have erased
his number: Saint Lucy holding a lamp
before her in the dark.

          I lay me down,
to dream of the lofty Madonna
of my assumptions. I take off my spectacles,
cross the side-arms, turn out the light.
Sisters, I pray, let your glances
trespass in my direction.
I renounce old Hydra and his many eyes.

Celebration for the Cold Snap

Pre-dawn's pilot lights
glow under the burners
like the vigil lamps of runways. Not one
but has kept the faith all night.

At six the window squares
go blue, the first commuter
trains clang by, full
of people with bills to pay,
important telephones to answer,
custom-made ornaments
for their office tree.

I labor alone, draping tinsel
on my foot-high pine,
turning the world news
down to a simmer. I parse words
together, make lists of things
I can do without: gifts
and their impossible demands.

Old lovers' faces rise and set
in my dreams. Their hands
reach for me, toadstools
that spring up in one rain.
I glue their greeting cards
to the windows, the year's
discarded printouts.

I wrap presents to myself.
Free of the Big World
and its confusion of envies,
I stand at the window,
watch trains crawl past: everyone
I've had to let go of,
sleepwalkers lost in the heart's
subzero weather.

Josie Bliss, October 1971

> "Nombre definitivo que cae en las semanas
> con un golpe de acero que las mata."
> —Pablo Neruda, *Residencia en la tierra.*

When they brought me the newspaper
headlines with your name translated
to the round dark petals of our script,
I knew you'd finally found
your love. I'm happy for you,
Pablo. After all these years, silence
between us like seabottom jewels,
the Bay of Bengal with jellyfish
armadas patrolling the beachheads
from which I could wage no campaign
against loss, your face in the photo
grown heavier—faithful, at last, to the body's
vows with earth. Our season of mangoes
and brainfire, the paraffin lamp
guttering out on the other side
of the curtain, white jasmines
in my hair and naked feet
you said you loved.
Forget those foolish nights
I circled the bed with a knife,
a dance the old women showed me—
panther's ritual, incense I burned
to weaken your instinct for betrayal.
I was your first love, wasn't I? No spell
bound with camphor and inflections
missing for thousands of years
in our mouths can change that. Remember
how I said my fears would end
with your death? When you gave death
the slip, boarding the westbound
freighter, leaving your freshly ironed shirts
to fend for themselves, and books
like a row of hostile witnesses, in languages
you returned to every morning, every night
you cried out in your sleep—it was I
who died: into the betel leaf and fringed
anxiety of palm, sarongs and Malay silks
stacked like jute bales in the courtyard.

405

Airless nights and the ache of salt
between my thighs, my body closed up
like a village in wartime.
No steamer passage across an ocean
littered with telegrams and the summons
of fair-skinned women, no hampers
of saffron rice and clear plum wine
to remind you, no conjures of sweet oil
and scimitars could break the spell of flesh
I lost you to. You wouldn't recognize me
now, Pablo. I've blurred with age
and sons and the long war in the East.
And the one daughter they took from me,
whose secret name meant Heartbreak
in our tongue, and in your language,
Song. Veiled in blue silk for the voyage,
she vanished from the docks at Singapore
into abject air, water the color
of a beating. Now I'm alone, refugee
of the blood's terrain, memory's
backhanded apologists. No husband
to uproot the strangle-vine called
afternoon, no one to put a stop
to these voices, bright calligraphy
giving me my share of messages
you could never bring yourself
to send. What else remains
of what we called our lives?
The house with the jagged bamboo fence
went back to the tribe of liana
and baobab and climbing fern. My brothers
in their blood-colored pagodas
came for me, snake bracelets on their arms,
their tongues heavy as bronze bell
clappers. In Mandalay market
they sold my true name: a powder against suspicion
and English ways. Since then
I am married to quarry stone and razor-
palm green air, desire that honeycombs
the brain like limewater, fool's gold
gleam in passageways of no return.
Gone the parrot's emerald laugh,
the incantations of monkey flower
you used against the shadows. Gone

the history of broken clay you told,
gone the hard fruit wrapped in tilak
skin that began our countries' sad,
metallic generations. Gone your tongue
in my mouth, sweet anarchy of the hands.
Don't look for me, Pablo,
if you come. I am the first wife
and widow of my own refusals—
in this neighborhood of narrow doors
and shadow longings, the retreating
steps of my blue daughter, machine
gun voices of my sons, I have forgotten
how to open dawn's orange fan. No more
do I search through books full of dreams'
high-water marks, no more glide from room
to room, listening to your pale breath,
my own lost pulse along the heartwire.
No more do I throw myself down and kiss
the chalk feet of the bearded god.
Stay in your land of stone's tremor
and women like the avalanche's blessing.
I couldn't bear the hidden fault
lines in your beauty, and I no longer
answer to the empty net, the long-knived
moon—warnings between the hand
and its caressing, names you gave me
for my fury and my joy.

Under the Sign of Cancer

Born under the sign of Cancer,
I knew I'd die of it.
Horoscopes were against me,
and sky maps in the newspaper
featured the Crab stars every Sunday.

That was the hushed-up Fifties,
after Bikini Atoll and the Big C,
and they'd just found strontium-
90 in the milk. It smelled
like weapons. I tried to figure out

the tropics, running their 23½
degree circles around the globe.
The one up north
would get me. I envied my father
his Capricorn birthday.

Later, I read Henry Miller
for a clue, until my father came in
one night, pulled back the bedsheets
and snapped the flashlight off.
I still seek that known latitude.

I boycott Replogle products,
wear Linus Pauling T-shirts
and teach my parrot to say
Ban the Bomb.
I telephone Madame Noor,

my chartmaker, for a reading.
She tunes in the celestial sphere,
my stars line up.
She shakes her head, warns me
not to read the *National Enquirer*

for a cure. She says, "Think of the thing
you're most afraid of, dream yourself
dying, healed of it forever."
I imagine myself empty
between collarbone and hip,

sunlight falling in long arcs
where an arm was. I say things
about the nuclear family,
buy mushrooms and make detonation
noises as I slice them, never use

words like *metastasize* and *remission,*
even when I'm going through a change
of subject, or trying to move out
on sin. To date, I have no symptoms.
I have nothing in common with children

lying in their tents of pure breath
at the Mayo Clinic,

their charts fixed at the angles
of declining stars, Three Mile Island
glowing through their sleep.

Jon Anderson (1940) was born in Somerville, Massachusetts, and attended Northeastern University and the Iowa Writer's Workshop where he earned an M.F.A. He has taught Creative Writing at several colleges, and has been the recipient of N.E.A. and Guggenheim Fellowships, the Shelley Memorial Award, and other notable awards. Currently, he teaches at the University of Arizona in Tucson.

Looking for Jonathan (University of Pittsburgh Press, 1968)
Death & Friends (University of Pittsburgh Press, 1970)
In Sepia (University of Pittsburgh Press, 1974)
Counting the Days (Penumbra Press, 1975)
Cypresses (Graywolf Press, 1981)
The Milky Way: Poems 1967-1982 (Ecco Press, 1983)

George Barlow (1948) was born in Berkeley, California. He received an M.F.A. from the Iowa Writer's Workshop, and has taught at the University of California at Berkeley and, currently, teaches at De Anza College in California. He has been awarded a Woodrow Wilson Fellowship, a Ford Foundation Fellowship, and was selected for inclusion in the 1981 National Poetry Series.

Broadside Series No. 66 (Broadside Press, 1973) broadside
Gabriel (Broadside Press, 1974)
Gumbo (Doubleday & Co., 1981)

Michael Burkard (1947) was born in Rome, New York, and has earned degrees from Hobart College and the Iowa Writer's Workshop. He has taught at a number of universities, and is currently teaching at the Writer's Voice in New York City and at Sarah Lawrence College.

In a White Light (L'Epervier Press, 1977)
None, River (Ironwood Press, 1979)
Ruby for Grief (University of Pittsburgh Press, 1981)

Peter Cooley (1940) was born and raised in Detroit. He attended the University of Chicago and earned his Ph.D. at the University of Iowa. He has taught at the University of Wisconsin at Green Bay and currently teaches at Tulane University in New Orleans. He has received fellowships from the Louisiana Division of the Arts and the Breadloaf Writers' Conference. Since 1970 he has been the Poetry Editor of the *North American Review*.

The Company of Strangers (University of Missouri Press, 1975)
The Room Where Summer Ends (Carnegie-Mellon University Press, 1979)
Nightseasons (Carnegie-Mellon University Press, 1983)

Philip Dacey (1939) was born in St. Louis and received his M.F.A. from the Iowa Writer's Workshop. He has taught at Southwest State University in Marshall, Minnesota since 1970, and has been the recipient of two N.E.A. grants, the YMHA Discovery Award, and other awards of recognition. He is currently at work on a book-length sequence of poems entitled *The Movie: A Book of Poems*.

How I Escaped from the Labyrinth and Other Poems (Carnegie-Mellon University Press, 1977)
The Condom Poems (Ox Head Press, 1979)

411

The Boy Under the Bed (Johns Hopkins University Press, 1981)
Gerard Manley Hopkins Meets Walt Whitman in Heaven and Other Poems (Penmaen Press, 1982)
Fives (Spoon River Poetry Press, 1984)
Strong Measures: Contemporary American Poetry in Traditional Forms (Harper & Row, 1985) anthology

Stephen Dobyns (1941) was born in Orange, New Jersey and has received degrees from Wayne State University and the Iowa Writer's Workshop. In 1971 his first book won the Lamont Award. Currently, he lives in Watertown, Massachusetts, and teaches in the M.F.A. Program at Warren Wilson College.

Concurring Beasts (Atheneum Pub. Co., 1972)
A Man of Little Evils (Atheneum Pub. Co., 1973) novel
Griffon (Atheneum Pub. Co., 1976)
Saratoga Longshot (Atheneum Pub. Co., 1976) novel
Heat Death (Atheneum Pub. Co., 1980)
Saratoga Swimmer (Atheneum Pub. Co., 1981) novel
The Balthus Poems (Atheneum Pub. Co., 1982)
Dancer with One Leg (E.P. Dutton, 1983) novel
Black Dog, Red Dog (Holt, Rinehart & Winston, 1984)
Saratoga Headhunter (Viking Press, 1985) novel

Mark Doty (1953) was born in Tennessee and raised in the South and West. He studied at the University of Arizona and at Goddard College, and has edited *Blue Buildings* journal and Press. He currently lives in Boston and teaches in the M.F.A. Program at Vermont College.

An Introduction to the Geography of Iowa (Great Raven Press, 1978) co-author
Climbing the Wet Islands (Moondance Press, 1979) co-author
An Alphabet (Alembic Press, 1979)
The Empire of Summer (Thunder City Press, 1981)

Rita Dove (1952) was born in Akron, Ohio, and received an M.F.A. from the Iowa Writer's Workshop. She was a Fulbright Scholar studying European Literature in West Germany and was also a guest at the International Working Periods for Authors in Bieleford, Germany. She has taught at Tuskegee Institute and currently teaches Creative Writing at Arizona State University. She is the recipient of both N.E.A. and Guggenheim fellowships.

Ten Poems (Penumbra Press, 1977) chapbook
The Only Dark Spot in the Sky (Inland Boat, 1980)
The Yellow House on the Corner (Carnegie-Mellon University Press, 1980)
Mandolin (Ohio Review Poetry Series, 1982) chapbook
Museum (Carnegie-Mellon University Press, 1983)

Norman Dubie (1945) was born in Barre, Vermont, and attended Goddard College and the Iowa Writer's Workshop. He has taught at the University of Iowa, Ohio University, and, currently teaches at Arizona State University. He has been the recipient of a Guggenheim fellowship and the Bess Hopkin Award.

Alehouse Sonnets (University of Pittsburgh Press, 1971)
Prayers of the North American Martyrs (Penumbra Press, 1974)
In the Dead of the Night (University of Pittsburgh Press, 1975)
The Illustrations (George Braziller, 1977)

The City of Olesha Fruit (Doubleday & Co., 1979)
A Thousand Little Things (Abbattois Editions, 1978)
Odalisque in White (Porch Publications, 1978)
Popham of the New Song (Graywolf Press, 1975)
The Window in the Field (The Razorback Press, 1981)
Comes Winter, the Sea Hunting (The Maguey Press, 1979) chapbook
The Everlastings (Doubleday & Co., 1980)
New and Selected Poems (W.W. Norton, 1983)

Russell Edson (1935) lives in Connecticut and has been the recipient of two N.E.A. grants and a Guggenheim fellowship and has published the following partial list of collections:
A Stone Is Nobody's (Thing Press, 1961)
Appearances (Thing Press, 1961)
The Bound(a)ry (Thing Press, 1964)
The Brain Kitchen (Thing Press, 1965)
What a Man Can See (The Jargon Society, 1969)
The Clam Theatre (Wesleyan University Press, 1973)
The Childhood of the Equestrian (Harper & Row, 1973)
The Very Thing That Happens (New Directions Publ., 1974)
The Falling Sickness (New Directions Pub., 1975) four plays
The Intuitive Journey (Harper & Row, 1976)
The Reason Why the Closet-Man Is Never Sad (Wesleyan University Press, 1977)
Gulping's Recital (Guignol Books, 1981)
The Wounded Breakfast (Wesleyan University Press, 1985)

Carolyn Forché (1950) was born in Detroit. She has taught at the University of Virginia among other places, and has been the recipient of an N.E.A. grant, a Guggenheim fellowship, the Yale Series of Younger Poets Award, and the 1981 Lamont Award from the American Academy of Poets. Currently, she lives in New York and teaches at New York University.
Gathering the Tribes (Yale University Press, 1976)
The Country Between Us (Harper & Row, 1981)

Alice Fulton (1952) was born in Troy, New York, and received her B.A. from Empire State College and her M.F.A. from Cornell. She has won the 1982 Associated Writing Programs Award in poetry, the Emily Dickinson Award, and has been a Fellow at The Fine Arts Work Center in Provincetown. Current-ly, she teaches at The University of Michigan.
Anchors of Light (Swamp Press, 1979) chapbook
Dance Script with Electric Ballerina (University of Pennsylvania Press, 1982)

Tess Gallagher (1943) was born and raised on the Olympic Peninsula in Wash-ington, and she attended the University of Washington and the Iowa Writer's Workshop. She has written film scripts and short stories, and has been the re-cipient of numerous grants and awards. She has taught at St. Lawrence Univer-sity, Syracuse University, and currently lives in Washington state.
Stepping Outside (Penumbra Press, 1974)
Instructions to the Double (Graywolf Press, 1976)
Under Stars (Graywolf Press, 1978)
Willingly (Graywolf Press, 1984)

Albert Goldbarth (1948) was born in Chicago and earned his M.F.A. from the Iowa Writer's Workshop. He has lived in Iowa, Utah, New York, and Austin, where he is teaching Creative Writing at the University of Texas. He has received two Texas Institute of Letters Awards in poetry, two N.E.A. fellowships, a Guggenheim grant, and numerous other awards.

Under Cover (The Best Cellar Press, 1973)
Curve (New Rivers Press, 1973)
Coprolites (New Rivers Press, 1973)
Opticks (Seven Woods Press, 1974)
Jan. 31 (Doubleday & Co., 1974)
Keeping (Ithaca House, 1975)
A Year of Happy (North Carolina Review Press, 1976)
Comings Back (Doubleday & Co., 1976)
Different Fleshes (Hobart & Wm. Smith Colleges Press, 1979) novel/poem
The Smuggler's Handbook (Chowder Chapbooks, 1980) chapbook
Ink Blood Semen (Bits Press, 1981)
Eurekas (St. Luke's Press, 1981)
Who Gathered and Whispered Behind Me (L'Epervier Press, 1981)
Faith (New Rivers Press, 1981)
Goldbarth's Book of Occult Phenomena (Blue Buildings Press, 1982)
Original Light: New & Selected Poems 1973-1983 (Ontario Review Press, 1983)
Collection (Trilobite Press, 1984) chapbook

Barry Goldensohn (1937) was born in Brooklyn, New York, and attended Oberlin College and the University of Wisconsin where he earned an M.A. He has taught at Goddard College, the University of Iowa, Hampshire College, and currently teaches Creative Writing at Skidmore College.

St. Venus Eve (Cummington Press, 1972)
Uncarving the Block (Vermont Crossroads, 1978)
he, Marrano (forthcoming)

Lorrie Goldensohn (1935) is a native of Manhattan but has spent most of her life living in New England. She was educated at Oberlin College and earned her Ph.D. at the University of Iowa. She has taught at Goddard College, Mount Holyoke College, Hampshire College, and currently teaches at Vassar College. Her essays on poetry and reviews of poetry books have appeared in numerous literary journals.

Dreamwork (Porch Publications, 1980)
The Tether (L'Epervier Press, 1982)

Jorie Graham (1951) was born in New York City and grew up in Italy where she attended French schools and, later, the Sorbonne in Paris. After moving to the United States, she studied at New York University, Columbia University, and the Iowa Writer's Workshop where she earned her M.F.A. She has received an Ingram Merrill Foundation grant, a Bunting Fellowship, an N.E.A. and a Guggenheim Fellowship. She is a permanent member of the Iowa Writer's Workshop.

Hybrids of Plants and of Ghosts (Princeton University Press, 1980)
Erosion (Princeton University Press, 1983)

Linda Gregg (1942) grew up in rural Northern California, and earned degrees from San Francisco State University. In 1983, she was awarded a Guggenheim Fellowship. Currently, she is teaching at the Iowa Writer's Workshop, and has recently completed a new book of poems entitled *The Scent of White.*

    Too Bright to See (Graywolf Press, 1981)

Daniel Halpern (1945) was born in Syracuse, New York, and raised in Los Angeles and Seattle. He has taught at Princeton University, The New School for Social Research, and currently is Chairman of the graduate Writing Division at Columbia University. He has won the YMHA Discovery Award, an N.E.A. grant, and a Robert Frost Fellowship. He is editor of *Antaeus* and the Ecco Press.

    Traveling on Credit (Viking/Penguin Press, 1972)
    Borges on Writing (Dutton, 1973) co-editor
    The Songs of Mririda (Unicorn Press, 1974) translation
    The Lady Knife Thrower (The Bellevue Press, 1975)
    Street Fire (Viking/Penguin Press, 1975)
    The American Poetry Anthology (Avon Pub. Co., 1975) editor
    Orchard Lamps (Sheep Meadow Press, 1978)
    Seasonal Rights (Viking/Penguin Press, 1982)

Patricia Hampl (1946) was born in St. Paul, Minnesota, and earned degrees from the University of Minnesota and the Iowa Writer's Workshop. In 1981, she was awarded a Houghton Mifflin Literary Fellowship, and has been commissioned by the Arkansas Opera Theatre to write librettos. Currently, she lives in St. Paul and teaches at the University of Minnesota.

    Woman Before an Aquarium (University of Pittsburgh Press, 1978)
    A Romantic Education (Houghton Mifflin, Co., 1981) prose memoir
    Resort (Houghton Mifflin, Co., 1983)

Robert Hass (1941) was born and raised in San Francisco, and attended St. Mary's College in Oakland and Stanford University. He has taught at the State University of New York at Buffalo and currently teaches at St. Mary's College. He has won numerous awards for his work, among them a MacArthur Foundation grant and the Yale Series of Younger Poets Award, and he has contributed essays on poetry and poetics and a number of literary journals.

    Field Guide (Yale University Press, 1973)
    Praise (Ecco Press, 1978)
    The Separate Notebooks (Ecco Press, 1983) co-translator
    20th Century Pleasures (Ecco Press, 1984) essays

William Hathaway (1944) was born in Madison, Wisconsin, underwent early schooling in Italy and Switzerland, attended the American College in Paris, Cornell University, University of Montana, and the Iowa Writer's Workshop where he received his M.F.A. Since 1970 he has taught at Louisiana State University in Baton Rouge where he directs the Creative Writing Program and hosts the PBS radio program, "Writers Voices."

    True Confessions and False Romances (Ithaca House, 1972)
    A Wilderness of Monkeys (Ithaca House, 1975)
    The Gymnast of Inertia (Louisiana State University Press, 1982)
    Fish, Flesh & Fowl (Louisiana State University Press, 1985)

Edward Hirsch (1950) was born in Chicago, and educated at Grinnell College, the University of Iowa, and the University of Pennsylvania, where he earned his Ph.D. He is the recipient of awards from the American Academy of Poets, the Ingram Merrill Foundation, the N.E.A., and has been a Fellow at Breadloaf. Currently, he lives in Detroit and teaches at Wayne State University.

For the Sleepwalkers (Alfred A. Knopf, 1981)
Wild Gratitude (Alfred A. Knopf, forthcoming, 1986)

Terry Hummer (1950) was born in Prairie Point, Mississippi, and earned his M.A. from University of Southern Mississippi and his Ph.D. from University of Utah. He has worked in the Mississippi Arts Commission, the Poets-in-the-Schools Program, has edited *Quarterly West, Cimarron Review,* and has taught at Oklahoma State University. Currently he teaches at Kenyon College where he is on the staff of the *Kenyon Review.*

Translation of Light (Cedar Creek Press, 1976)
The Angelic Orders (Louisiana State University Press, 1982)
The Passion of the Right-Angled Man (University of Illinois Press, 1984)
The Imagination as Glory: The Poetry of James Dickey (University of Illinois Press, 1984) criticism, co-editor

Mark Jarman (1952) grew up in Southern California and Scotland. He earned his M.F.A. from the Iowa Writer's Workshop, and has been the recipient of two N.E.A. fellowships. Currently, he teaches at Vanderbilt University in Nashville, and co-edits, with Robert McDowell, the journal *The Reaper.*

North Sea (Cleveland State University Press, 1978)
The Rote Walker (Carnegie-Mellon University Press, 1981)

Denis Johnson (1949) was born in Munich, Germany, and raised in Tokyo, Manila, and Washington, D.C. He received his B.A. and M.F.A. from the University of Iowa, and has been the recipient of a number of awards for his work. Currently, he lives in Wellfleet, Massachusetts, where he works as a freelance writer.

The Man Among the Seals (Stone Wall Press, 1969)
Inner Weather (Graywolf Press, 1976)
The Incognito Lounge (Random House, 1982)
Angels (Alfred A. Knopf, 1983) novel
Fiskadoro (Alfred A. Knopf, forthcoming) novel
Resuscitation of a Hanged Man (Alfred A. Knopf, forthcoming) novel
The Veil (Random House, forthcoming)

Richard Katrovas (1953) spent most of his childhood on the road, and his high school years in Sasebo, Japan. He attended San Diego State University, the University of Virginia, University of Arkansas, and the Iowa Writer's Workshop where he earned his M.F.A. He currently lives in the French Quarter in New Orleans and teaches at the University of New Orleans.

Green Dragons (Wesleyan University Press, 1983)
Snug Harbor (Wesleyan University Press, forthcoming)

Sydney Lea (1942) was born in Pennsylvania and has lived in Grafton County, New Hampshire, since 1969. He earned his Ph.D. from Yale University, and is founder and co-editor of *New England Review.* He has been a recipient of a

Fulbright Fellowship. Currently, he teaches at Middlebury College and its Breadloaf Writers' Conference.

Searching the Drowned Man (University of Illinois Press, 1980)
The Floating Candles (University of Illinois Press, 1982)
Gothic to Fantastic (Arno Press, 1980) criticism

Larry Levis (1946) was born in Fresno, California. He has taught at the University of Missouri, where he edited *The Missouri Review,* and he is currently teaching in the writing program at the University of Utah. In 1976 he won the Lamont Award, and, subsequently, he went on to receive two N.E.A. fellowships and publication in the National Poetry Series.

Wrecking Crew (University of Pittsburgh Press, 1972)
The Rain's Witness (Southwick Press, 1975)
The Afterlife (University of Iowa Press, 1977)
The Dollmaker's Ghost (E.P. Dutton, 1981)

Robert Long (1946) was born in New York City, and studied at Long Island University, in Ireland on a Yeats Fellowship, and at Vermont College where he earned his M.F.A. He lives in Easthampton, New York, and New York City, and since 1978 has taught literature and Creative Writing at Southampton College.

Getting Out of Town (Street Press, 1978)
What It Is (Street Press, 1981)

Thomas Lux (1946) was born in Massachusetts and attended Emerson College in Boston and the Iowa Writer's Workshop for a year. He has taught Creative Writing at Emerson College, Columbia College (Chicago), Oberlin College, Columbia University, the University of Iowa, and is currently teaching at both Sarah Lawrence College and the Warren Wilson M.F.A. Program.

The Land Sighted (Pym-Randall Press, 1970)
Memory's Handgrenade (Pym-Randall Press, 1972)
Almost Dancing (Pym-Randall Press, 1975)
The Glassblower's Breath (Cleveland State University Press, 1976)
Sunday (Houghton Mifflin Co., 1979)
Massachusetts (Pym-Randall Press, 1981) chapbook
Tarantulas on the Lifebuoy (Ampersand Press, 1983) chapbook

Morton Marcus (1936) was born in New York City. He has traveled and read his work throughout the country, and has been active in the Poetry-in-the-Schools Program on both coasts. Currently, he lives in Santa Cruz, California, and teaches at Cabrillo College.

Origins (Kayak Press, 1969)
Where the Oceans Cover Us (Capra Press, 1972)
The Santa Cruz Mountain Poems (Capra Press, 1972)
The Armies Encamped in the Fields Beyond the Unfinished Avenues: Prose Poems (Jazz Press, 1977)
The Brezhnev Memo (Dell Pub. Co., 1980) novel
Big Winds, Glass Mornings, Shadows Cast by Stars: Poems 1972–1980 (Jazz Press, 1981)

Mekeel McBride (1950) was born and raised in Pittsburgh, Pennsylvania, and attended college in California and Indiana. She has taught at Wheaton College,

Harvard University, Princeton University, University of New Hampshire, and in the Vermont College M.F.A. Program. She has been a fellow at the Radcliffe Institute, the Bunting Institute, and has been an N.E.A. fellowship recipient.

A Change in the Weather (Chowder Press, 1979) chapbook

No Ordinary World (Carnegie-Mellon University Press, 1979)

The Going Under of the Evening Land (Carnegie-Mellon University Press, 1983)

Heather McHugh (1948) was born and raised on both coasts and attended Radcliffe College. She earned her M.A. from Denver University in 1972, and has received an N.E.A. fellowship. She has taught in the Warren Wilson M.F.A. Program, Columbia University, among other places, and is currently Writer-in-Residence at the University of Seattle in Washington.

Dangers (Houghton Mifflin Co., 1977)

A World of Difference (Houghton Mifflin Co., 1981)

D'Apres Tout: Poems by Jean Follain (Princeton University Press, 1981)

Sandra McPherson (1943) is a native of San Jose, California. She has been the recipient of grants from the N.E.A. and the Ingram Merrill Foundation, and has taught at the Iowa Writer's Workshop and the University of California at Berkeley. Currently, she lives in Portland, Oregon, where she teaches part-time at the Oregon Writer's Workshop in the Pacific Northwest College of Art.

Elegies for the Hot Season (Indiana University Press, 1970)

Radiation (Ecco Press, 1973)

The Year of Our Birth (Ecco Press, 1978)

Sensing (Meadow Press, 1980)

Patron Happiness (Ecco Press, 1983)

Susan Mitchell (1942) grew up in New York City and attended Wellesley College and Georgetown University where she earned an M.A. She has been a Fellow at the Fine Arts Work Center in Provincetown and Poet-in-Residence at the University of Virginia. Her honors include the Discovery/*The Nation* prize, an N.E.A. grant, as well as grants from the Artists Foundation in Boston. Currently, she teaches at Middlebury College in Vermont.

The Water Inside the Water (Wesleyan University Press, 1983)

Jack Myers (1941) was born in Lynn, Massachusetts, and grew up in the ocean town of Winthrop, Massachusetts. He earned his M.F.A. from the Iowa Writer's Workshop, and has been teaching Creative Writing since 1975 at Southern Methodist University in Dallas and in the Vermont College M.F.A. Program since 1980. He is a recipient of awards from the Texas Institute of Letters and the N.E.A.

Black Sun Abraxas (Halcyone Press, 1970)

Will It Burn (Falcon Pub. Co., 1974) epigraphs/photography, co-author

The Family War (L'Epervier Press, 1977)

I'm Amazed That You're Still Singing (L'Epervier Press, 1981)

A Trout in the Milk: A Composite Portrait of Richard Hugo (Confluence Press, 1982) festschrift, editor

New American Poets (Wampeter Press, 1984) anthology, co-editor

Coming to the Surface (Trilobite Press, 1984) chapbook

The Longman Dictionary of Poetry (Longman, Inc., 1985) co-editor

As Long as You're Happy (L'Epervier Press, forthcoming)

Naomi Shihab Nye (1952) was born in St. Louis to a Palestinian refugee father and American mother. She graduated from Trinity University and has worked in the Texas Poets-in-the-Schools program for ten years. She has also taught at the University of California at Berkeley and, currently, at the University of Texas at San Antonio. She was a winner in the 1982 National Poetry Series, the Texas Institute of Letters award, and has traveled abroad under the auspices of the U.S. Information Agency's Arts America Program.

Tattooed Feet (Texas Portfolio Press, 1977) chapbook
Eye-to-Eye (Texas Portfolio Press, 1978) chapbook
Different Ways to Pray (Breitenbush Books, 1980)
On the Edge of the Sky (Iguana Press, 1981) chapbook
Hugging the Jukebox (E.P. Dutton, 1982)

Steve Orlen (1942) was born in Holyoke, Massachusetts, and attended the University of Massachusetts and the Iowa Writer's Workshop. He has been awarded two N.E.A. fellowships, and currently lives in Tucson where he teaches at the University of Arizona.

Sleeping on Doors (Penumbra Press, 1975)
Separate Creatures (Ironwood Press, 1975)
Permission to Speak (Wesleyan University Press, 1978)
A Place at the Table (Holt, Rinehart and Winston, 1982)

Greg Pape (1947) was born in Eureka, California, and spent his formative years in the West, Southwest, and Florida. He attended California State University at Fresno and earned his M.F.A. at the University of Arizona at Tucson. He has been a Fellow at the Fine Arts Work Center in Provincetown, worked for the Commission on the Arts and Humanities, and has taught most recently as Poet-in-Residence at the University of Louisville.

Border Crossings (University of Pittsburgh Press, 1978)
Little America (The Maguey Press, 1984)
Black Branches (University of Pittsburgh Press, 1984)

Robert Pinsky (1940) was born and raised in Long Branch, New Jersey, and attended Rutgers University and Stanford University. He has served as Poetry Editor of *The New Republic* since 1978, and has received awards from the Guggenheim Foundation and the National Institute and Academy of Arts and Letters. He currently teaches at the University of California at Berkeley.

Landor's Poetry (University of Chicago Press, 1968) criticism
Sadness and Happiness (Princeton University Press, 1975)
The Situation of Poetry (Princeton University Press, 1977)
An Explanation of America (Princeton University Press, 1979)
The Separate Notebooks (Ecco Press, 1983) co-translator
History of my Heart (Ecco Press, 1984)

Stanley Plumly (1939) was born in Barnesville, Ohio, and grew up in the lumber and farming regions of Virginia and Ohio. He received an M.A. from Ohio University, and has taught at a number of universities. He has received two N.E.A. grants, the Delmore Schwartz Memorial Award, and a Guggenheim fellowship. Currently, he co-directs the University of Houston Creative Writing Program, and is at work on a book about the last year-and-a-half in the life of John Keats.

In the Outer Dark (Louisiana State University Press, 1970)

How the Plains Indians Got Horses (Best Cellar Press, 1973)
Giraffe (Louisiana State University Press, 1974)
Out-of-Body-Travel (Ecco Press, 1977)
Summer Celestial (Ecco Press, 1983)

Bin Ramke (1947) was born in Port Neches, Texas, attended Louisiana State University, and earned his Ph.D. at Ohio University. He won the 1977 Yale Series of Younger Poets Award, and is currently teaching at Columbus College in Georgia. He has recently completed a new manuscript of poems entitled *Night Baseball.*
Any Brass Ring (The Ohio Review Poetry Series, 1977) chapbook
The Difference Between Night and Day (Yale University Press, 1977)
White Monkeys (University of Georgia Press, 1981)

Alberto Ríos (1952) was born in Nogales, Arizona, and earned his M.F.A. at the University of Arizona. He has worked extensively for the Arizona Commission on the Arts, and has received the Walt Whitman Award, the 1984 Western States Book Award in fiction, and an N.E.A. grant. Currently, he teaches at Arizona State University in Tempe.
Whispering to Fool the Wind (Sheep Meadow Press, 1981)
The Iguana Killer: Twelve Stories of the Heart (Blue Moon Press, 1984)

Pattiann Rogers (1940) was born and raised in Joplin, Missouri, and earned her M.A. in Creative Writing from the University of Houston. She has been the recipient of an N.E.A. grant, a Texas Institute of Letters award, the Theodore Roethke Prize, and a Guggenheim fellowship. She lives in Stafford, Texas, and will be Visiting Lecturer in poetry this spring at Southern Methodist University.
The Expectations of Light (Princeton University Press, 1981)
The Only Holy Window (Trilobite Press, 1984) chapbook

Kenneth Rosen (1940) was born in Boston and has lived in York and Philadelphia, Pennsylvania. He attended both Penn State and the Iowa Writer's Workshop where he earned his M.F.A. Since 1965, he has been living in Portland, Maine, and teaching at the University of Southern Maine, and directing the Stonecoast Writers' Conference.
Whole Horse (George Braziller, 1973)
Black Leaves (New Rivers Press, 1980)

Michael Ryan (1946) was born in St. Louis and grew up in Allentown, Pennsylvania. He earned his M.F.A. and Ph.D. from the University of Iowa, where he edited *The Iowa Review,* and in 1974 won the Yale Series of Younger Poets Award. He has been a recipient of an N.E.A. grant and a Guggenheim fellowship, and was selected to be included in the 1981 National Poetry Series. He has written and had produced a one-act off-Broadway play, and since 1979 has been writing essays about poetry and poets, and about his experience as a guest of the Sandinistas in Nicaragua. Currently, he is a faculty member of the Warren Wilson M.F.A. Program.
Threats Instead of Trees (Yale University Press, 1974)
In Winter (Holt, Rinehart and Winston, 1981)

Sherod Santos (1948) was born in South Carolina and attended the University of California and the University of Utah, where he earned his Ph.D. He has been the recipient of many awards, including the 1982 National Poetry Series, the Discovery/*The Nation* Award, the Delmore Schwartz Award, an Ingram Merrill grant, and a Guggenheim fellowship. Currently, he teaches at the University of Missouri at Columbia.

Accidental Weather (Doubleday & Co., 1982)

Herbert Scott (1931) was born in Norman, Oklahoma, and grew up there on a farm near Guthrie. He attended Fresno State College and the Iowa Writer's Workshop, and in 1984 received an N.E.A. grant. Currently, he lives in Kalamazoo, Michigan, where he teaches in the M.F.A. Program at Western Michigan University.

Disguises (University of Pittsburgh Press, 1974)
Groceries (University of Pittsburgh Press, 1976)
Durations (Louisiana State University Press, 1984)

Michael Sheridan (1943) grew up along the Mississippi River in Fort Madison, Iowa. He received his M.F.A. from the Iowa Writer's Workshop, and he has received awards from the N.E.A. and the Illinois Arts Council. Currently, he is teaching at Geneseo High School in Illinois.

Days (Ohio Review Poetry Series, 1978)
The Fifth Season (Ohio University Press, 1978)

John Skoyles (1949) was born in Queens, New York. He earned his M.F.A. from the Iowa Writer's Workshop, and has taught Creative Writing at Southern Methodist University, Sarah Lawrence College, and has served as Chairman of the Writing Committee at the Fine Arts Center in Provincetown. He has received grants from the N.E.A. and the New York State Arts Council and currently directs the Warren Wilson M.F.A. Program.

A Little Faith (Carnegie-Mellon University Press, 1981)

Gary Soto (1952) was raised and educated in Fresno, California. His work has earned him the Discovery/*The Nation* Award, the U.S. Award of the International Poetry Forum, a Guggenheim fellowship, and an N.E.A. grant. Currently, he is a Professor of Chicano Studies and English at the University of California at Berkeley.

The Elements of San Joaquin (University of Pittsburgh Press, 1977)
The Tale of Sunlight (University of Pittsburgh Press, 1978)
Father is a Pillow Tied to a Broom (Slow Loris Press, 1980)
Where Sparrows Work Hard (University of Pittsburgh Press, 1981)
Black Hair (University of Pittsburgh Press, forthcoming 1985)

Maura Stanton (1946) was born in Evanston, Illinois, and attended the University of Minnesota and the Iowa Writer's Workshop, where she earned her M.F.A. and Ph.D. She won the 1975 Yale Series of Younger Poets Award, two N.E.A. grants, and the *Michigan Quarterly Review* Lawrence Foundation Prize for the short story. She has been Distinguished Writer-in-Residence at Mary Washington College, and has taught at a number of universities. She currently is on the faculty of Indiana University.

Snow on Snow (Yale University Press, 1975)
Molly Companion (Bobbs-Merrill, 1979) novel
Cries of Swimmers (University of Utah Press, 1984)

Pamela Stewart (1946) was born in Boston and attended Goddard College and the Iowa Writer's Workshop, where she earned her M.F.A. She has taught at Arizona State University, the University of Arizona, the University of California at Irvine, and at the Women's Division of the Arizona State Prison. In 1982, she received a Guggenheim fellowship.

The St. Vlas Elegies (L'Epervier Press, 1977)
Half-Tones (The Maguey Press, 1977)
Cascades (L'Epervier Press, 1979)
Silentia Lunae (Chowder Chapbooks, 1981) chapbook

Susan Stewart (1952) was born in York, Pennsylvania, and attended Dickinson College, The Johns Hopkins University Writing Seminars where she earned her M.F.A., and the University of Pennsylvania where she was awarded a Ph.D. in Folklore Studies. She lives in the Germantown section of Philadelphia and teaches at Temple University.

Nonsense (Johns Hopkins University Press, 1980) literary theory
Yellow Stars and Ice (Princeton University Press, 1981)
On Longing, Narratives of the Miniature, the Gigantic, the Souvenir, the Collection (Johns Hopkins University Press, 1984) literary theory

David St. John (1949) was born in Fresno, California, and studied at Fresno State College and the Iowa Writer's Workshop, where he worked as a poetry editor for *The Iowa Review*. He has been the recipient of grants from the N.E.A., the Ingram Merrill Foundation, the Guggenheim Foundation, and the American Academy and Institute of Arts and Letters. Currently, he teaches in The Writing Seminars at Johns Hopkins University.

For Lerida (Penumbra Press, 1973)
This (The Cassiopeia Press, 1975)
Hush (Houghton Mifflin Co., 1976)
The Shore (Houghton Mifflin Co., 1980)
No Heaven (Houghton Mifflin Co., forthcoming)

James Tate (1943) was born in Kansas City, Missouri, and earned his M.F.A. from the Iowa Writer's Workshop. He was awarded the 1966 Yale Series of Younger Poets Award, a National Institute for the Arts and Letters Award, a Guggenheim fellowship, and an N.E.A. grant. Currently, he teaches at the University of Massachusetts in Amherst.

The Lost Pilot (Yale University Press, 1967)
Notes of Woe (Stone Wall Press, 1968)
The Torches (Unicorn Press, 1968)
Row with your Hair (Kayak Press, 1969)
Wrong Songs (Halty Ferguson Press, 1970)
The Oblivion Ha-Ha (Atlantic-Little, Brown, 1970)
Hints to Pilgrims (Halty Ferguson Press, 1971)
Absences (Atlantic-Little, Brown, 1972)
Hottentot Ossuary (Temple Bar Press, 1974)
Viper Jazz (Wesleyan University Press, 1976)
Riven Doggeries (Ecco Press, 1979)
Constant Defender (Ecco Press, 1983)

Richard Tillinghast (1940) was born and raised in Memphis, Tennessee, and earned his M.A. and Ph.D. at Harvard. He has taught at the University of California at Berkeley, the College of Marin, Sewanee, Harvard, and the University of Michigan where he currently directs the M.F.A. Writing Program. In addition, he has taught in the college program at San Quentin Prison, and has been a poetry reviewer for several major periodicals. He has received an N.E.A. fellowship and a grant from the Mary Roberts Rinehart Foundation, and has been a Staff Associate at the BreadLoaf Writers' Conference. Recently he has guest-edited an issue of *Ploughshares* magazine, and been a poetry consultant for Wesleyan University Press.

The Keeper (Pym-Randall Press, 1968)
Sleep Watch (Wesleyan University Press, 1969)
The Knife and Other Poems (Wesleyan University Press, 1980)
Sewanee in Ruins (The University Press, Sewanee, Tenn., 1981)
Our Flag was Still There (Wesleyan University Press, 1984)

Leslie Ullman (1947) was raised in the Mid-west and attended Skidmore College and the Iowa Writer's Workshop where she earned her M.F.A. She has taught in a number of Mid-west colleges, and was a guest Editor of *Mademoiselle* magazine. She has received a 1976 N.E.A. fellowship, the Great Lakes College Association New Writers Award, and the 1978 Yale Series of Younger Poets Award. Currently, she is teaching at The University Texas at El Paso and in the Vermont College M.F.A. Program. Other recent activities include stints at the Bennington Summer Workshop, and essay writing on and about poetry.

Natural Histories (Yale University Press, 1979)

Michael Waters (1949) was born in New York City, and earned his M.F.A. from the Iowa Writer's Workshop, and his Ph.D. from Ohio University. He has taught at Ohio University, University of Athens (Greece), and has recently been awarded an N.E.A. fellowship. Currently, he teaches Creative Writing at Salisbury State College in Maryland.

Fish Light (Ithaca House, 1975)
Not Just Any Death (B.O.A. Editions, 1979)

Bruce Weigl (1949) was born in Lorain, Ohio, and served a tour of duty in Vietnam with the 1st Cavalry. He earned his M.A. from the University New Hampshire, and his Ph.D. from the University of Utah, where he co-edited *Quarterly West*. He has received a Breadloaf fellowship and a Pushcart prize. Currently, he lives in Virginia where he teaches at Old Dominion University in Norfolk, and is completing work on a new book of poems, tentatively entitled *Monkey Wars*.

Executioner (Ironwood Press, 1976) chapbook
Like a Sackfull of Old Quarrels (Cleveland State University Press, 1977)
A Romance (University of Pittsburgh Press, 1979)
The Imagination as Glory: Essays on the Poetry of James Dickey (University of Illinois Press, 1984) co-editor

Roger Weingarten (1945) was born and raised in Cleveland, Ohio, and educated at Goddard College and the Iowa Writer's Workshop where he earned his M.F.A. He has taught at Western Michigan State University, Arizona State University, Goddard College, and Vermont College, where he currently directs and teaches in the M.F.A. Program. He has received an N.E.A. grant and a Vermont Council on the Arts grant, and has been the Poetry Editor of *Fiction International*, among others.

What are Birds Worth (Cummington Press/Abbattois Editions, 1975)
Ethan Benjamin Boldt (Alfred Knopf, 1975)
The Vermont Suicides (Alfred Knopf, 1978)
The Love & Death Boy (W.D. Hoffstadt & Sons, 1981)
Tables of the Meridian (Blue Buildings Press, 1982)
Love Stories/Love Poems (Fiction International Press, 1983) co-editor
New American Poets (Wampeter Press, 1984) anthology, co-editor
Night Signals (forthcoming, 1985)

C.K. Williams (1936) was born in Newark, New Jersey, and is a contributing editor of *The American Poetry Review*. He is a recipient of a Guggenheim fellowship, and is currently teaching in the Writing Division of Columbia University and at George Mason University in Virginia.

Lies (Houghton Mifflin Co., 1969)
I Am the Bitter Name (Houghton Mifflin Co., 1972)
With Ignorance (Houghton Mifflin Co., 1977)
Sophocles' Women of Trachis (Oxford University Press, 1978) translation
The Lark, the Thrush, the Starling (Burning Deck Press, 1983) translation
Tar (Vintage Books, 1983)

David Wojahn (1953) was born in St. Paul, Minnesota, and attended the University of Minnesota and the University of Arizona where he received an M.F.A. He has worked for the Poets-in-the-Schools Program and is the recipient of the 1981 Yale Series of Younger Poets Award, a fellowship from the Fine Arts Work Center in Provincetown, the William Carlos Williams Book Award, and an N.E.A. grant. He has taught at the University of New Orleans, and, currently, is Poetry Editor of *Crazy Horse* and teaches at the University of Arkansas and in the Vermont College M.F.A. Program.

Icehouse Lights (Yale University Press, 1982)

Carolyne Wright (1949) grew up in Seattle, Washington, and earned her M.A. and Ph.D. from Syracuse University. She has taught at a number of colleges and is currently teaching at Whitman College in the Seattle area. She has received a Fullbright-Hayes grant, the Pablo Neruda Prize, the Maesfield and Wagner awards from the Poetry Society of America, a New York CAPS grant, an N.E.A. grant, and the AWP Book award in poetry. Currently, she is working on a memoir of her experience in Chile.

Stealing the Children (AshahtaPress, 1978)
Returning What We Owed (Owl Creek Press, 1980) chapbook
Premonitions of an Uneasy Guest (Hardin-Simmons University Press, 1983)
From a White Woman's Journal (Water Mark Press, 1984) chapbook

ACKNOWLEDGEMENTS

JOHN ANDERSON: "Each Day Does That," "The Face of Durer," "The Cypresses," "The Time Machine," and "In Sepia" are reprinted from *The Milky Way: Poems 1967–1982* by permission of The Ecco Press and the author. Copyright © 1983 Jon Anderson. "Ye Bruthers Dogg" is used by permission of The Ecco Press and the author.

GEORGE BARLOW: "Stacademia," "Old Man Sweeping," and "Little Half-Brother, Little Star" are reprinted from *Gumbo* by permission of Double & Company, Inc., and the author. Copyright © 1981 George Barlow.

MICHAEL BURKARD: "A Feeling From the Sea," "Time When the Day Ended," and "The Story of Marie" first appeared in *The American Poetry Review* and are reprinted by permission of the author. Copyright © 1983 Michael Burkard. "Your Voice" first appeared in *Pequod* and is used by permission of the author. Copyright © 1984 Michael Burkard. "Strangely Insane" first appeared in *The Black Warrior Review* and is used by permission of the author. Copyright 1983 Michael Burkard.

PETER COOLEY: "For Alissa," "Such Comfort as the Night Can Bring Us," "The Sparrows," "The Unasked For," "The Last Gift," and "The Other" are reprinted from *Nightseasons* by permission of Carnegie-Mellon University Press and the author. Copyright © 1983 Peter Cooley.

PHILIP DACEY: "Skating" first appeared in *Lake Street Review* and is used by permission of the author. Copyright © 1982 Philip Dacey. "Wild Pitches" first appeared in *The Minneapolis Review of Baseball* and is used by permission of the author. Copyright © 1983 Philip Dacey. "The Winter Thing" first appeared in *Crazy Horse* and is used by permission of the author. Copyright © 1982 Philip Dacey. "Crime" first appeared in *Milkweed Chronicle* and is used by permission of the author. Copyright © 1984 Philip Dacey. "The No" first appeared in *The Iowa Review* and is used by permission of the author. Copyright © 1979 Philip Dacey. "Pac-Man" first appeared in *Poetry Northwest* and is used by permission of the author. Copyright © 1983 Philip Dacey.

STEPHEN DOBYNS: "Bleeder," "Black Dog, Red Dog," and "Under the Green Ceiling" are reprinted from *Black Dog, Red Dog* by permission of Holt, Rinehart and Winston, Inc., and the author. Copyright © 1984 Stephen Dobyns.

MARK DOTY: "Gardenias" first appeared in *The Iowa Review* and is used by permission of the author. Copyright © 1984 Mark Doty. "Late Conversations" first appeared in *The Mississippi Review* and is used by permission of the author. Copyright © 1982 Mark Doty.

RITA DOVE: "The Oriental Ballerina" first appeared in *The New England Review* and is used by permission of the author. Copyright © 1984 Rita Dove. "Pomade" first appeared in *Poetry* and is used by permission of *Poetry*. Copyright © 1984 The Modern Poetry Association. "Parsley" is reprinted from *Museum* and is used by permission of Carnegie-Mellon University Press and the author. Copyright © 1983 Rita Dove.

NORMAN DUBIE: "Einstein's Exile in an Old Dutch Winter," "Lord Myth," "The Sketchbook Ashes of Jehoshaphath" are reprinted from *The Everlastings*

428

433